Gender, Sex and Sexuality

Contemporary Psychology Series: 9

Gender, Sex and Sexuality: Contemporary Psychological Perspectives

Gerda Siann

40431

Taylor & Francis
Publishers since 1798

UK   Taylor & Francis Ltd, 4 John Street, London WC1N 2ET
USA   Taylor & Francis Inc., 1900 Frost Road, Suite 101, Bristol, PA 19007

First published 1994

A catalogue record for this book is available from the British Library

Library of Congress Cataloging-in-Publication Data are available on request

ISBN 0 7484 0185 7
ISBN 0 7484 0186 5 (pbk)

Cover design by Amanda Barragry

Cartoon used on cover reproduced by kind permission of Jacky Fleming and Abner Stein.

Typeset in 10/12 pt Garamond
by Graphicraft Typesetters Ltd., Hong Kong

Printed in Great Britain by Burgess Science Press, Basingstoke on paper which has a specified pH value on final paper manufacture of not less than 7.5 and is therefore 'acid free'.

Contents

Preface		vi
Acknowledgments		viii
Chapter 1	Gender and Sexuality	1
Chapter 2	Tarzan, Jane and Boadicea	22
Chapter 3	Gender Differences and Biological Determinism	41
Chapter 4	Sugar and Spice; Frogs and Snails	64
Chapter 5	Poles Apart? Abilities, Attributes and Social Behaviour	88
Chapter 6	Structuralism, Feminism and Post-feminism	116
Chapter 7	Fatal Attractions	150
Afterword		178
References		179
Index		195

Preface

In his book on Gender, Ivan Illich draws a sharp distinction between gender and sex. He defines gender as that which distinguishes 'places, times, tools, tasks, forms of speech, gestures, and perceptions that are associated with men from those associated with women'. He goes on to say that this definition of gender designates a duality that in the *past* was too obvious even to be named. He reserves the term 'sex' on the other hand to indicate a 'polarisation in those common characteristics that, starting with the late 18th century, are attributed to all human beings'. In other words sex unlike gender is immutable and not subject to a local material culture. The concept of sex, being based upon an anatomical division of types of reproductive organs, carries connotations of an unchangeable dichotomy between men and women. In fact even a cursory contemplation of men and women, reveal that not only in characteralogical terms but also in physical terms there is an enormous overlap in the traits that each displays. A biological male may be short and softly rounded, without facial hair, caring considerate and emotional. A biological female may be tall and strong, assertive and aggressive.

It has taken psychologists a long time to realise the importance of drawing a distinction between sex and gender, and even longer to pay sufficient attention to the significance of drawing this distinction. There have been many studies in the history of psychology of 'sex differences' in behaviour which have looked to see whether men or women were more or less intelligent, more or less aggressive, had more or less spatial ability, or were more nurturent than each other. These kinds of studies carried two implications. First that biological sex was a meaningful basis for dividing people into distinct groups. Secondly, an assumption that the human norm was male. Which implied that female characteristics are, in some way distant, or deviant from the human norm.

Many psychologists now prefer to reserve the word 'sex' to describe specific biological mechanisms or structures and to routinely use the term 'gender' when they are discussing social and psychological aspects that are characteristic of men and women or which are assumed to be appropriate to men and women. Thus we have the terms, 'gender-stereotype', 'gender-roles' and 'gender-identities' which imply that these are subject to social and cultural influences and are only minimally, if at all, influenced by sexual characteristics such as hormones, chromosomes and sex organs.

It is still more recently that psychologists have come to accept that there is a perfectly legitimate and interesting view of human behaviour, and indeed gender-roles, that can be taken from a women's perspective. Undoubtedly much of contemporary psychology is still male dominated and essentially and androcentric, but a significant number of women psychologists (and a few men psychologists) are deliberately taking a different point of view. This paradigm shift was produced partly by the rise of feminist perspectives in society at large, but also by an increase in dissatisfaction with what traditional psychology was delivering in terms of explanations and understandings of gender differences and gender relations. The movement in this direction was also undoubtedly accelerated by the increase in popularity of the study of psychology among women to the extent that most undergraduate classes in psychology now have 2 or 3 times as many women as men students in them.

In her book Gerda Siann does not suggest that men and women are basically the same – to do so would be nonsense. If you look around you at men and women you can quite plainly see that they differ. They look differently, they dress differently, they walk differently, they speak differently and they behave differently. What is important is not that these differences exist, but to ask why they exist and to what extent these differences are important.

Gender, Sex and Sexuality takes us through the most significant theoretical approaches to gender contemporary psychology and looks at the way in which gender identities develop and influence perspectives on the self, others, relationships, and society. Gerda Siann's book does not ignore the possibility that there are biological determinants of gender differences in abilities and behaviour but puts the research from this tradition into a perspective which reveals the subsidiary nature of biological influences compared to the overwhelming impact of social expectations and social traditions. Finally the book tackles the important, timely and difficult topic of violence against women in all its forms and the relationship of this disturbing phenomenon to gender identities.

The book is designed, as are all others in this series, for readers who will not necessarily have any previous acquaintance with psychology but who are prepared to meet challenging ideas and new concepts in what they read, be prepared to grapple with the methodology and findings of contemporary psychological research and to move on to a deeper understanding not only of the psychology of gender but of their own position in a very gender structured world.

Reference

ILLICH, I. (1993) *Gender.* London: Marion Boyars.

Raymond Cochrane,
Birmingham, January 1994.

Acknowledgments

I would like to thank the editor of this series, Ray Cochrane for his unfailing kindness and assistance while I was writing this book and I would also like to express my appreciation for the assistance I was given by Francis Bock, Marian Miller and Pamela Milliken.

I would also like to thank the following people for their help: Halla Beloff, David Bell, Vince Brennan, Rinelle Cere, William Connolly, Linda Croxford, Charlie Ennis, Douglas Forbes, Alexa Hepburn, Carol Jackson, Comfort Jegede, Myra Macdonald, Mary Marsden, Paul Morton, George Newbigging, Tanya Siann, Willie Thompson, Iain Wilkie, Cathy Wright and Alastair Young.

I am grateful to Jacky Fleming and Abner Stein, and *The Spectator* for giving Henry Martin and me permission to use their cartoons and I would also like to thank the following for permission to quote from their work:

Gerald Duckworth & Co. Ltd. to reproduce from *Collected Dorothy Parker*.

Warner Chappell Music Ltd. by Permission of International Music Publications Limited for the reproduction of Lyric extracts from *Back off Bitch* and *Why can't a woman be more than a man*.

Faber and Faber Ltd. and Harper Collins Publishers for use of Sylvia Plath's poem in Ted Hughes (Ed), *Selected Poems*.

Virago Press for permission to reproduce from Maya Angelou (1992) *And still I rise*.

The man is the peak of the house;
That is what we have understood.
It is the women who make the pinnacle
On top of the roof.
Initiation song of Bemba girls translated by Audrey Richards.

Chapter 1

Gender and Sexuality

. . . how touching, how pliantly feminine this most masculine and re-
sourceful of women could be.
(Lawrence Durrell)[1]

If a woman can't make her mistakes charming, she is only a female.
(Oscar Wilde)[2]

Holly came from Miami FLA
Hitchhiked her way across the USA
Plucked her eyebrows on the way
Shaved her legs
Then he was a she . . .
Lou Reed, *Walk on the Wild Side*

Feminine/masculine, male/female, women/men, boy/girl – terms of sexual
and gender division like these permeate the way we think and talk about
ourselves and each other. On most occasions we find their use non-problematic
and we employ them easily. At other times, however, particularly if we are
interested in psychology, we may wonder whether this ease is illusory. We
may speculate, for example, whether being a woman necessarily implies being
'feminine'. We may question why young women are often referred to as girls
while young men are seldom referred to as boys. When we consider the
relationships between gender, sex, sexuality and appearance we may encounter
more conundrums. For example, is dressing in a stereotypically feminine manner
a reliable indication that a woman is heterosexual? And what about cross-
dressing? Are we likely to consider a man in drag at a fancy-dress party as
more stereotypically masculine than a transvestite who dresses as a woman in
the privacy of his bedroom? And why is it that cross-dressing is more easily
tolerated in women than men. It is not unusual, for example, for fashion
features to show female models in men's clothes, but how often do we see the
reverse?

We might also wonder at the fascination these topics appear to hold for
the media. Aside from the large numbers of documentaries, chat shows and
features that are directly concerned with gender issues, there is also far more
flexibility in the manner in which individuals are encouraged to display their
experimentation with gender than there has been in the past. Is it likely that
a celebrity like Julian Clary would have been as acceptable hosting game

'I assure you, Mr Wilburton, that wearing an apron in the kitchen is not cross-dressing.'

shows in the seventies or even in the eighties as he is in the nineties? Why does Madonna exercise such a grip on the popular imagination and why do we care about what one reviewer has called 'her warm chaotic world of (presumably) multi-gendered . . . bliss' (Worth, 1992)?

This chaper is concerned with the issues of gender, of gender labelling and of sexuality. The manner in which the following chapters will further develop such issues is also discussed.

Distinguishing between sex and gender

With remarkably few exceptions people identify themselves quickly and easily as either male or female and consequently filling in the category labelled sex on a questionnaire, or ticking a box labelled male or female rarely presents problems. As chapter 3 will indicate, this apparent unambiguity is sometimes illusory and in a small minority of cases sexual assignation is not straightforward. However, for the time being, we will make the assumption that we are all born as either male or female and we will go on to look at the manner in which that sexual identification interacts with another identification – that of gender.

For some time it has been customary for social scientists to make the following distinction between sex and gender. **Sex** is defined as the biological differences between males and females and **gender** is the manner in which culture defines and constrains these differences; not only differences in the manner in which women, in general, live their lives compared to men in general, but also differences in the manner in which individuals view both themselves and others, in terms of the female/male dichotomy. Obviously then, gender and the labels associated with it, primarily those two descriptors, 'feminine' and 'masculine', are neither fixed nor immutable depending as they do on cultural constructions.

This is not to imply that the sexual distinction itself is absolute and immune from subjective biases. For, as we shall see in chapter 3, even biologists and endocrinologists (Lorber and Farrell, 1991) have discovered that not everyone fits as neatly into the categories male and female as once was assumed. Rather it is to make the point that if the concept of sex is no longer seen as absolute because distinctions about it are made by people living in particular cultures at particular times, how much less absolute must be distinctions concerned with gender.

In this chapter we will look at three major ways in which gender as a category system can be thought of as operating and then we will consider the cultural context in which sexuality is viewed. Before starting to look at gender as a category system, however, let us place the discussion within the context of the basic inequality that has until recently dominated established thinking about gender. This inequality has reflected the opinion of men rather than women and the reason for this inequality lies in the fact that, until very recently, in most societies power and status have been very unequally apportioned between the sexes. Many of these inequalities are on the wane but others have remained obstinately persistent. Looking specifically for the moment at the UK, it is clear that the battle for female equality is not over. For while women have won some spectacular victories, such as for example the right to be ordained as priests in the Church of England, progress at other more mundane but particularly vital levels has been slow, laborious and in some cases static. Women continue to be massively under-represented at all levels of government (O'Reilly, 1992); continue to earn less than men both in general and, in many instances, compared to men in similar positions (Equal Opportunities Commission, 1992); continue to experience bias in promotion to management (Institute of Management, 1992) and at times continue to see their experience of sexual and physical abuse trivialized and minimized (Scully, 1990).

Throughout this book I will be concerned with the effect that such inequalities, and the battle to remove them, have had on the psychologies of both men and women. At this stage, let us examine the reflection of these inequalities in literature and folklore.

Misogyny and mystification

Until very recently, in the very great majority of cultures,[3] men as a social group have exerted power over women as a social group – over how they lived and how they were regarded, not only by men but also by women themselves, who very often internalized men's views about themselves as a sex. In general, in this relationship between the sexes, women were regarded as the 'other', the weaker and the second sex – all terms that have been echoed in discussions of gender. This of course, is not to deny the existence of love between the sexes or that the great majority of men have loved individual women and been concerned with their welfare. But, as Tavris and Wade (1984) put it, man's concern about woman has been, and perhaps, continues to be, marked by both passion and paradox.

By passion in terms of emotional relationships whether familial, sexual or somtimes social, as in friendship. By paradox in terms of the mystery that men have imputed to women which has resulted in ambiguity and contradiction in their conceptions of women. Thus women, for most heterosexual men, are both desirable and, at times, feared. Feared not in their possession of economic and social power but because in essence for most men, women as the 'other' are essentially unknowable. Feared also, perhaps, because it is women who have control over men when they are at their most vulnerable in infancy and early childhood. And individually many men will have experienced the paradoxical feelings of exercising power over women in their public life while simultaneously feeling in thrall to the mysterious nature of an individual woman's sexual allure. It is perhaps this complex interaction between power, desire and fear that accounts for another emotion commonly voiced by men about women, that of contempt.

These conflicting emotions of desire, fear and contempt felt by men about women are reflected in most recorded references to gender. Women's musings about men are less well documented because, as it is men who have held social and economic power it is their voices that we find reflected not only in written records but also in oral tradition. Many such references reflect antagonism, distrust and belittlement and the documentation of such misogynistic references can be found in recent collections like Joan Smith's *Misogynies* (Smith, 1993) and Tama Starr's *In her Master's Voice* (Starr, 1991). Such as these, for example:

> One volume could never contain
> All the insults and satires against women.
> De Fonseca, C., 1614, in Starr (1991)

She was maintaining the prime truth of woman, the universal mother;
that if a thing is worth doing, it's worth doing badly.
G. K. Chesterton, 1910

And finally, woman! one half of mankind is weak, chronically sick,
changeable, shifty . . .
F. Nietzsche, 1888

A woman has the form of an angle, the heart of a serpent, and the
mind of an ass.
German proverb, quoted by Starr (1991)

The place of a horse and a women is under the thighs
Hindi folk saying[4]

Barley and millet improve by addition of salt, women through a beating
by a pestle.
Gujarati folk saying[4]

But men's emotions about women are not univalent and consequently the
way men write and speak about women reflects not only contempt and deni-
gration but also a fascination and a guarded respect. For example:

As you are woman, so be lovely;
As you are lovely, so be various,
Merciful as constant, constant as various,
So be mine, as I yours forever.
Robert Graves (1927)

Women are stronger than men – they do not die of wisdom
They are better than men because they do not seek wisdom
They are wiser than men because they know less and understand
more
Stephens (1912)

Women are like tricks by sleight of hand,
Which to admire, we should not understand
Congreve *Love for Love* (1689)

On the other hand, women's views on men, have until very recently
seldom been documented and it is this inbalance that lies, In believe, at the
centre of the documentation of male – female relations. In the recorded discussion of gender it is the male view that, until very recently, has prevailed.

Gender as a category

. . . the notion of gender distinction constitutes a ubiquitous intellectual
and moral lens through which we perceive and evaluate the world.
Billig *et al.* (1988, p. 127)

Although the term gender has been in general use for some time it has mainly been used in the context of grammar because most languages employ particular syntactical terms to indicate sex (e.g. his, hers, etc). More recently the term has been used to draw attention to the social, rather than biological, construction of sex differences. The term 'construction' is employed to highlight the fact that the differences between the way men and women are thought about and treated owe less to their biological differences than to the manner in which each society organizes their lives.

However, even if the wider use of the term 'gender' has only been current in recent years, distinctions based on gender have dominated most societies for centuries (Billig, 1988). What Billig's quotation encapsulates is the notion that values and beliefs about femininity as opposed to masculinity permeate all aspects of day to day life. Hare-Mustin and Maracek (1990) have suggested that within psychological theory this dichotomy has been 'construed' in three ways: as structural differences between males and females; as behavioural attributes of males and females and as essential male and female nature. Each of these facets is discussed briefly below and in detail in chapters 2 and 3 (essential nature), chapters 4 and 5 (behavioural attributes) and chapter 6 (structural differences).

Essential Nature

> Man is the hunter, women is his game:
> The sleek and shining creatures of the chase,
> We hunt them for the beauty of their skins;
> They love us for it, and we ride them down.
> Alfred, Lord Tennyson *The Princess* (1847)

This view that females and males are essentially different in nature has deep historic roots in both western and non-western cultures and permeates mythology, folk-lore, literature and philosophy in most cultures. It is not surprising then, to find that such views (which Hare-Mustin and Maracek refer to as 'essentialist') are reflected in some approaches to the psychology of sex and gender notably in two contrasting approaches.

The first approach is related to psychoanalysis and the second to biology. These approaches will be pursued further in chapters 2 and 3.

The next chapter will also look at the psychoanalytic perspectives on gender. Such approaches to gender locate the source of gender differences in the familial relationships of the very early years of life. Although, as we shall see, psychoanalytic approaches to gender have been developed in different ways at different times and by different theorists, all have been heavily influenced in their views on gender by the 'essentialist' approach of the founder of psychoanalysis, Sigmund Freud.

Freud's approach to gender was not without ambiguities and contradictions but nevertheless the general tenor of his writing suggested that there were identifiable and consistent personality differences between men and women. The differences that he identified reflected the ethos of nine-teenth century Europe – women were by nature more passive than men and thus less well suited to life outside the family circle. Men, on the other hand, were by nature active and more suited to dealing with the world outside the family.

As we shall see his male successors working in the psychoanalytic tradi-tion largely endorsed this viewpoint which, in most ways, regarded men as the standard and women, in a phrase that we shall return to frequently, as the 'other'. His female successors have taken very divergent viewpoints and we will explore these as well. What unites most psychoanalysts however, are the twin beliefs that personality is rooted in the experiences of infancy and early childhood and that it is very difficult to modify personality in later life. Consequently they believe that sex differences, rooted as they are in the earliest years, are an essential part of human nature.

The second 'essentialist' viewpoint is that emerging from a biological perspective. This viewpoint locates the major source of sex and gender dif-ferences in nature, arguing that these differences are largely innate. As we shall see in chapter 3 this perspective rests on two propositions which are:

1. there are commonalities running through time and across all cultures in female as compared to male behaviour;
2. these commonalities within the same sex, and differences between the sexes, are due in a major part to 'human nature'.

In other words, sexual differences in human behaviour exhibit some constancies and these can be attributed to nature rather than nurture. The term **biological determinism** is often used to describe this viewpoint and two versions of this stance will be considered.

The first of these, which has emerged directly from the field of biology and more recently from socio-biology (Wilson, 1978), draws on evolutionary theory to argue, in essence, that human society has evolved in such a way that men have the innate qualities and attributes of the hunter, whereas women's innate predispositions are towards domesticity.

A great deal of empirical research in biology has been adduced in support of these claims which produce a rather similar viewpoint to that postulated by Freud, in that men are seen as–by nature–active, dominant and rational, while women are seen as passive, submissive and emotional.

More recently a second version of biological determinism has appeared. This viewpoint has emerged in certain feminist positions which have tended to 'idealize femininity' (Squire, 1989) but which, like socio-biology, attribute fundamental and consistent sex differences to nature rather than nurture. This perspective neatly inverts most other perspectives on sex differences in that it treats women as the standard and man as the 'other'. Women by nature are seen as compassionate, empathic and flexible, men by nature as tending to-wards domination, violence and over-rationality. This viewpoint rests, as will be shown in chapter 3, on a rather different version of biological determinism than that proposed by the socio-biologists just referred to.

While essentialist approaches have dominated psychoanalytic views on gender, they have had very little influence on the views of gender held within psychology in general. Views within mainstream psychology have tended to reject psychoanalysis as unscientific and, as a result, psychoanalytic views on gender have, until recently, had little influence on most psychological approaches to sex and gender. Instead, mainstream psychological approaches have rested largely on the results of psychological experiments into human behaviour and studies of how individuals 'learn' to play the role proscribed for their particular gender.

Behavioural attributes and sex-role theories

Chapters 4 and 5 will describe in some detail how mainstream psychologists have, in general, approached the study of gender but at this stage the parameters of these chapters are sketched out.

Initial approaches to the study of gender within psychology were rather indirect in that they derived from the tendency within psychology to focus on variables that might account for the 'individual differences' displayed by 'subjects' in psychological experiments and studies. Amongst individual differences studied were such variables as intelligence, personality attributes and, as the subject pool enlarged away from the traditional one of male undergraduates, sex.

Sex, rather than gender, was the main focus of these early studies and, as we shall see in chapter 5, as fewer and fewer areas of investigation concentrated only on one sex, no major study was reported without some investigation of sex differences between the subjects.

Changes in the sex ratio of those studies were also reflected, though to a lesser extent, in changes in the sex ratio of those carrying out the studies and the advent of more female psychologists led to changes in the focus of psychological investigations of gender. In the first instance this was because female psychologists like Carole Jacklin (1981) began to challenge the methodologies and techniques that had been used in sex difference studies and, in the second instance, this was because other female psychologists, such as Carole Gilligan (1982), began to question the content of such studies.

Chapter 4 will detail the manner in which such critiques led to a movement away from the concentration on gender differences and towards an emphasis on the acquisition of sex role and gender identity. At this stage it should be pointed out that it was the interaction of this movement in psychology with the re-emergence of feminism that sparked off major discussions in the ranks of female psychologists about the bias in psychology towards male-centred views – sometimes referred to as **androcentric**. This debate was influenced as well by major movements within the social sciences in general, in particular by that of 'structuralism' and it is to this movement that we now turn.

Structural differences between males and females
The social sciences in the twentieth century have been heavily influenced by the movement of structuralism with its dual roots in the work of the French anthropologist Henri Levi-Strauss (1969) and in the field of linguistics.

Levi-Strauss' anthropological studies lead him to suggest that the nature of the human mind, operating universally in all cultures, produces a disposition to organize the representations or models we make of the world around fundamental distinctions. Applying this general principle to kinship systems with which anthropologists were at that time chiefly concerned, Levi-Strauss proposed that women provide an object of exchange which consolidates and differentiates kinship relations. This, he argued, was because women, as brides, are exchanged from one clan to another through the institution of marriage. In this way he relegated women to a subordinate status (as opposed to men whose status was dominant) within the cultural reality, not only of the societies he was describing, but also by implication in his further discussion on societies in general (Butler, 1990). As will be shown in chapter 6, his viewpoint has been energetically challenged by contemporary feminist anthropologists who cite a number of instances of non-western societies in which women have not, and in some cases do not, play a subordinate role (Sanday and Goodenough, 1990).

Levi-Strauss extended his argument to suggest that, in many ways, gender relations could be seen as 'bipolar opposites', each sex on either side of a dichotomy. But this was not the only dichotomy that he proposed. Indeed it could be argued that his whole approach suggested that there was an 'oppositional logic' to most representations human make of the world. That is we tend to conceptualize in terms of opposites.

This oppositional logic is also reflected in the work of certain linguists who have argued that linguistic features can best be represented in terms of structures and systems based on networks of opposites (Scott, 1990), and by certain psychologists, like George Kelly (1955), who have also claimed that the way human beings represent the world is in terms of dichotomies. Thus, according to Kelly, we think about ourselves and others in terms of dichotomies such as good/bad, warm/cold, beautiful/ugly, etc.

Applying such dichotomous structuralist approaches to gender, provides us with a structural principle of social relations which can be seen as underpinning the relations between the sexes in all cultures, and which allows for the division of human behaviour and our thinking about it into the basic dichotomy, male-female.

This dichotomy is not, however, equally balanced. As the discussion in chapter 6, will make plain the dichotomy can be seen as operating as masculine (normative) versus feminine (the 'other') in such a way that the feminine pole is always seen as less desirable. For the moment let us anticipate this discussion by noting the suggestion made by Hare-Mustin and Maracek (1990, p. 4) that there are three major mechanism through which the dichotomising principle operates – how children are brought up, how society is structured in terms of the different facilities offered to the two sexes and how meaning is generated when we talk or write about the differences between men and women. According to Hare-Mustin and Maracek, though these mechanism differ in detail from society to society in nearly all cultures their operation has resulted in the relative disadvantage of women because power has been in the hands of men.

One of the primary ways in which cultural values permeate notions of gender is, of course, in the approach to sexuality and the remainder of this chapter presents a historical overview of sexuality and describes the terms and terminology which are used when we think and talk about sex and gender differences in sexuality.

Sexuality and gender

The most important first step in studying sexuality is to differentiate it from gender.
Caplan (1987, p. 2)

The notion that humans have an innate sexual urge that propels them towards sexual activity is one we are all familiar with. It is a belief which is characteristic of all societies although the manner in which individuals feel able to give expression to their sexuality varies across societies and across time. This is because all societies prescribe and codify sexual activity and in this way legitimize some sexual practices and not others. While in all cultures this codification of sexuality has been linked to gender, the nature of the link between gender and sexuality is by no means universal as will be shown.

Historical aspects of sexuality in the west

Woman is the lesser man, and all thy passions, match'd with mine
Are as moonlight into sunlight, and as water into wine.
Alfred, Lord Tennyson *Locksley Hall* (1842)

A vulgar opinion prevails that (women) are creatures of like passions with ourselves . . . Nothing is more utterly untrue. . . . Only in rare instances do women experience one-tenth of the sexual feeling which is familiar to most men.
George H Napheys, MD (1878)

That women are less motivated by sexuality than men is a belief that has long been held in the west and it can be argued that the belief owes far more to the unequal status of the sexes than to any scientific study of sexuality. Indeed the attempt to document and understand the nature of sexuality in any sense is characteristic only of the twentieth century. Which is not to say that empirical investigations into sexuality in the last century have not been coloured by attitudes towards gender.

Williams (1987) suggests that the major historical influence on western ideas about sex differences in sexuality lay in the value of women to men as items of property and primarily as items of exchange. As an item of exchange a woman should of course be above reproach.

> Authorities both old and recent
> Direct that women must be decent
> Jonathan Swift *Strephon and Chloe* (1731)

Thus for both girls and women the essential attribute was chastity. As a girl, because on marriage her bridegroom would want to feel assured that she had never belonged to another man. As a wife, because her sexual fidelity would ensure that her husband's property would not be passed down to the children of another man.

This concept of woman as the sexual property of men was reinforced in Europe in the period before the Reformation by intepretations of the Bible which merged asceticism with holiness and which associated sexuality, even within marriage, largely with procreation. The devout man was urged to protect himself from the dangerous devices of the unchaste woman who might divert him from his familial and social duties. Devout women were required to bow before their lot and as wives to:

> submit yourselves unto your husbands. . . . as unto the Lord. For the husband is the head of the wife, even as Christ is the head of the church
> Ephesians, 5:22–23

After the Reformation attitudes towards sex became less censorious in that it was accepted that, for men at any rate, celibacy was a demanding condition. Marriage, however, continued to be seen as the appropriate location for containing and controlling sexual feelings which continued to be seen as demeaning to both sexes. It was, however, only in the middle of the eighteenth century with the growth of romanticism and its emphasis on freedom and individuality, that sexuality began to be associated with love and emotional fulfilment. Then for a short period, for a privileged section of the population, loving and overtly sexual relations between men and women were celebrated both within and indeed outside marriage. These attitudes were exemplified by the fascination exercised in Europe and in the USA by romantic figures like Byron and Shelley who were renowned as much for their erotic and passionate relationships as for their poetry or their politics.

As the nineteenth century advanced, however, the influence of romanticism waned to be replaced as a dominant ethos by the repressiveness of the post-romantic movement and in Britain and in America by what is termed the Victorian era.

As is well known the Victorian era was characterized by a severe and extremely puritanical approach to all overt manifestations of sexuality, particularly for women of the middle classes. At the same time the sexual desires of upper and middle class men were catered for by a network of brothels and bordellos. Child prostitutes of both sexes were not uncommon and the boundary between the protected, if repressed, lives of economically privileged children and the exploited, if somewhat more permissive, lives of the children of the poor was marked and seldom, if ever, crossed.

The repression of overt sexuality both reflected and reinforced an ideology of sexual relations which reflected earlier pre-romantic themes. Pamphlets, child rearing manuals, articles on health and hygiene all promoted the virtues of self-control, continence and chastity. Sexual intercourse was only approved of in the context of marriage and primarily for procreation; anything that might stimulate what were regarded as 'the sexual appetites' was frowned upon. In many middle class homes activities, particularly for girls, that might lead to the transgression of the stringent moral code were strictly controlled. The reading of romantic novels, dancing and close emotional relationships, even with the same sex, were monitored and sometimes even forbidden, and young girls were expected to be passive and modest. Their destiny was to be pursued but not to pursue. Once married, women were expected to endure sexual relations passively and desire and pleasure were to be avoided.

Masturbation, 'the solitary vice' was heavily censored for both sexes and was associated with the threat of madness, blindness and general physical and mental degeneracy. Masturbation was regarded as a sure sign of ungovernable sexual impulses and such impulses were of course regarded as extremely threatening to the lives of women and were thought to be directly associated with insanity. So convinced was one medical practioner (Dr Isaac Baker Brown) that strong sexual impulses in women were associated with insanity that he carried out sexual surgery – removal of the clitoris and sometimes the labia – on patients as young as ten because it was suspected that their well being was threatened by their sexuality. Such rampant sexuality could, he believed, first be detected in puberty when girls became 'restless and excited . . . and indifferent to the social influences of domestic life'. There might also be depression, loss of appetite, a 'quivering of the eyelids and an inability to look one in the eye' (Dr Isaac Baker Brown in Showalter, 1987). Even the desire to leave home and become a nurse or a sister of charity could be regarded as a clue to the over-excitement and general instability which presaged the insanity deriving from disorderly and unfeminine impulses.

At the turn of the century, however, such avid policing and control of sexuality began to lose force. As the themes of passionate and erotic love began to be explored again in literature (for example in the novels of Thomas Hardy); as pioneering women moved into professions like medicine, and as particularly after the first world war during which women had begun to perform many jobs that had previously been regarded as suited only to men, it began to be generally accepted that women, like men, had sexual impulses which were neither unnatural nor unhealthy.

Twentieth century western perspectives on sexuality
Although the systematic and large scale documentation of sexuality only began in the middle of the twentieth century with the surveys of Alfred Kinsey and his associates, pioneering investigations were carried out much earlier in the century primarily by Havelock Ellis. Ellis, published six volumes on sexuality between 1897 and 1910 drawing both on biological studies and western and non-western data in which he emphasized that sexuality was natural, healthy and variable. Arguing for sexual equality for women, he countered the generally held belief that women's sex drive was weaker than men's and he also challenged the still prevailing view that masturbation was unhealthy and unnatural. But, although Ellis argued for sexual equality for women, he did not question the prevailing view that there was a qualitative sexual difference in response to sexuality, endorsing the prevailing view that in courtship men should initiate and women respond. The relationship was ultimately one of the female at first resisting, and in this way increasing the man's ardour, and then yielding. Because Ellis's model was based on this model of necessary and unequal power relations which derived from his belief that human courtship, like animal courtship, was based on conquest, he also claimed that for women pain and sexual pleasure were sometimes indistinguishable: 'the normal manifestations of a women's sexual pleasure are exceedingly like pain' (Ellis, 1913).

In this manner, despite promoting women's right to sexual satisfaction, Ellis endorsed a biological determinism with respect to sexuality. It was in the nature of men to enjoy conquest and of women to enjoy submission.

This view of the nature of courtship dominated much that was written by both women and men about sexuality in the early years of this century. For example, Marie Stopes who pioneered birth control clinics for women despite promoting women's sexual rights, nevertheless wrote about human sexuality in the context of man's innate hunting instincts and in a book called *Education for Marriage*, Estelle Cole advised young women that:

> Man is a hunter by nature. He likes to chase his game. His pleasure lies in the pursuit. With capture and possession there often comes lack of interest; so that the wise woman restrains herself at such passionate moments, in order that he may be kept eager in his pursuit.
> Cole (1938)

Nevertheless, despite this prevailing model of sexual differences in the enjoyment of sexuality, attitudes towards women's sexuality had moved on enormously from the repressive puritanism of the previous century. In no way, was this more apparent in the English speaking world than in the enormous success of a sex manual which had originally been published in Dutch. This was *The Ideal Marriage* written by a gynaecologist called Van der Velde (1928). In this book Van der Velde was concerned with the sexual satisfaction of both partners and of the woman's right to orgasm. Like Ellis, however, he saw the, presumably more experienced, male as the initiating partner whose duty it was to stimulate the virginal bride who was by nature slower to be aroused. Van der Velde frequently used the analogy of a sensitive musician who by the appropriate techniques could bring both himself and his partner to glorious climax:

> Woman is a harp who only yields her secrets of melody to the master who knows how to handle her . . . the husband must study the harp and the art of music . . . this is the book of rules for his earnest and reverent study . . . his reward comes when the harp itself is transformed into an artist in melody, entrancing the initiator.
> Van der Velde (1928)

Van der Velde's model of sexual relations reflected the continuing double standard, which also prevailed in numerous other sex manuals, and which was based on a belief that sex was ideally to be enjoyed within a marriage that was entered into by a man who had had some sexual experience and a bride who had not.

That such was the theory, but not necessarily the practice, was revealed by empirical studies which began to be conducted in the middle of the twentieth century. Foremost amongst these was that of Kinsey in the USA. Kinsey and his collegues interviewed over 10 000, mainly middle class men and women. Their findings created a furore because they indicated that the great majority of males and over three-fifths of females had masturbated, that about 50 per cent of both sexes had had sexual intercourse before marriage and that over a third of men had some sexual experience of a homosexual nature (Kinsey, *et al.* 1948, Kinsey, *et al.* 1953).[5]

By 1960 Kinsey's interviews were supplemented in the USA by the laboratory research of Masters and Johnson who studied the physiological sexual responses of large samples of heterosexual subjects nearly all of whom were white and middle class although their later work included some studies of gay men and lesbian women.

During the later years of the twentieth century, the large scale and 'scientific' study of sexuality in the USA began to be supplemented by a large number of enquiries into sexual practice. For example by Nancy Friday's (1991) investigations into sexual fantasies and Sheryl Hite's (1976) documentation of how both men and women felt and thought about their own sexual experience.

These American studies created a climate of opinion in the USA which not only legitimized female as well as male sexuality and acknowledged the widespread practice of masturbation, premarital and postmarital sex but also, for the first time, accepted that for a substantial minority sexuality was not necessarily heterosexual.

Attitudes towards sexuality had always been rather more repressive in the USA and to some extent in Britain than they had been in other western countries. In those countries there has been, for some time, open acknowledgement not only of the similarity of the levels of male and female sexuality, but also of the diverse nature of sexual behaviour whether hetero or homosexual. More recently with the advent of Aids, open discussion of sexuality in all its diversity has become characteristic of all western societies. Before, however, looking at the diverse nature of sexuality in the west today, I would like to turn briefly to non-western views of sexuality.

Non-western models of sexuality

As the discussion above indicates the fact that females have as active an interest in sex as males has only recently been acknowledged in the west. This acknowledgement is obviously linked to the changes in the status of women that have occurred as women begin to play a more equal role in society in general. Extrapolating from this link between power and the social endorsement of sexuality, it could be argued that, in general, the more equal the social status of the sexes, the more likely it is that their level of sexuality will be viewed as similar.

This is a point of view that has been advanced by some anthropologists and has recently been put very forcibly by Helen Fisher. In general she makes the point that the relatively equal status of the sexes in hunting and gathering societies was, or in some cases still is, accompanied by an acceptance of very similar levels of sexual activity. Looking specifically at individual societies, she highlights traditional Australian Aboriginal society. Initially, she writes, this had been investigated by anthropologists, predominantly male, who had argued that practices such as the betrothal of infant girls to men 30 years their senior illustrated the subordinate nature of women in that society and also that Aboriginal women were 'pawns in the marriage manipulations of men'. More recently, however, she writes:

> Today we know that this picture of aboriginal life is distorted. Women ethnographers have gone into the Australian outback and talked to women . . . and have established that Australian aboriginal women politick avidly in the betrothal poker game and begin to choose their own new husbands by middle age. Women regularly engage lovers . . .
> Fisher (1992)

Similar patterns of sexuality emerge in other non-western societies. Not only in hunting and gathering societies but also in some pastoral societies where women own and inherit land and live with their own kin after marriage. In such societies, for example, in the case of the Vanantinai people of New Guinea, where there is little gender inequality in social roles, there is little evidence of differences in attitudes to male and female sexuality and 'sexual activity in Vanatinai is regarded as a pleasurable activity appropriate to both men and women from adolescence to old age' (Lepowsky, 1990).

On the other hand, in many non-western societies, where women have tended to be accorded lower social status than men, this inequality has had inevitable repercussions on attitudes to sexuality and marriage. This issue will be returned to later but in the interim it should be noted that cross-cultural data do not support the 'essentialist' position, which will be explored in the next two chapters, that female sexuality is innately more passive than male sexuality.

Aspects of sexuality

Open discussion of sexuality only really started to take place during the present century. Such discussions were, until very recently, dominated by both explicit and implicit assumptions that 'normal sexuality' is always heterosexual in nature. It was only with the publication of the Kinsey reports that the general public began to accept that a substantial minority of society rejected this assumption in terms of both inclination and practice. The remainder of this chapter discusses some of the terms used to discuss sexuality which could not be described as heterosexual.

Homosexuality and lesbianism

> Homosexuality, same-gender-sex, needs no introduction. From pre-Christian times, it has troubled, terrified – and inspired – the western mind and culture. Sodom and Gomorrah, the Cities of the Plain, were supposedly destroyed because of it; Paul warned the early Christians against it; leading scholars of the Church wrote eloquently opposing it; English kings were assassinated on suspicion of it; and countless common people have been victimized, blackmailed and persecuted because of it.
> Ruse (1988, p. ix)

As the quotation above indicates very powerfully, sexual preference is not, of course, only a matter of sexuality. Sexual orientation, if it is not heterosexual and if it is made overt, has implications that extend far beyond sexual relations because, in very many cultures, until recently such an orientation could lead not only to stigmatization and social rejection but also to imprisonment and sometimes persecution.

Yet the practice of homosexuality has been reported in almost all cultures (Shepherd, 1987), although the concept of a 'homosexual' is a relatively recent one and the term 'homosexual' was only coined in 1869 and did not come into common usage until the 1880s and 1890s (Weeks, 1987). This is because, although individuals might have formed same-sex sexual relations and indeed been persecuted for it, the concept of a homosexual 'identity' in the manner we think of it now did not exist.

Today, however, as Ruse (1988, p. ix) puts it, 'for various reasons, homosexuality seems particularly an obsession of our own age'. This is partially because homosexuals have been actively campaigning for their rights, partially because of the relatively greater openness about sexuality in general and partially because of the dread of Aids which, when it first appeared in the west, afflicted the homosexual rather than the heterosexual community.

The term, homosexual, is now usually taken to refer not only to a male who is attracted to members of his sex, but also to one who *identifies* with other males who feel the same way. The term is sometimes used in this way to include women who are erotically attracted to their own sex and who identify with other women who do so, but this usage is not common and such women are usually described as lesbians.

Both homosexuality and lesbianism have however, as the quote from Ruse indicates, emerged as issues with social, political and historical dimensions and we will be returning to the discussion of such issues. In doing so I will be looking at different accounts of lesbianism and homosexuality although my own position on it is well summed up by the following remarks made in 1987 by Celia Kitzinger:

> I no longer believe that there is a single 'correct' account of lesbianism (or any other social phenomenon) that will stand revealed once we have peeled away the layers of prejudice, special pleading and personal bias that form a veil between us and the 'facts'.

In other words, how and why individuals come to regard themselves as homo rather than heterosexual will differ from individual to individual. Similarly as we shall see, the reasons that are advanced by scientists and social scientists to account for the fact that sexual orientations vary, differ considerably and it is important to bear in mind that such accounts are not mutually exclusive. Different accounts may be needed if we are to come to some understanding of individual sexuality and sometimes we may need to view sexuality from more than one perspective.

Bisexuality
The term bisexual is used to describe individuals of either sex who feel erotic attachments to members of both sexes. Some researchers and clinicians maintain that there is no such thing as a 'true' bisexual only individuals, homo and heterosexual, who have confused identities (Unger and Crawford, 1992). This contention is also advanced by some members of the lesbian and homosexual communities and within these communities bisexuality is often an extremely contentious issue. Nevertheless, many individuals undoubtedly regard themselves as bisexual, either in orientation or in practice, or in both

orientation and practice. This is illustrated by a survey carried out by Carla Golden with 95 American Psychology of Women students in which 65 per cent identified themselves as heterosexual, 26 per cent as bisexual and 9 per cent as lesbian. Their sexual experience, however, was not reported as consistent with the survey in that 72 per cent reported that this was exclusively heterosexual, 20 per cent reported that it was bisexual, 4 per cent as lesbian while 4 per cent reported no sexual experience. As Golden (1987) put it, 'every possible permutation of feelings and activities existed within each sexual identification category'.

Bisexuality has been documented at other times in both western and non-western cultures. In the West, bisexuality was clearly practised extensively in ancient Greece, where it was customary for heterosexual married men to form strong erotic bonds with other younger men. In contemporary times bisexuality has been documented in some anthropological studies. For example, in the study carried out by Gillian Shepherd who worked amongst a Swahili community in Mombasa and described how homosexual relationships within this group are almost without exception between a younger, poorer partner and an older, richer one. However, both or either partner may also have had, or may in future continue to have, heterosexual relations. To take one example, a young woman, who was divorced by her husband, became the lover of an older, richer woman in order to gain financial security for herself and her children. Shepherd (1987) argues that within this particular community, where the existence of homosexuality is generally acknowledged by all, some individuals may move between sexual orientations in search both of social rank and of economic well-being.

For centuries the community Shepherd worked with in Mombasa has had close contact with the Gulf state of Oman. Bisexuality has also been reported there by Wikan (1977) in her discussion of a group of homosexuals she studied who were known as the Xanith. These individuals, who were biologically men and retained men's names, nevertheless dressed differently from other men and functioned differently in their association with women, in that they could talk with women and sit with women at segregated events and thus were able to violate the restrictions of purdah. (Purdah is the term used to describe the system whereby women, for reasons of modesty, are secluded from the company of men who are not of their immediate family.) Xanith, however, did not always retain the same gender role in that some of them married and became heterosexual and then in some cases after marriage reverted to homosexuality.

In general, in line with the studies just described, research on bisexuality indicates that for a minority of individuals sexuality is fluid. This fluidity has, however, seldom been explicitly acknowledged or permitted in the past. Recently, however, with increasing openness in the discussion of sexuality, individuals who regard themselves as bisexual have felt able to write and talk frankly and candidly about it. Furthermore novels and biographies now deal far less secretively with the issue as can be seen, for example, in the recent biography of the writer Daphne du Maurier which explores her emotional and sexual relationships with both sexes (Forster, 1993). Books such as this reflect the relatively greater latitude in the construction of both social and sexual identities that people now have in comparision to the past. We are indeed far less the prisoners of both the social class we were born into or the rigid sexual stereotypes of the past.

Transsexuality

Chapter 3 will look at the physiological aspects of sexual identity and will discuss in some detail the physiological conditions which make the assignation of sexual identity complicated as, for example, in the case of babies who are born with ambiguous sexual organs, or in the case of individuals with particular physical conditions which affect their levels of sex hormones. Such physiological conditions are bound to affect the formation of gender identity and in some cases the individuals concerned frequently have problems of gender identity. These problems are obviously related to their physical conditions.

Occasionally, however, certain individuals who differ in no physical aspect from others of their sex, feel convinced that they are trapped in the wrong-sexed body. Such individuals have been termed 'transsexuals' and this conviction is more common amongst males than females. It has been suggested the reason for this gender disparity lies in the different status of males and females in most societies. Because the male role is overvalued compared to the female, men who feel that they do not conform to masculine stereotypes are more likely to feel conflict than women who feel that they do not conform to feminine stereotypes. Thus, as Unger and Crawford (1992, p. 221) put it, 'men who deviate in some ways may come to believe that they are not men at all'. In any event there is no disputing the gender imbalance in transsexualism which is variously estimated to be between four to one, and eight to one.

The condition has been very well documented by Jan (formerly James) Morris (1974) in her book *Conundrum* in which she describes how, from earliest childhood, although her appearance was stereotypically male, she was unhappy with her identity as a boy. This unease culminated in an active desire to physically change her identity from male to female despite a career as a successful foreign correspondent and despite marriage and fatherhood. In order to make this change, she underwent extensive surgery and now lives and works unambiguously within a female identity.

It has been estimated that there are 30 000 transsexuals in the world, 10 000 of whom are believed to live in the United States (Grimm, 1987). Clinics, which provide the transformational surgery that transsexuals usually want, frequently make it a requirement that the person concerned lives and 'passes' as a member of the other sex for a specified period of time.

The outcome of such surgery is currently a matter of great controversy in that while some studies have indicated positive outcomes after surgery, other studies indicate that some transsexuals appear less well adjusted after surgery than before (Blanchard *et al.*, Lindemalm *et al.* 1986).

Transvestism

Transvestism is used to describe the practice of dressing in the clothes, and taking the appearance of, members of the other sex and more recently has tended to be termed 'cross-dressing'.

The history of transvestism can be traced both in individual biographies and in the impersonation of one sex by the other in the theatre and more recently through the mass media. Turning first to a discussion of the former, there are many documented instances of women living their lives in the persona of men in order to escape the limitations of the traditional female role. A notable example of this is the case of Deborah Sampson, an eighteenth century American woman, who served in the army, was decorated and was only discovered to be a woman when she was hospitalized (Williams, 1987).

The impersonation of the other sex in the theatre is, of course, rooted in the fact that until the eighteenth century, in the west, women were seldom permitted to appear on the stage. But even after women began to play most female roles in the theatre the impersonation of the opposite sex has continued in a number of genre. These impersonations are sometimes satirical as in the pantomine dame or as in Barry Humphrey's portrayal of the Australian suburban housewife and self-styled superstar, Dame Edna Everidge. At other times, gender impersonations are camped up as in the 'glamour' portrayals of performers like Danny La Rue and in the tongue-in-cheek 'gender-bending' of Madonna. Gender impersonation is also still to be found in the serious theatre, for example, in some of the productions of the Glasgow Citizens Theatre when males play female roles.

Transvestism is also practised by some individuals within the privacy of their homes and sometimes in social groups with other transvestites. The stigma previously associated with it has indeed been so eroded that a chain of shops catering to the fashion needs of male transvestites has recently been established in Britain (*Today*, Radio 4 3.3.1993) and it has been the subject of a number of plays and films.

In general, most transvestites are not homosexual in orientation. Indeed Ruse (1988, p. 4) maintains that they are 'if anything' heterosexual 'to a more extreme degree than usual'. Nevertheless there is a considerable minority of homosexuals who do cross-dress.

In a recent book, devoted to the subject of cross-dressing, Marjorie Garber (1993) has claimed that the individual who cross-dresses poses a challenge to cultural certainties about gender. Reviewing the history of cross-dressing, she argues that society has always tended to regard cross-dressers as 'male or female manque' (aiming at, but not successfully achieving, the other gender). She contends, however, that cross-dressers should be seen more appropriately as simply individuals who subvert and challenge social conventions by their appearance and sometimes, but not necessarily, by their behaviour.

It could be argued that in recent years more open attitudes to sexuality, and less restricted views of stereotyped male and female behaviour, have permitted a degree of experimentation for all of us in our self-presentation. These tendencies are obvious, not only in the increasing numbers of cross-dressers but also in the phenomenon of unisex fashions and hairstyle. As with sexuality, there is more acceptance of flexibility in the way we dress and look.

Summary

This chapter has been concerned with the definition and discussion of gender and sexuality in general. The discussion was first located in the context of the unequal status that has until very recently characterized males and females. Following these preliminary observations three modes of gender categorization were introduced. These will be followed up in the next five chapters. They are 'essentialist' gender categorization (chapters 2 and 3), social and behavioural categorizations (chapters 4 and 5) and structural categorizations (chapter 6).

This outline of categorization systems was followed by a survey of historical aspects of the study of sexuality. The chapter concluded with the discussion of a number of terms concerned with sexuality, i.e. homosexuality, lesbianism, bisexuality, transsexuality and transvestism.

Notes

1. Durrell (1963) writing about Justine in the book of that name.
2. In Lord Arthur Savile's Crime in Borges (1966).
3. See chapter 6 where anthropological studies show that in some societies which were, or are, relatively egalitarian in nature, sexual inequalities were, or are, negligible. See for example (Lepowsky, 1990).
4. Sayings quoted in Kakar's (1990) book about sexuality in India by an Indian psycho-analyst.
5. More recent figures give rather different estimates. For example, a recent Harris survey, reported that 4.4 per cent of American males and 3.6 per cent of American females have had homosexual sex in the past five years (Guardian, 26 April 1993, p. 22).

Chapter 2

Tarzan, Jane and Boadicea

Woman wants monogamy;
Man delights in novelty.
Love is woman's moon and sun;
Man has other forms of fun.
Woman lives but for her Lord;
Count to ten, and man is bored.
With this gist and sum of it,
What earthly good can come of it?

Dorothy Parker, General Review of the Sex Situation (1989) reproduced by permission
of Gerald Duckworth & Co Ltd.

In the last chapter, it was suggested that many people feel intuitively that
the observed differences in the behaviour of the sexes are very easy to explain:
these differences are due to differences in the nature of the sexes and because
of this such differences are not only universal but extremely difficult, if not
impossible, to eradicate. This essentialist perspective has been developed in
two ways. One of these, the approach that derives from psychoanalysis, will
be considered in this chapter.

Freud's perspective on gender differences

Maleness combines (the factors of) subject, activity and possession of
the penis, femaleness takes over (those of) object and passivity.

Sigmund Freud (1923 in Strackey, 1977)

The origins of psychoanalysis

Sigmund Freud (1856–1939), the founder of the movement called psychoanalysis, has had a unique impact on western understanding of the human
mind. He was born into a middle class Jewish family in Moravia and later
moved with his family to Vienna where he was educated. After studying physiology, he eventually qualified as a doctor in 1881 but it was not until 1885
when he went to Paris to study with the famous neurologist, Jean Charcot, that
he first became interested primarily in the mind. This interest was precipitated
by Charcot's work with what was termed hysterical patients who were primarily

female. The term 'hysteria' was used to describe conditions like paralysis, loss of speech and blindness which had no apparent physiological causes. It derived from the Greek word, *hystera*, meaning uterus, because ancient Greek physicians believed that its symptoms were caused by the wandering of the uterus through the body.

Although Charcot believed that hysterical symptoms did have some roots in neurological pathology, he also believed that the symptoms could be alleviated by using hypnotic sessions during which patients were induced to believe that their symptoms would be relieved when they emerged from the hypnotic sessions. Returning to Vienna, Freud integrated Charcot's approach to hysteria with the approach of an older Viennese physician, Josef Breuer, who claimed that hysterical conditions could be alleviated by what one of his patients called 'the talking cure' during which the patient, in a trancelike state, spoke both about her symptoms and about unpleasant events she associated with them. Freud developed these techniques further into a particular approach to dealing with problems of the mind which he called **psychoanalysis**.

Psychoanalysis is based on Freud's conviction that the roots of human motivation and consequently the causes of human behaviour lie in deeply submerged and suppressed memories of early emotional relationships. According to Freud such memories are characteristically both very intense and very painful. The pain arises, according to Freud, from the depth of unresolved conflicts with parents which are almost invariably experienced during the early years of life. He believed that as a result of these painful associations many memories of our early years tend to be heavily suppressed and to become unavailable to conscious thought. Instead, according to Freud, such memories become lodged in a kind of mental repository which Freud called the **unconscious**.[1] During psychoanalysis, the analyst's task is to bring the memory of these conflicts to the fore, by taking them out of the unconscious and making them accessible to conscious thought. This retrieval is carried out by means of the twin psychoanalytic techniques which Freud had developed from Breuer's 'talking cure'. The two techniques are **free association** and the **interpretation of dreams**. In the former, patients are required to talk about anything that comes into their minds, in the latter to recount their dreams and fantasies. In both cases patients are encouraged to report all their thoughts, feelings, dreams and fantasies freely and without reservation.

Freud believed that by thus freely associating and recounting their dreams patients are able to allow the analyst an access into their unconscious. The task of the analyst is then to interpret the material that has emerged from the patient's unconscious, that is to expose the hidden meanings underlying the associations and dreams. The psychic conflicts thus interpreted were seen by Freud to have arisen primarily in very early childhood from the interactions of family dynamics and, consequently, he believed that it was important for the patient and analyst to go beyond the stage of interpretation. This is achieved by the process of **transference**. During transference, the psychoanalyst attempts to allow the patient to displace on to the analyst the unresolved conflicts with his or her parents which had arisen during early childhood. As can be imagined, because the material the psychoanalyst has to work on emerges only indirectly, psychoanalysis has traditionally been a very time consuming process. Psychoanalytic sessions typically take place two or even three times a week and often continue for years.[2] (Training as a psychoanalyst is even more time consuming in that all psychoanalysts are required to undergo extensive psychoanalysis themselves before being regarded as qualified to practice.)

It was from consideration of the material emerging from the psychoanalytic sessions with his patients, as well as from his research into some anthropological material (Freud, 1983), that Freud developed his body of theory. This is summarized briefly below with particular reference to Freud's complex and often contradictory views on masculinity and femininity. But before doing so let us look briefly at Freud's relationship with the women in his personal and professional life.

Freud's relationships with women

Freud's home life was marked both by predictability and stability. His marriage was reputedly very happy and he was a devoted father to a family of three sons and three daughters; indeed for the greater part of his life he lived in the same house and used the same consulting rooms until he was forced to flee to London when the Nazis took power in Austria.

Within his domestic sphere, it seems that his attitude to his wife was essentially one which reflected the conventional middle class of his time. In his early years he had reacted strongly against the feminist argument for the equality of the sexes and apparently thought the idea that some women could, in the future, earn as much as their husbands 'absurd'. Indeed his attitude towards the role of wives precluded such a notion as was reflected in the remarks made in a letter to his wife which has frequently been quoted:

> Law and custom, have much to give women that has been witheld from them, but the position of women will surely be what it is: in youth an adored darling and in mature years a loving wife.
> Williams (1987, p. 29)

His attitude towards his children largely reflected the conventional views of his time with respect to issues of gender. For example when his youngest daughter Anna was born he wrote to his close friend Wilhelm Fliess as follows:

> If it had been a son I should have sent you the news by telegram. But as it is a little girl . . . . . . you get the news later.
> (Sayers, 1992)

The children were brought up in a very conventional manner and despite the obvious interest his younger daughter Anna showed in forging a career for herself, she was not sent to schools that would have prepared her for university entrance. Instead she went to the local cottage lyceum which, according to Janet Sayers (1992), she later described as 'quite stultifying'. Anna, nevertheless, did not follow the example of her older sisters and marry young. Instead, after a period of teaching and working with young children, she eventually underwent a training analysis and joined her father in the practice of psychoanalysis.

Despite his earlier lack of encouragement of Anna's aspirations it seems that once she joined him in practice Freud had no difficulty in working with her as a peer. Indeed Freud's relations with women psychoanalysts seems to have been far easier and less problematic than his relationships with male analysts which were frequently characterized by bitter disputes and considerable animosity (Masson, 1990).

It is probably fair to say, as the brief discussion above shows, that in his personal life Freud's relationships with women indicated considerable ambivalence. While clearly having some reservations about the extent to which women should be involved in professional as compared to domestic pursuits, he was nevertheless able to have excellent professional relationships with them.[3] As we shall now see, his theories about the differences between men and women reflected similar ambiguities.

Freud and psychosexual development

As is very well known, Freud placed an enormous emphasis on sexuality as a well-spring of human behaviour. In Freud's theories sexuality was mediated through an energizing force he called **libido**. The influence of libido according to Freud is felt even at birth and from then throughout the human life span this energy needs to be discharged or 'consummated' in some manner. Consummation of sexuality, however, is obviously not always easily attainable and in discussing how this need for consummation is controlled, Freud outlined three aspects of the human mind. The first, the **id**, is the actual seat of the instincts, which of course includes the libido or the sexual drive. The id represents the desire to attain pleasure and it operates largely in the unconscious. It is kept in check by two other aspects of the mind. The first of these, the **ego**, operates in the conscious and strives to keep the id under control by responding realistically to the demands of the external world. The other aspect, the **super-ego**, represents the part of the mind in which self observation and self criticism take place. As we shall see, Freud posited major differences between the sexes in the operation of the super-ego.

It is not possible, however, to understand Freud's conceptualization of sex differences without reference to his description of the development of the libido. In the earliest years, according to Freud, libido is undifferentiated and the young infant simply has a generalized propensity to sexuality which he termed **polymorphous sexuality**. Depending on the experiences of early childhood, this polymorphous sexuality develops through what Freud termed the **psychosexual stages** into either normal[4] heterosexuality or into less usual behaviours such as homosexuality or fetishes.

Freud referred to the first of these stages as the **oral** stage. In the oral stage, the infant's source of gratification and pleasure, and the discharge of libido, is associated with feeding and sucking, and the lips and mouth become the source of sexual pleasure. In the next phase, the **anal** stage, reached during the second and third years of life, sexual pleasure moves to the anal region as an erotogenic zone as the child becomes able to control his or her bowel activity. According to Freud there is no difference between the sexes during these first two stages but for both sexes, both the oral and anal stage can be the source of later sexual 'perversions'. For example the tendency towards masochism, in which pleasure is taken in the experiencing of pain, or sadism, in which pleasure is experienced in the administration of pain.

By the time the child is three or four, he or she has attained mastery over anal functions and, according to Freud, now discovers the potential of the genitals and of infantile masturbation.[5] Thus erotic attention now moves to the genitals and the child enters into the third stage, the **phallic** stage, and it is this stage which will prove crucial for his or her gender development.

As they enter this stage both boys and girls, according to Freud, have the mother as their most important love object. In the case of the boy this devotion to the mother starts to become problematic when he begins to perceive his father as rival for her favours. Simultaneously he discovers that women and girls do not have a penis as he does and he comes to the conclusion that theirs have been cut off. He now becomes extremely anxious that the same fate may befall him (a fear Freud termed **castration anxiety**). Fuelled by this anxiety and by terror of his more powerful rival (his father), the boy moves his emotional identification from the mother to the father and begins to identify with, and to model, the behaviour of his father. In this way the boy both appeases his rival and acquires a masculine gender identity. Identification with the father also involves taking on the father's moral values and it is in this way that the super-ego is developed.

Freud referred to this phallic period as the time of the **Oedipus complex**, because of the resemblance his analysis had to the Greek drama, **Oedipus Rex**, in which a young prince is abandoned at birth because of a prophecy that he will kill his father and subsequently marry his mother. The prophecy is fulfilled when the child is rescued and, unaware of his parentage, in early manhood kills his father and marries his mother.

During his earlier writings, Freud did not really explore the manner in which the girl experienced the phallic stage in much detail, apparently finding female sexuality very puzzling. He noted, for example, after a discussion of male sexual development that 'the corresponding processes in the girl are not known to us' (Freud, 1923 in Strachey, 1976). In later life, however, he wrote three papers (Freud, 1925, 1931 and 1933) in which he developed the following scenario for the girl's experience of the phallic stage. As she enters it she becomes aware of her own lack of a penis and, according to Freud, becomes from that stage on 'a victim to envy of the penis' (Williams, 1987, pp. 34–5). Further she believes that she has been castrated, and blames her mother for this. As a consequence she rejects her mother as her most important love object and replaces her by her father whom she comes to believe would be able to give her a baby, a son, who will in effect give her the longed for penis. As she grows older, she transfers this wish for the father into a wish for a husband. In this way the girl begins to develop her female sexuality. Her intense relationship with her mother also continues, however, and in identifying with her mother she also takes on feminine attributes. In a similar manner to the boy she also at this stage 'introjects' (or internalizes) her parents' moral values into her super-ego but for reasons that will be described below this process is, according to Freud, less intense for the girl than for the boy.

Following the phallic stage both sexes were seen by Freud as entering two further stages: the latency stage when sexuality is relatively dormant and then the genital stage where sexual desire in both sexes is directed towards members of the opposite sex.

This reading of sexual development rests crucially on three propositions:

1. that gender differences are forged in the phallic stage;
2. that for both sexes the possession or non-possession of the penis is central to the development of gender;
3. that both sexes perceive that the girl's genitals are not only different to the boy's but also inferior.

There is no doubt that this is rather a male biased viewpoint and as we proceed through this chapter we will look at the challenges that have been made by women theorists to this perspective. For the moment, however, let us look at the major implications for sex differences in psychological functioning that Freud drew from this theory (Mitchell, 1974).

Freud and sex differences

In the *first* instance, according to Freud, the sexes differ because women habitually feel inferior to men. This sense of inferiority derives directly from their envy of the penis:

> The psychical consequences of envy for the penis . . . are various and far reaching . . . she develops like a scar, a sense of inferiority.
> (Freud, 1925)

Men, on the other hand, feel no such generalized sense of inferiority to women.

Secondly, Freud believed that the sexes differ in their propensity to masochism. For, although he accepted that individual men could display masochism, he regarded the attribute of masochism as inherently 'feminine'. This is because masochism springs from the phallic stage during which, because of her perception that she lacks a penis, the girl forms a desire for passive intercourse with a sexually aggressive father as well as a desire for childbirth. Both these unconscious desires are seen by Freud as suggesting pleasure-in-pain and consequently as a direct result of the dynamics of this stage, women tend towards masochism and masochism, in either sex, was associated by Freud with femininity.

According to Freud a *third* aspect of sex difference also has its roots in the phallic stage when the boy is made more anxious by the threat of castration than the girls is by penis er.vy. The boy deals with this greater menace by a correspondingly deeper identification with the father and a correspondingly greater need to take over his moral standards in comparison to the girl's identification with the mother. As you may recall Freud located these aspects of human functioning in the super-ego and as a result Freud believed that men have a more active super-ego and a more compelling sense of justice than do women.

A *fourth* aspect of sexual difference, according to Freud, lies in women's greater tendency towards jealousy, narcissism (a preoccupation with self[6]) and vanity. Freud believed that these characteristics also derived from the phallic stage: jealousy from the girl's penis envy, narcissism and vanity from her desire to compensate for her lack of a penis by making her whole body into a 'proud substitute' (Mitchell, 1974, p. 116) for a penis.

The *final* aspect of sexual difference that Freud discussed is perhaps not only the most important in his eyes but also the one aspect which he located not only in the dynamics of the phallic stage but also in biology. This is the assertion that *masculinity is associated with activity and femininity with passivity* which he saw as deriving, to some extent, from nature. Primarily these were differences in aggressiveness, in physical strength and in intensity of libido, which characteristics he believed to be stronger in men than in women. In this respect his remark that 'biology is destiny' is often quoted (Freud, 1940). Freud also regarded this activity/passivity difference as partially due to the girl's need in the phallic stage to be loved by the father and her later need to be actively loved by her husband.

It was with respect to this attribute of agency that he showed most ambivalence because, while he clearly believed in innate differences between the sexes, writing that 'we are faced . . . by the great enigma of the biological fact of the duality of the sexes' (Freud, 1940), he also apparently believed that the infant is born bisexual and that it is only in the phallic stage, by means of 'identification' with the same sex parent, that the child enters on the pathway to man or womanhood. He also sometimes indicated that it was inappropriate to always identify males with activity and females with passivity because of the 'fact of psychological bisexuality'. Nevertheless, and despite his occasional reservations, he did regard men and women as essentially different. Even if he was ambivalent and sometimes contradictory in his discussion of the origins of this difference, he frequently wrote as though there were unambiguous sex differences in personality. For Freud, men were active, with a strong sense of morality and a keen 'social interest' (Mitchell, 1974, p. 52), women were weak, passive, vain and narcissistic.

In summary, then, there is no doubt that Freud believed that there were major differences between the sexes and these differences were inevitable and natural. To this extent his position is regarded as an essentialist one and this essentialist stance has been echoed by the great majority of post-Freudians. The next two sections will look at the views on sex differences of some of his followers and critics, and at contemporary feminist viewpoints on sex differences which derive from psychoanalysis.

Freud's followers and critics

Freud's ideas about sex differences were by no means universally accepted by his students and followers. Most, however, echoed his overall orientation in three ways.

1. They regarded the early years of life as of supreme importance in the moulding of gender as well as of other aspects of personality.
2. They placed a great deal of emphasis on the effect of the differences in genital physiology.
3. They believed that there were essential differences in the nature of men and women.

Erik Erikson, for example, who underwent a training analysis with Freud's daughter Anna, located the sources of sex differences, like Freud, in the human body. He argued that it is the physical design of the human body; the inner space of the womb and the vagina, which signifies the women's biological, psychological and moral commitment to motherhood, and the possession of the penis which predisposes men to be concerned with achievement and exploration. While Erikson believed that this led to women possessing, in comparison to men, some superior qualities e.g. greater sympathy, these qualities are all linked to her innate need to nurture. However women's inner space can, according to Erikson, lead to despair as well as to fulfilment, if she experiences any form of rejection:

> To be left for her, means to be empty, to be drained of the blood of the body, the warmth of the heart, the sap of life . . . such hurt can be re-experienced in each menstruation, it is crying to heaven in the morning over a child and it becomes a permanent scar in the menopause.
> Erikson (1968)

Men, on the other hand, as possessors of the active penis were both more concerned with achievements outside the family and more suited to life outside the family circle, although Erikson conceded that for both sexes the particular culture into which they were born could modify these sex differences to some extent.[7]

Thus, Erikson, though placing relatively little stress on the dynamics of the phallic stage, nevertheless continued the Freudian tradition of relating gender differences to physiological differences and regarding men and women as essentially different in nature.

While Erikson was critical of many aspects of traditional Freudian theory his work was very much within the classical psychoanalytic tradition. The eminent psychoanalyst Carl Jung, however, while retaining much of Freud's clinical methodology and insistence on the importance of the unconscious, rejected one of Freud's central contentions: that libido was the driving force in human life. While any detailed discussion of Jung is beyond the scope of this book, it is perhaps relevant to look very briefly at Jung's understanding of gender differences. Jung (1953) contended that a very important role in the unconscious is played by two fundamental components, the **anima** and the **animus**. The anima is the repository of feminine characteristics that exists in the male unconscious and the animus is the repository of male characteristics that exists in the female unconscious. Thus the behaviour of women can sometimes be influenced by the masculine components of their unconscious and vice versa. What is interesting, however, from the viewpoint of sex differences is that Jung took as indisputable the idea that there are two opposing styles of psychological functioning – the feminine and the masculine. The feminine style embraces the caring, the nurturing and the passive; the male, the adventurous, the striving and the active. Thus although Jung differed from Freud in many ways, he concurred in his acceptance of essential differences in the nature of masculinity and femininity.

It was not, however, only male analysts who continued the Freudian tradition with respect to sex differences. Helen Deutsch for example, who spent some time in analysis with Freud, also assumed that the nature of the physiological differences between the sexes predisposes them to different psychological functioning. In particular, according to Deutsch, women's anatomy and physiology provides a basis for their ultimate destinies as wives and mothers. Men's destinies are not so constrained and thus they are far more active than women in society at large.

Deutsch also followed Freud in accepting the role in the girl's development of penis envy, although, unlike Freud, she believed that boys could experience this as well. She also differed from Freud to some extent in her understanding of the balance of the role of the parents in the phallic stage. She ascribed far more importance to the mother, particularly in the case of the girl (Sayers, 1992), arguing that the girl's future development was more tied in with her early relationship with her mother than with her idolization of her father.

According to Deutsch, femininity was very clearly distinguishable from masculinity and was marked by a triad of personality factors already identified by Freud: narcissism, passivity and masochism. Her tendency towards passivity was, for Deutsch, the centre of femininity, as was the man's tendency towards activity the centre of masculinity. Deutch developed a position in which this basic difference predisposed women to being more intuitive and receptive and men to being more rational and aggressive.

Deutsch's rather extreme version of biological determinism has, not surprisingly, been heavily attacked by feminists and her own writing reveals that she experienced considerable conflicts in reconciling her own views of women with her own active professional life (Deutsch, 1973).

Karen Horney who was born in 1885, just one year after Helen Deutsch, was like Deutsch trained as a classical psychoanalyst. Unlike Deutsch, however, she was very critical of Freud's delineation of sex differences and particularly of the role of penis envy in the psychological development of women. She pointed out how much psychoanalysis had been influenced by the male bias of psychoanalytic observers and that psychoanalytic ideas about the phallic stage reflected a little boy's views rather than those of a little girl. In this way she threw doubt on Freud's hypothesis that the little girl believes she 'lost' her penis. There is no reason, she argued, to believe that little girls perceive themselves as lacking anything. While some girls may grow up feeling inferior, this derives not from their observed lack of a penis but from the fact that they are 'forced into a flight from womanhood' because masculine attributes are culturally accepted as more desirable than feminine ones.

Furthermore, she argued, boys are equally likely to suffer from envy of the opposite sex, of the events of motherhood, pregnancy and childbirth, and it is this envy which drives them, in some cases, into both denying the worth of women and into a ceaseless desire to be active and productive in the world outside the home.

While Horney was thus very critical of the male bias of Freudian psychoanalysis, for much of her life she placed an important emphasis not only on the phallic stage, but also on the influence of the sex differences in physiology on later sex differences in psychological functioning. As she grew older, however, she moved towards a position which ascribed less and less importance to 'biological destiny' and more and more importance to the role of the social environment (Horney, 1967). In this position her views on sex differences were very similar to those of another very influential early psychoanalyst, Alfred Adler.

Adler, was a doctor with a particular interest in psychological medicine, who joined Freud as one of the founder members of the Vienna Psychoanalytic Society. He was also one of the early collaborators with whom Freud was later to differ most bitterly. This was largely because, like Jung and like Horney in her later years, Adler rejected the all powerful role of libido in psychological development and was far more concerned with the role of the social environment. With respect to sex differences Adler (1954) argued that if a girl feels inferior to boys it is largely because she has been born into a society which is biased and 'robs her of her belief in her own value'. Unlike Freud who ascribed neuroticism in both men and women to the dynamics of their early relationships with their parents in the phallic stage, Adler ascribed neuroses to problems that both sexes experience in overcoming their infantile experience of powerlessness. This striving is more complicated for women, according to Adler, because:

> All our institutions, our traditional attitudes, our laws, our morals, and customs, give evidence of the fact that they (women) are determined and maintained by privileged males for the glory of male domination.
> Alfred Adler (Tong, 1992, pp. 147–8)

This is, of course, a view that is hardly controversial today but at the beginning of the century Adler's highlighting of the domestic social injustices experienced by women was relatively unusual within the psychoanalytic community, which on the whole, tended to concentrate attention on the impact on psychological functioning of biological differences between the sexes.

Adler's views on sex differences were very much in tune with the views of the growing academic schools of psychology within universities in both America and Europe where both theories and empirical studies began to centre on the importance of the social environment in the home in the creation of sex differences. These approaches will be discussed in detail in chapters 5 and 6, but we will conclude this chapter by looking at those twentieth century developments in psychoanalytic views of sex differences which have been influenced by feminism.

Recent trends in psychoanalysis

> Women were just about to take off on their own when a catastrophe befell them: Freud.
> Benoite Groult (Olivier, 1989)

Psychoanalytic views on sex differences continue to be very influential even towards the end of the twentieth century. In this section we will look at two of the major areas where their impact continues. The first of these is in the clinical practice of women who continue the Freudian tradition of ascribing sex differences to the crucible of the early years in the family.

Nancy Chodorow and the role of the mother

Nancy Chodorow (1979) retains in her work Freud's emphasis on the effect on sex differences of the experiences of infancy. In fact she traces these to a period before the phallic stage when, because the infant is small and helpless, it is totally reliant on its chief caretaker, whom Chodorow takes to be normally its mother. The child initially has great difficulty in differentiating itself from its mother, but with growing physical and cognitive maturation begins to define itself in relation to its primary caretaker.

This process develops differently for boys and girls. Girls grow up with a sense of similarity to, and continuity with, their mothers while boys have to learn a different sense of gender identity and, because fathers are less often present than mothers, they have a more precarious sense of gender identity. In order to compensate for this they become more concerned than girls with knowing what is 'masculine' and what is 'feminine' and in drawing the boundaries between these attributes. Mothers contribute to these growing differences, according to Chodorow, because they have themselves been girls and consequently they experience their daughters as an extension of themselves but their sons as 'male opposites'. In this way, they encourage girls to identify with them and boys to differentiate themselves from them.

Chodorow argues that these early gender differences in identity formation have important consequences for personality differences in later life. Girls emerge with a capacity for empathy and a set of emotional needs which are tied to the desire for being connected to other human beings, and which commit them to the destiny of nurturing others, notably their own children. Boys, on the other hand, who have learned to define masculinity as the opposite of femininity, grow into men who devalue women and who believe in the superiority of whatever qualities they define as masculine.

Thus, according to Chodorow, each generation, reproduces the traditional sex differences of caring, empathic women and rational, achieving men not because of their biology but because masculine – feminine differences are continually reproduced in the dynamics of early family life. Thus, while rejecting Freud's emphasis on the importance of the phallic stage and penis envy, she accepts his basic argument that later personality development, and consequent sex differences, depend crucially on the earliest years of life and their influence on unconscious processes.

Chodorow's influence can be traced in the work of a number of contemporary women therapists who are concerned particularly with working with women. For example in the work of Susie Orbach and Luise Eichenbaum (1982) who, while rejecting much of traditional psychoanalytic practice, retain in their approach Freud's stress on the importance of the experiences of early childhood within the nuclear family, and its continuing effect not only on unconscious motivation but also on the reproduction of gender differences.

Other contemporary women analysts base much of their work on the approach of Jung and his concepts of the anima and the animus. Thus, Young-Eisendrath and Wiedemann (1987), for example, continue the Jungian tradition of considering gender to be based on basic unconscious representations of masculinity and femininity (the **animus** and the **anima**) which are different from each other in fundamental ways, and which consist of aspects of gender identity covering images, ideas and feelings about the opposite sex. Although they accept that culture can modify the animus and the anima they, like Freud, Jung and the other theorists we have discussed in this section, make clear distinctions between the feminine and the masculine and regard these differences as 'essential'.

Although the influence of psychoanalysis was felt almost immediately in the English speaking world, in the twentieth century its influence has been nowhere more powerful than in France where it underwent a particular transformation in the work of Jacques Lacan and his followers.

Lacan and sex differences

In order to understand Lacan, who is a notoriously difficult writer, it is important to relate him to the contemporary intellectual debate about gender in France which has been very much concerned with three concepts.

The first of these is relatively straightforward and derives largely from the writing of Simone de Beauvoir to whose work we shall return in chapter 6. This is that in almost all the social, psychological and philosophical thought of the western world, the viewpoint has been male rather than female. In the phrase de Beauvoir made famous, the female is 'the other'. The second and third of these concepts are often referred to as central to 'Deconstuctionism'.[8] The first of these is that, despite our subjective feeling that we have a unified sense of self, this notion of a unified core is deceptive because our self is fundamentally split between its unconscious and conscious dimensions. The second is that reality is not absolute but relative, and that our understanding of it is affected by the language we think in and the values that we have unconsciously absorbed from our culture. As Tong (1992) notes, these ideas are fundamentally unsettling because they imply that there is neither self-identity nor absolute truth.

Lacan drew on all three constructs in his discussion of the differences between males and females. Arguing that both sexes develop in a symbolic world in which the accepted reality is that of the male, he claimed that both sexes had to fit into a society which reflected a male view — the 'Law of the Father'.

Lacan based his views of child development on those developed by Freud, accepting both the important influence of infancy and early childhood on the unconscious and also the notion of psychosexual stages.[9] However, he outlined them somewhat differently although, like Freud, he thought that there were no differences between the sexes in the first phase.

He labelled the first stage the *imaginary* phase and he claimed that in the beginning of this phase the child has no sense of where his or her boundaries begin or end, because the child is totally tied up psychologically with the mother. In the second part of the imaginary phase, which Lacan called the *mirror* phase, the child begins to realize that his or her reflection in a mirror is a representation of him or herself. Lacan believed that this recognition is very significant because it is the precursor of all our understanding of ourselves, in that the self can only find itself through reflection (in this case the mirror) and later in the way we are reflected in others. As the child leaves the mirror phrase he or she takes away the realization that although the mirror represents him or herself, the image is not its real self. Henceforth self is split.

According to Lacan, sex differences are forged in the next phase which Lacan, following Freud, called the *Oedipal* phase. As the child enters the Oedipal phase he or she leaves the world of the 'imaginary' and enters the *symbolic order* – the system of social relationships embodied in language into which we must all fit and which is dominated by the 'Law of the Father'. Sex differences, as has been noted above, originate here as well. To begin with, in the case of both sexes, the child disassociates itself from the mother. The boy, fearing symbolic castration,[10] separates from his mother and in exchange, identifies with the male symbolic order, primarily through language. In a similar way to Freud, Lacan then sees the boy taking over the role of the male. This role is far more powerful than the female role and its power is evident in that the male point of view permeates language, law and custom. It is characterized by the phrase already referred to and for which Lacan is famous, the Law of the Father. In the case of the girl, Lacan argued, identification with the powerful male role is impossible, because of her anatomy, and she is excluded from a powerful role in society and is forced to take the role of 'the other' – in all spheres of life including the sexual. Lacan believed that women's sexual pleasure is, of necessity, more repressed than men's. As Tong (1992, p. 222) notes, 'women were for Lacan permanent outsiders'.

Not surprisingly, women theorists in France have found Lacan's conclusions very unpalatable. The best known refutation of his views by a woman psychoanalyst is found in the work of Luce Irigary. Irigary focuses on the Oedipal phase in her disagreements with Lacan, arguing that it is more difficult for girls than boys to leave this phase because the 'symbolic order' is so male dominated and, as a result, women tend to remain in the 'imaginary'.

But according to Irigary 'rather than viewing this entrapment as sheer negativity (Tong, 1992, p. 226) women can develop fuller lives by following three strategies. The first of these is to reclaim and reshape male dominated language. The second is to subvert the way men regard women by overplaying the stereotyped feminine role and the third is to regard her sexuality as superior, not inferior, to men. Like other French female psychoanalysts she celebrates the fact that sexuality in women is not tied to the 'big dick' (Irigary, 1985) but envelops her whole body:

> So woman does not have a sex organ? She has at least two of them,
> but they are not identifiable as ones. Indeed she has many more. Her
> sexuality is always at least double, goes even further: it is plural.
> Helen Cixous (Tong, 1992)

In their celebration of the superior erotic potential of women, psychoanalysts and other women theorists in France (for example, Julia Kristeva and Helen Cixous) draw closer to the ideas of some contemporary feminist writers who argue, not only that there is an innate biologically determined feminine core that is different to the innate masculine core, but also that it leads to more compassionate and less violent behaviour. This approach will be discussed briefly in the next chapter.

Issues of dominance

Everywoman adores a Fascist
The boot in the face, the brute
Brute heart of a brute like you
Sylvia Plath *Daddy* 1985

As we have seen central to psychoanalytic notions of sex difference is the passive/active dimension, and related to this dimension is the concept of masochism. The majority of psychoanalytic writers have argued that, because of her relatively passive role in sexuality, it is normal for a women to exhibit masochistic tendencies. Indeed, Helen Deutsch contended that masochism, passivity and narcissism are the three key characteristics of the female personality. The most extreme portrayal of female masochism by psychoanalysts is probably that of the analyst Marie Bonaparte (1953) who characterized sexual intercourse as follows:

> The woman, in effect, is subjected to a sort of beating by the man's penis. She receives its blows and often, even, loves the violence.

Karen Horney, who was far more critical of Freud's notions about feminity, rejected the notion that female masochism derives from the sexual act, arguing that it could far better be explained by cultural conditioning in a society where women are treated as inferiors. Nevertheless, the notion that women enjoy sexual subjugation has lingered in psychoanalysis together with belief, first proposed by Freud, that masochism in men is evidence of a degree of feminization.

More recently, Jessica Benjamin (1988) in a reinterpretation of psychoanalytic approaches to masochism has argued that two fantasies predominate in the very young child. The first of these fantasies concerns an image of an all-powerful mother who can and will do everything for the child, controls the child, and who may never let it go with the possible end result that the child may never attain autonomy and may indeed be destroyed. The second fantasy is of the omnipotent child who will totally control the mother and the end result of this might be that the mother could in effect 'disappear' and as a result be lost to the child. Thus for Benjamin, unlike for most psychoanalysts, the mother may at times be a very powerful figure.

According to Benjamin these fantasies of domination and subjugation remain in the unconscious and often play a vital part in healthy sexuality which according to Benjamin often 'plays' with notions of domination and subordination. She believes that both sexes have the capacity for playing either the subordinate or dominant role but that, because of the Oedipal phase, men tend towards escape from the powerful mother, hence adopting the dominant role, while girls tend towards identification with the mother and hence adopt the passive role.

Psychoanalysts were not of course the first people to propose that the activity dimension – men are active, women passive – is basic to gender differences. This notion, with particular reference to sexuality, has dominated western literary works from the early novels of Samuel Richardson (1980) to those of many contemporary authors like Ian McEwan (1982) and Norman Mailer (1991). And indeed as the quote from Sylvia Palth's poem <i>Daddy</i> (above) indicates, the work of certain women authors as well. Further, as we have seen in chapter 1, it is only recently that medical opinion has accepted that women's sexuality is not essentially passive.

Empirical studies, however, as we shall see in the next chapter reveal few, if any gender differences in levels of sexuality. And, indeed, parallel with the notion that women are passive and difficult to awaken sexually, there are also reflections through the ages of the reverse notion – women are predatory and filled with active sexuality.

Every woman loves more than a man does, but out of shame she hides the sting of love, although she be mad for it.
Nonnus, Dionysiaca (ca AD 500) in Starr (1991)

By 'woman' is meant sensuality itself, which is well signified by woman, since in woman this naturally prevails.
Peter Lombard, <i>Senterntiae</i>, 1155, in Starr (1991)

Men, some to Business, some to Pleasure take:
But every woman is at heart a Rake'
Alexander Pope, <i>Of the Characters of Women</i>, 1732–33, in Starr (1991)

Further, as the following quote from the personal column of <i>The List</i>, an Arts Listings magazine dated 11 March 1993, indicates it is clear that not all heterosexual men wish to dominate either socially or indeed in sexual relations:

Athletic, Compliant
yielding, submissive, male (29 years)
seeks imperious, sexy, haughty, dominant female

Indeed, as Horowitz and Kaufman (1987, p. 199) write of sexually explicit material used by some heterosexual men: 'much pornography shows an active, sexually aggressive, vampish woman. Some shows the subjugation of men: the classic photo of a man under her stiletto heel'.

Nevertheless for most heterosexual men, masculinity is tied to a notion of sexuality in which men's needs are seen as more direct, more simple and less complicated than women's. Hence for the majority of heterosexual men the onus is on them both to initiate and to satisfy sexuality in both partners (Tiefler, 1988). As we shall see in chapters 4 and 5 these perceptions owe as much, if not more, to social expectations than they do to innate differences between the sexes on the dimension of activity/passivity.

Psychoanalytic perspectives on homosexuality

Although Freud held open the possibility that a contributing factor to an individual's sexuality might be constitutional (Ruse, 1988), he regarded the Oedipal stage as most important in the determination of sexual orientation. However he believed events later in life could also influence sexuality. For example, in an analysis of a girl with lesbian tendencies, he regarded the birth of a sibling when the girl was 16 as partially leading to her rejection of men because he believed the girl saw the baby's birth as evidence of her father's betrayal of her, showing that he loved her mother more (Freud, 1955).

Freud also indicated that the fear of female genitals might play a significant part in homosexual orientation in men, because women remind men of the possibility of castration. In a similar manner he thought that the sight of male genitals might frighten girls because girls could perceive them as a source of potential harm, not only in intercourse but also because of the damage they might suffer in childbirth as a result of intercourse. He also believed that the sight of the penis could set up uncomfortable feelings of envy in girls.

Following on from Freud a number of psychoanalysts have theorized about the nature of homosexuality, in most cases regarding the psychodynamics of the Oedipal stage as most important in the determination of sexuality.

Evaluating psychoanalytic aproaches to gender

Neither Freud nor any of the other early psychoanalysts were centrally concerned with gender or gender differences. Nevertheless, as we have seen, by placing so much emphasis on the dynamics of the Oedipal stage, with its differing implications for the sexes, they were inevitably led to discuss the nature of the resulting sex differences in psychological functioning.

Most psychoanalysts regarded the Oedipal stage as being dominated by the young child's reactions to the genital differences between the sexes and, because of this, they were led to an essentialist view of sex differences resting on biological determinism. The boy centres on his biology and his possession of his penis, the girl on her biology and her lack of a penis and these early preoccupations continue to dominate their psychological functioning.

There is, however, another reason for regarding psychoanalysts as essentialist in their view of sex differences. This is because they place so determining an influence on the first few years of life. Gender identity and gender attributes are fixed in the unconscious in early childhood and continue to exert their influence throughout life.

In common with many developmental psychologists (Bee, 1992), I believe that psychoanalysts are mistaken in their belief that very young children are dominated by their interest in their genitalia. Empirical studies of child development which we will look at in chapter 4 do not indicate such an overriding interest. In addition, few contemporary psychologists find it easy to accept that children's perceptions of their bodies and those of their siblings or peers determine their later psychological development (Unger and Crawford, 1992).

Even if it is conceded that psychoanalysts are correct in their claims that it is the perception of genital differences in early childhood that leads to gender differences in psychological functioning, it is still possible to question the stance adopted by the great majority of psychoanalysts whereby males are seen as the norm and women are, in general, viewed far less positively than are men (Williams, 1987).

However, while psychoanalysis has attracted considerable criticism from psychologists in general, not only with respect to its approach to gender differences, but also more importantly with respect to its methodology and to its neglect of social and cultural influences on psychological functioning (Tavris and Wade, 1984), it is generally conceded by most psychologists that in turning our attention to the role of unconscious processes psychoanalysis has illuminated our understanding of the human psyche (Archer and Lloyd, 1985).

Notes

1. Freud was not the first person to make use of the term unconscious but he was the first person to write extensively about it.
2. Some psychoanalysts still conduct their sessions on orthodox Freudian lines, but in general few people are able to afford the kind of lengthy and frequent sessions that were characteristic of the early years of psychoanalysis. Most psychoanalysts, however, continue to refer to their analysands as 'patients'.
3. For an example of the relatively easy relationship Freud had with women analysts see Andreas-Salome (1987).
4. Although Freud, did not regard homosexuality as 'normal', untypically for his time he displayed no condemnation of homosexuality.
5. As the last chapter indicated, masturbation in childhood had been very heavily condemned and indeed punished in the nineteenth century. A more enlightened approach was fostered with the spread of psychoanalytic concepts.

6. So named after the Greek mythological figure Narcissus who fell in love with his own reflection.
7. Unlike Freud, and many other earlier psychoanalysts, Erikson did take into account the effects of culture. See for example, Erikson (1963).
8. Deconstructionism is the term used to describe contemporary intellectual movements which are concerned with the relationships between meaning and power and the role of language in these relationships. See for example, Jamieson (1982).
9. Lacan, however, was less interested than Freud in the physical aspects of the penis, placing more emphasis on its symbolic representation, for which he used the term phallus.
10. Lacan can be very difficult to follow, but by the term symbolic castration, he appears to refer to the potential loss of the gratifications emerging from the possession of the phallus.

Chapter 3

Gender Differences and Biological Determinism

Male and female – the dichotomy based on sex

The term **sex** is assumed to be a biological category that stands for an understanding of what is 'natural', what cannot be changed. However, biologists, endocrinologists and social scientists have started to examine the categories of 'female' and 'male' more closely, because they have found that not everyone fits into one or other as neatly as had been previously assumed.
Lorber and Farrell (1991, p. 7)

In the last chapter we considered an essentialist position which argued that there are basic differences in male and female nature deriving from sex differences in biology interacting with the very early experiences of childhood. In this chapter we will examine a rather more straightforward essentialist position which regards gender differences in psychological functioning as arising directly from **biological** sex differences. As indicated earlier in chapter 1, this position has been labelled 'biological determinism' and it springs from the following two propositions:

1. there are commonalities running through time and across all cultures in female as compared to male behaviour;
2. these commonalities within the same sex, and differences between the sexes, are due in major part to our inborn physiological make-up.

This view has twin roots in biology and in evolutionary theory and we shall be examining the scientific evidence that has been adduced in support of such biological determinism.

Generalizing about the behaviour of males as compared to females is something we become accustomed to from a very early age. For example, in a recent classroom study with children in their first year at school, Lloyd and Duveen (1992) reported that both boys and girls, echoed the tendency of their teachers to expect boys to be naughtier than girls, and girls often used boys' naughtiness as an excuse to complain to the teacher about boys monopolizing toys. Boys retaliate both in their conversation by stereotyping girls as 'sissies' and in their behaviour by complying with the demands of other boys and ignoring those of girls.

If you ask children at this age to account for their different treatment of the sexes they are likely to respond with generalizations about the opposite sex, like the little girl in Lloyd and Duveen's study who said that 'boys are horrible'. Implicitly children appear to locate these differences in behaviour in nature: boys and girls are different because they are born that way. Biological sex is seen as shaping difference and for children, and indeed for most adults, the dichotomy of male/female appears to be universal and the decision as to whether a baby is male or female appears to be simple and uncomplicated.

In fact recent research shows both these assumptions to be incorrect in that the biological categories of male and female are neither as universal nor as fixed as most people assume.

Are there always two separate sexes?

Sexual dimorphism, or the existence of two different forms which is characteristic of most species, is regarded by biologists as a way of increasing diversity within species because it provides two sets of genetic material out of which individuals may be created. It is not, however, universal. Many invertebrate species, such as earthworms and oysters, show no sexual dimorphism and individuals in those species possess male and female gonads – the organs that manufacture sperm and eggs – either simultaneously or in sequence.

Some species of fish also show considerable inconsistency in sexual behaviour. For example, Yamamoto (1969) cites the case of a Red Sea fish which changes spontaneously from fertile female to fertile male in the absence of any other males of the species. Should a male appear, however, this transformation is reversed.

Even within vertebrates there are some rare exceptions of species that reproduce parthogenetically, that is by means of an unfertilized egg. In certain bird species unfertilized eggs in the female can develop into birds without the influence of sperm from a male (Blackwelder and Shepherd, 1981). Exceptions such as these to the sexual dimorphism of male/female may be extremely rare but they do lead us to question how universal and fixed the existence of two sexes is in the animal world. Turning to humans, we may ask the same two questions. First, how universal is the clearcut division of individuals into male and female and, second, how fixed is such a division?

In the very great majority of human births, the unambiguous assignment into one of the categories, female/male, is clearcut but, as all societies have been aware, occasionally individuals are born who prove exceptions to this general rule and who have the sexual characteristics of both sexes. It is the existence of such exceptions that has led to much of the scientific investigation into how sexual differentiation occurs in human development. In the next sections we shall first look briefly at how sexual differentiation is affected by two areas into which there has been a great deal of investigation – the sex chromosomes and hormones. This will be followed by a discussion of individuals whose sexuality is physiologically ambiguous.

The chromosomes

As most people know, the transmission of hereditary characteristics in human beings is carried on the chromosomes which form part of the nuclei of cells. In humans there are 23 pairs of chromosomes. One member of each pair is contributed by the mother and one by the father when the egg and the sperm unite at conception. Twenty-two of these pairs carry the genes which determine various features of the individual, the remaining pair are termed the **sex chromosomes**. While the rest of the chromosomes are roughly identical in shape, the two forms of the sex chromosomes, known respectively as X and Y chromosomes, differ considerably in shape and size. The first of these, the X chromosome is larger and carries more genetic material. These sex chromosomes are produced by organs called the **gonads**, the ovaries in females and the testes in males. The ovaries can produce only X chromosomes but the testes can produce both X and Y chromosomes. If an X unites with another X, the chromosomal sex of the baby will be female (XX), while if an X unites with a Y, it will be male (XY) so that it is the father who determines the chromosomal sex of the child.

While the Y chromosome is much smaller than the X and while, as noted above, it carries relatively little genetic information, it does contain a gene (or possibly genes) which cause the production of hormones and these hormones transform the XY baby's originally undifferentiated gonads into testes. In the case of the XX baby, the gonads develop into ovaries.

The nature of the baby's sex chromosomes can be very easily determined by a simple test and in the very great majority of cases, the sex chromosomes will be shown to be either XX or XY. Some very rare individuals, however, do have other chromosomal patterns and we will look at such patterns later in the chapter. For the moment I want to look at another important determinant of sexual differentiation – the sex hormones.

The role of the sex hormones

As the embryo of either sex develops, the pre-natal sex hormones notably testosterone in males and oestrogen in females continue to be secreted and the external and internal sex organs continue to develop. After birth the level of sex hormones remains relatively stable until puberty when there is a marked increase in their circulation in both sexes. It is important to note, however, that throughout the life cycle both males and females secrete the sex hormones of the other sex although, of course, to a far lesser extent.

In order to understand the role of the sex hormones in sexual differentiation in humans, it is helpful to look first at their role in sexual differentiation
in other mammals and to explore the extent to which such differentiation
affects **behavioural dimorphism** in animals. (Behavioural dimorphism is a
term used to describe differences in behavioural patterns between the sexes.)

Behavioural dimorphism

If we look for the moment at sexual behaviour in rats, we will note that adult
male rats show **mounting** behaviour (climbing on the back of another animal
and performing pelvic thrusts) and female rats show **lordosis** (arching the back
and permitting another animal to mount). If male rats are castrated after birth,
even though they have developed male organs pre-natally because of the
action of pre-natal sex hormones, because they no longer secrete male hormones
they will not show mounting behaviour in adult life unless they are given
artificial male hormones. This indicates that sexual behaviour in rats is affected
by hormone levels after birth as well as before birth. However, dimorphism in
sexual behaviour is not *determined* by the sexual differentiation produced by
sex hormones because under some circumstances male rats show lordosis and
female rats show mounting – for example in the absence of rats of the opposite
sex. In other words rats of either sex can sometimes exhibit the sexual behaviour
of the opposite sex.

Indeed it is important to note that in all species sexual differences in
behaviour are not absolute but relative. For example, one of the most commonly observed behavioural differences between male and female mammals
is that young male mammals show more rough and tumble play than females.
However, in some primate species young females living in mixed sex groups
show more rough and tumble play that young females living in single sex
groups (Goldfoot and Neff, 1987, pp. 179–195). In effect this shows an interaction between social environment and behaviour in areas with established
sex differences.

The fact that rough and tumble behaviour is more characteristic of males
than females has often been associated with claims that, across all species,
males are more aggressive. However, this generalization about sex difference
in levels of aggressive behaviour does not hold for a large number of animal
species where either there are no differences in aggressive behaviour, as in
some primate species (Tiger, 1980) or where females behave more aggressively
than males, for example with hamsters (Johnson, 1972) and eagles (Cowden,
1969).

Furthermore, even within species sex differences in behaviour are not
invariant across all species members. For example, while in most primates,
large and conspicuous males are most dominant, in several macaque species
dominance hierachy in young animals is affected by the mother's position in
the hierachy (Lancaster, 1973).

The discussion above indicates that in animals sexual differences in behaviour, while obviously affected by hormones and physiological sex differences, are neither fixed nor invariant even in reproductive behaviour. It is not surprising, when we consider how much more complex human behaviour is, to find that in human beings sexual dimorphism in behaviour is even less fixed and invariant. Consider, for example, how the social environment affects the manner in which males and females live their lives and the extent to which time and place constrain the kind of behaviour expected of women and men respectively. Not only are there differences in the kinds of behaviour expected from the sexes across cultures at different times, but there are also differences within cultures at different times. In addition, the extent to which sexual difference in behaviour is a characteristic of social life also varies considerably. To take an example suggested by Williams (1987): in hunting and gathering societies, such as the !Kung in southern Africa there are minimal sex differences in social roles with both sexes caring for the young and taking responsibility for gathering food; in contrast 'the frail corseted Victorian lady in England' both played a very different role from her spouse and was regarded as very different in temperament and capabilities.

It is thus not open to argument that culture affects sex differences in behaviour, but this conclusion does not rule out the possibilities that if we scrutinize the evidence from relevant biological studies we may show that biology does, to some extent any way, at least constrain psychological development. In effect we may show evidence for some elements of biological determinism. Hence it is convenient to look at studies in six related areas. These are:

1. studies of individuals with abnormalities in sex hormones;
2. studies of individuals with abnormalities in their chromosomal make-up;
3. studies of the relationship between hormones and behaviour;
4. studies of sex differences in the brain;
5. studies that draw on evolutionary theory;
6. studies that investigate the effect of biology on sexual orientation.

As the various research findings are looked at, comments will be made on the implications the findings have for biological determinism or for what is sometimes termed the nature/nurture issue. However, it is only at the end of this chapter that we shall try to evaluate, in the light of these studies, the claims about sex differences made by biological determinists.

Abnormalities in sex hormones

As stated earlier, the first stage in the development of the embryo's sex is initiated by the action of the Y sex chromosome which starts the process of modifying the XY embryo in a male direction. Very occasionally foetuses that are genetically, chromosomically masculine (XY) develop genitals that are ambiguous or that look more like a clitoris than a penis[1] and, equally occasionally, female embryos because of hormonal conditions may develop genitalia with masculine characteristics.[2] Individuals with these sorts of conditions are often referred to as **hermaphrodites**.[3] The term hermaphrodite originates in Greek mythology where it is used to refer to the offspring of Hermes and Aphrodite who were believed to have the attributes of both sexes.

Recent advances in knowledge about gonadal and chromosomal structures now assist in the decision as to whether such individuals are to be brought up as girls or boys, but in the past, sexual assignation was made largely on the appearance of the external genitalia. No matter how assignations were, or are, made, individuals with such conditions have been, and continue to be, subject to a great deal of both medical and psychological investigation because it has been argued cases such as theirs allow conclusions to be drawn about the claims of biological determinism.

Hormonal abnormalities in XX individuals

In this subsection let us look at research data on individuals whose chromosomal make-up is XX (female) but who have been 'masculinized' by being subjected to relatively large amounts of masculine hormones when their mothers were pregnant with them, either because of hormonal abnormalities or because their mothers were given high doses of male hormones in order to prevent miscarriages[4] (a practice that is no longer employed). A number of studies have followed these individuals in later life.

In general these studies have reported that the individuals concerned identified themselves as girls and showed developmental patterns in gender identity and sexuality that were not very different from girls with no hormonal abnormalities. In two areas, however, some differences have been reported. The first of these concerned social behaviour and interests that were labelled by the researchers as 'tomboyism', a term used to refer to these girls' relatively high level of interest in outdoor sports and games, lesser interest in babysitting and dolls and greater preference for wearing trousers rather than dresses. The second area of difference was concerned with sexuality in that the girls were reported as showing developmental delays, compared to their non-androgynized peers in dating, petting and heterosexual intercourse. In addition one study (Ehrhardt and Meyer-Bahlberg, 1981) suggested androgynized women reported relatively high levels of homo or bisexual behaviour and erotic dreams and fantasies.

These studies have been severely criticized on methodological grounds on a number of counts. First because the reports of interests and activities were supplied by individuals – the girls themselves, their mothers and their teachers – who were aware of the girls' medical history and who were likely to have been influenced by this (Bleier, 1984). Second because of the un-warranted assumption in some studies that these girls' higher level of tomboyism could be unproblematically ascribed to the pre-natal influence of hormones rather than cultural factors. As Williams (1987) points out, interest in sports and outdoor activities has increased sharply in recent times and rejection of tra-ditional feminine interests in areas like babysitting in favour of following careers is by no means unusual.

Williams has also been particularly critical of the implicit assumption in many studies that these masculinized girls displayed high levels of disturbance of their sexual identity as a result of their pre-natal experiences, noting that:

> If they had displayed a high level of erotic interest in other girls, similar to that displayed by adolescent boys, or if they had identified with the male sex and had wished to change their sex as transsexuals do, then the effect of the fetal androgenization would be more impres-sive.
> (Williams, 1987, p. 116)

In other words, despite the fact that they had been exposed to male hormones pre-natally these girls apparently showed little disturbance in their gender role development and, as a result, provide little support for biological determinism with respect to the development of gender.

Hormonal abnormalities in XY individuals

In this subsection we shall discuss two conditions in which individuals who are chromosomally male (XY) exhibit unusual sexual development resulting from inherited conditions which affect their hormonal secretions. In the first of these conditions, **testicular – feminization syndrome**, embryonic tissues are not able to respond to the male hormone, testosterone, and as a result when the babies concerned are born, despite having internal male organs, their genitalia appear female and they are therefore assumed to be female. Their condition is usually only discovered in puberty because they do not menstruate or because testes are found in their groins. Such testes can often become malignant and they are usually removed. Hormonal treatment further reinforces a female identity and the individuals concerned develop feminine breasts and bodily contours.

There have been relatively few studies of such individuals because of the rarity of the condition but those studies that have been made (Money and Ehrhardt, 1972) indicate two things. First that the individuals concerned appear to have no problems with their sexual assignation as female although they are not able to have children; second they are unusually attractive. This second finding has been partly ascribed to the fact that their feminine shape is associated with male height.

From the point of biological determinism it could be suggested that these individuals present a strong case for the influence of biology on social development in that feminine identity can be unambiguously related to lack of testosterone but, as Unger and Crawford (1992) point out, there is an equally plausible alternative argument which is that because the appearance of these individuals is that of extremely attractive women their social role as women is reinforced and very rewarding. In other words, studies of this condition provide no strong evidence for or against biological determinism.

If the existence of individuals with the syndrome just discussed presents ambivalent evidence in the nature/nurture debate about sex differences, the next hormonal deficit to be discussed presents even more complex and contradictory data. In this condition, **alpha – reductose deficiency**, individuals with XY chromosomes lack enzymes for the conversion of testosterone and thus when they are born, although their internal reproductive organs are male, externally their genitals closely resemble those of girls and consequently, in the past, they have tended to be classified as girls. At puberty, however, such individuals become masculinized because of the increase in testosterone and their voice deepens, their penis enlarges and becomes capable of erection, and they become able to ejaculate. In this way we have the situation of individuals, brought up as girls although their chromosomal structure is male, i.e. XY, who at adolescence become unambiguously male in appearance, consistent with their chromosomal sex. If their social behaviour then becomes more similar to male rather than female patterns, it could be argued that this provides strong support for 'nature' and biological determinism in that their social behaviour is shown to be consistent with their male biology rather than their rearing as females.

Research studies of individuals with this condition are, however, both contradictory and very difficult to interpret and, as we shall see, allow no definitive conclusions to be drawn. The first set of data was reported by Imperato-McGinley and her associates (1976 and 1979) and relates to a group of 38 related individuals with this condition who lived in a rural area in the Dominican Republic where the condition is so common that it has a name 'penis at 12' (*guevedoce*). Imperato-MacGinley reported that for a large majority of these individuals the transition from being brought up as girls and then at puberty, as they began to look like boys, the adoption of male roles was relatively unproblematic in that 17 of the 38 assumed a heterosexual identity and 15 married. The researchers interpreted the data as showing that nurture (being brought up as girls) was less important than nature (being biologically XY) because the individuals concerned were able to move easily into a masculine role at puberty. The researchers suggested that this was because their 'brains had been masculinized pre-natally as well as at puberty' even though their bodies only became masculine at puberty.

Whether there are differences in male and female brains is a very controversial question as will be seen later in this chapter, but even if it were proved that such brain differences exist, the results from the Dominican Republic have been reassessed by other investigators who have contested the claims that the transition from 'girl' to boy was as easy as reported by Imperato-MacGinley and her colleagues. Later studies, for example by Rubin *et al.* (1981), showed that most of the individuals concerned had realized at early ages that they were different from other girls and, in a society with a relatively high degree of sex segregation in domestic tasks and play, had started associating with boys rather than with girls before the onset of puberty (i.e. their nurture was not like that of other girls). Furthermore, critics argued that Imperato-McGinley and her colleagues had not explored the implication of the fact that such physiological transformations were known to occur in this locality (as mentioned above the condition even had a name) and the impact of such knowledge on individuals and their families who must have seen that their genital organs, while appearing more female than male, did not look like those of other girls. Thus critics like Rubin argue it is not possible to equate the social experience before puberty of such individuals with 'normal' girls.

A more recent study by Herdt and Davidson (1988) of a rural population in New Guinea where this condition is relatively common has indicated that it is recognized at birth and the society even has a linguistic term for the condition as a sexual identity. This population having three terms for sexual identity – female, male and a third term which emphasizes the quality of transformation into male. In nine out of 14 individuals studied, child rearing was as boys (though these individuals did not take part in male initiation rites) and in five cases as girls. In later life, those raised as girls moved to a masculine role but with considerable conflict and difficulty showing that despite their masculine 'nature', their feminine 'nurture' had affected them.

The condition has also been documented in the USA and, in such cases, the individuals have tended to be reared as girls and have undergone feminizing hormone treatment at puberty. They have apparently not had any difficulties in the female role in adulthood (Rubin, *et al.* 1981).

If we look across all three studies for evidence that would support biological determinist claims, it would seem that while the study in the Dominican Republic appeared originally to offer strong support for biological determinism, later inspection of the data offers less as do the other two studies in New Guinea and the USA. Or to put it another way, evidence from studies of individuals with this hermaphroditic condition does not indicate that sex hormones are the determining factors in the manner in which individuals develop gender roles. Instead there is a complex interrelationship between hormones and the individual's social and cultural environment in that the ease of the transition from being reared as a girl to living as an adult male varies from case to case in the Dominican Republic and New Guinea, while in other cases, notably in the USA, the transition from female sex role to male sex role does not even occur. Studies of individuals with abnormalities in their chromosomal make-up also show this complex interaction as the next subsection indicates.

Chromosomal abnormalities

Most individuals, as indicated above, possess 46 chromosomes, 22 pairs of autosomes and one pair of sex chromosomes: in the case of females XX, and in the case of males XY. Occasionally during the development of the egg or sperm, an extra chromosome is developed or one is deleted. Of such abnormalities the three most common are the conditions 45XO, 47XXY and 47XYY.

Individuals with 45 XO chromosomes are termed, **Turner girls**, and as this label suggests, they are identified as females. This is mainly because their external genitalia are female at birth although they remain immature because they do not secrete any sex hormones. As a result of this absence they do not menstruate nor do they develop breasts or pubic hair at adolescence unless they are given female sex hormones. However, even with the administration of such hormones, these individuals remain sterile.

As indicated above, people with this condition are always reared as girls and so psychologists have been able to observe gender development before adolescence in individuals who will have been influenced by rearing but not by sex hormones (i.e. by nurture but not by nature). Such studies (Money and Ehrhardt, 1972) have indicated that the people concerned develop very strong female gender identification differing, before adolescence from their female peers, only in their relative lack of ability at certain cognitive tasks.

We thus have the finding that even in the complete absence of sex hormones, gender identification in childhood and early youth is unproblematic and this must suggest that normal gender development can take place without the action of sex hormones on the brain. In other words 'normal' sex role identification can occur under the influence of nurture without much contribution from nature.

'Turner girls' have never captured the popular imagination but individuals with another chromosomal abnormality certainly have. These are 47 XYY males who differ from other males in their possession of an extra Y chromosome leading to them being labelled in the popular press as **supermales**. Early studies of 47XYY males suggested that the incidence of such men in prisons was higher than their incidence in the general population. Some of these early studies also suggested that these men were more likely to have been convicted for crimes of violence, thus it could be argued, providing strong evidence for biological determinism in that an extra male chromosome was shown to be linked to violent behaviour. (Violent behaviour is more characteristic of males than females in most societies, although, as the discussion in chapter 5 will indicate, there is no clearcut evidence that men behave more aggressively, as distinct from violently, than women.) However, as indicated above, the notion of supermales predisposed to violence, became a folk myth and at the time of the first studies, notorious criminals were (erroneously) identified as having an extra Y chromosome and in the USA proposals were made that all newborn male babies be screened for this chromosomal abnormality.

Later and more systematic studies of XYY individuals indicated that the link between this abnormality and violence was extremely tenuous. One study, in particular, indicated how complex such interactions are. This was a study conducted in Denmark by Witkin *et al.* (1976) which investigated the levels of violence not only in 47 XYY males but also in males with 47XXY chromosomal abnormalities and compared these levels of violence to those of their XY peers. These comparisons were made because individuals with 47XXY syndrome (known also as Klinefelter's syndrome) have an extra X, or 'female' chromosome, and following the logic of biological determinism could be expected to be less rather than more violent than both XYY males and normal males as a consequence of being more 'female' than other males.

In the Witkin study the records of a representative sample[5] of 4139 men were inspected of whom there were 12 XYY and 13 XXY men. One of the major findings was that men with both chromosomal abnormalities had significantly lower intelligence scores than their peers. This is of relevance because, throughout the world, studies of prison populations indicate that convicted men tend to measure lower than the general public on such tests and this may be partially related to the link between economic disadvantage and the relative inability to score well on conventional tests of academic and cognitive ability. It has thus been argued (Siann, 1985) that one of the reasons for some studies showing higher levels of XYY men in prisons than in the general population is because of the relationships between economic disadvantage, scoring relatively poorly on intelligence tests and suffering from physical abnormalities. In other words, if you are poor, you are also likely to do relatively badly at school and at tests, and you are also more likely to be born with physical abnormalities.

To return to the Witkin study, the rate of criminal conviction for both chromosomal abnormalities was greater than for their peers. In the case of XYY males being 42 per cent, in the case of XXY males 19 per cent, and in the case of XY males 9 per cent, thus confirming earlier findings of a higher incidence of XYY men in prisons than in the general population, possibly for the reasons suggested in the paragraph above. But the link between an extra Y chromosome and violence was definitely not supported in that only two of the XYY men were habitual criminals and neither had convictions for violent or aggressive behaviour. In fact the only man with a chromosomal abnormality who had been convicted for a crime of violence was a man with the XXY syndrome. This study then provides little support for biological determinism and the link between Y chromosomes and 'supermale' behaviour.

Neither, indeed, do studies of other and rarer chromosomal abnormalities such as XXX females and XXYY males. These studies indicate that chromosomal abnormalities have little direct effect on gender identity or sexual orientation. Instead gender identity in such cases appears to be closely related to the appearance of the external genitalia which influence child rearing (Unger and Crawford, 1992) thus mirroring the findings concerning gender identity in hermaphroditic conditions which were reviewed in the previous section.

It could be argued, however, that the cases discussed so far are all of individuals with hormonal or chromosomal abnormalities of one sort or another and so it is perhaps not legitimate to generalize from them. If this is the case is there any evidence of a link between sex hormones and behaviour in the life development of normal individuals? To answer this question we shall be looking at two issues, first the relationship between male hormones and aggression, and second the relationship between female hormones and mood.

The relationship between hormones and behaviour

Aggression and androgens

One of the most heavily researched aspects of the relationship between sex hormones and behaviour has been the link between male hormones, particularly testosterone, and aggression. Proponents of biological determinism have argued that the reason that males are in general more violent and aggressive than females (a claim which we shall look at critically later) is that the male hormone, testosterone, is linked to aggressive behaviour in that the higher the level, the greater the tendency to behave violently. Evidence for this contention is usually cited as coming from three sources:

1. studies of the relationship between abnormal pre-natal levels of hormones and aggression in later life;
2. the effect of castration on aggression;
3. the relationship between levels of aggression and the levels of circulating hormones.

Studies of abnormal pre-natal levels of hormones and their effect on aggression fall into two groups: individuals with hermaphroditic conditions (see above); and individuals whose mothers were given artificial sex hormones in pregnancy because the pregnancies were perceived to be at risk and this treatment was thought to offer protection.

Reviews of these studies have not shown that girls who were exposed to high levels of 'male' hormones are more aggressive than their peers[6] or that boys who were exposed to high levels of 'female' hormones are less aggressive than their peers (Money and Schwartz, 1976, pp. 19–30).

If there is little evidence for a link between pre-natal levels of sex hormones and aggression what of post-natal levels of sex hormones and aggression? At the most extreme this can be investigated by looking at before and after studies of castration in men. Amazingly some men have, in the past, been castrated in both Europe and America in an attempt to curb behaviour that was regarded as antisocial by law enforcement agencies. As might be expected, studies of such men have been concerned with sexual rather than violent behaviour but where levels of violence has been investigated, results are inconsistent. Bremer (1959), for example, reports that castration of such men had no pacifying effects while Hawke (1950) describes some cases where after castration, generally aggressive men became less likely to create disturbances. These studies, whatever one may think of the ethics of castration, do not present any conclusive evidence of the link between violence and hormones because castration in human males is generally accompanied by such enormous changes in the manner in which such individuals think about themselves that the origin of behavioural changes becomes very difficult to ascertain. In any event it is worth noting that castration in other primates produces no changes in dominance hierachies (Kedenberg, 1979).

The third area bearing on the link between hormones and aggressive behaviour comes from studies of circulating testosterone and levels of aggression. Results of such studies are inconsistent; some showing men with higher levels of testosterone demonstrating higher levels of aggression (Kreuz and Rose, 1972) while others show no such link (Mattsson *et al.* 1980). In any event these studies are difficult to interpret for two reasons. The first because it is very difficult to obtain reliable estimates of circulating testosterone levels and the second because there is ample evidence that subjective mood influences testosterone, and that the social environment can affect mood states. Thus a number of studies show that when men become depressed their testosterone levels drop (Tavris and Wade, 1984).

The discussion above of the link between aggression and hormones seems to indicate that there is no simple link between male hormones and aggressive behaviour, and consequently the claim that men are more violent than women because their sexual hormones predipose them to violence is not substantiated. At this stage, however, let us examine another link that has been suggested between hormones and behaviour – the effect of 'female' hormones on behaviour, particularly in the period before menstruation, at childbirth and at menopause.

PMT, menopause and behaviour

Women become insane during pregnancy, after parturition, during lactation; at the age when the catamenia (menstruation) first appear and when they disappear . . . the sympathetic connection between the brain and the uterus is plainly seen by the most casual observer.

G. Blandford, 1871, in a treatise on insanity, in Ussher (1989)

For women the periods in which they experience major hormonal changes, such as at puberty and the menopause, are also periods in which they are also likely to experience major changes in life events. Consequently, attributing mood changes during such periods only to the effect of hormones is unwarranted. Nevertheless, such attributions have frequently been made, chiefly by male clinicians who have claimed that, in effect, women's behaviour is commonly influenced by their 'raging hormones'.

The period at which women are generally regarded to be most affected by their physiological make-up is that shortly before their monthly periods when it is commonly argued that their behaviour is adversely affected by the premenstrual syndrome. Moyer (1974) for example put it this way:

> . . . there is now good evidence that there is a periodicity to the irascibility of women and that it is related to the hormonal changes occurring over the course of the menstrual cycle . . . Emotional instability is characteristic of a number of women during the premenstrual period.

The term, premenstrual syndrome, refers to the fact that some, but not all, women report various symptoms premenstrually. The symptoms may include a variety of physical changes ranging from headaches to oedema (swelling of tissues because of increased fluid content) and weight gain. Simultaneously many women report a subjective feeling of increased emotionality. The emotions experienced are nearly always unpleasant ranging from depression and anxiety to hostility and irritation (Parlee, 1976). The percentage of women reporting these psychological symptoms varies from 25–100 per cent depending on the survey (Williams, 1987), but that women are more at risk psychologically in the period before menstruation is widely believed; the belief being epitomized by the term premenstrual tension (PMT).

PMT has been linked with a wide variety of phenomena including poor performance in the workplace, poor academic performance, greater propensity to have accidents and greater propensity to attempt suicide (Ussher, 1989). PMT has also been cited as a defence in a case of manslaughter on the grounds that the woman accused was suffering from diminished responsibility due to PMT.

Reviews of research on PMT (Parlee, 1973) have shown that many studies suffer from methodological shortcomings and reviewers tend to agree that in general the results of such studies are 'sparse and inconclusive' (Ussher, 1989, p. 67) and that there is little definitive evidence that women either perform more poorly during this period or are at more risk psychologically. This is not to deny the subjective experiences of discomfort many women suffer at this time.

Tavris and Wade (1984) have argued that at least some of the distress that women report premenstrually results from their own beliefs and expectations. In one study, they report that both men and women filled out questionnaires concerned with how they were feeling on that day. The male subjects and half the female subjects filled out forms headed 'Menstrual Distress Questionnaire', the other female subjects filled out identical forms without any title having been told that the study was concerned with daily fluctuations in health. In the first group of women, premenstrual women reported more general distress than either women who were between their periods or men, but in the second group of women (for whom the questionnaire had not been associated with menstruation) there were no differences in reported distress level between premenstrual women and women between their periods. The scores of all the women in the second group did not differ overall from those of the men.

Even if much of the data concerned with PMT is seriously flawed, the fact remains that many women experience the premenstrual period as relatively unpleasant. However, the link between such distress and hormonal fluctuations is by no means straightforward. To begin with there is considerable controversy between people making such claims as to which particular hormone or chemical messenger is chiefly responsible. Secondly, it is extremely difficult to disentangle the social and psychological aspects of menstruation from the biological and this is compounded by the fact that emotional tension can affect the menstrual cycle and that emotional stress can cause irregularities in womens' cycles (Dunbar, 1985).

While menstruation is natural and for many women non-problematic there is also little doubt that at the most practical level menstruation, particularly if it is associated with heavy bleeding, can present problems and very often these problems are worst at the age when women have the least experience of the world. For example, while most women may face practical problems with access to facilities during sports activities, this is often even more difficult for adolescent girls at co-ed schools who cannot simply leave, or be excused from such activities, without drawing attention to themselves. Again, at the most practical level, schoolgirls often have to deal with menstruation in schools with female toilets that allow very little privacy. So it is not surprising that menstruation becomes associated with feelings of stress.

At the symbolic level, as we shall see in chapter 6, most women grow up in cultures in which there are many negative associations with bleeding and particularly menstrual bleeding. The very term many women use for menstruation 'the curse' exemplifies this. On the other hand in cultures where no such negative associations are reported, women do not report menstrual symptoms and in one particular culture women only began reporting symptoms after the arrival of western female missionaries (Tavris and Wade, 1984).

In general it seems fair to conclude that for many women in western culture tension associated with mentruation is a fact. Whether this tension can be regarded as a well defined medical syndrome is less clear and the link between such tension and hormonal levels is even more tenuous. For as Williams (1987, p. 125) notes 'if the syndrome itself is not well established or clearly defined, identifying causative factors is a difficult enterprise'.

If women are thought to be at the mercy of their hormones during the years of youth and early maturity, when they are menstruating, they are also regarded as suffering severely from the lack of such hormones in later life, particularly during menopause. That women experience major physical changes shortly before and during the cessation of their periods is undeniable but the extent to which these physical changes are neccessarily associated with psychological stress has been vociferously debated as the discussion below will indicate.

The physical changes occurring in menopause, notably the fluctuations in hormonal levels, cause many women to suffer from well documented physical symptoms such as hot flashes or flushes during which they experience sensations of rapidly changing temperatures and levels of perspiration. Other physical symptoms commonly reported are dizziness and rheumatic pains. The reported incidence, however, of such experiences varies both across studies and across cultures (Kronenberg, 1990) which has sometimes led to the conclusion that such symptoms are 'all in the mind'. This conclusion is now regarded as mistaken because, although psychological and cultural factors undoubtedly affect how individuals interpret bodily sensations, it has been established that there are connections between the reduction in oestrogen level and the temperature regulation centres of the hypothalamus.

Probably far more important for women facing the onset of menopause, however, is the belief that at and during menopause physical changes in hormone level are inevitably linked to negative aspects of psychological functioning. That such a direct link existed was undisputed by the male medical establishment of the last century. Typical of their view of menopause was this pronouncement by Morrison in 1848:

> The ... 'change of life' as it is commonly called, frequently leads to periods of insanity ... because certain functions then cease, and the constitution is thereby always more or less deranged.
> Ussher (1989)

Such extreme views are not, of course, characteristic of this century but there is no doubt that as Ussher puts it, 'in popular consciousness' menopause is associated with unpleasant and negative aspects of mood and even with mental instability, as in the case of the 19-year old woman who put it this way:

> my grandmother went almost insane, she almost didn't make it through menopause.
> (Martin, 1987)

Or the situation, in parts of Ireland in the 1960s where women believed that

> menopause can induce insanity; in order to ward it off, some women have retired from life in their mid-forties and in at least three contemporary cases, have confined themselves to bed until death three years later.
> Unger and Crawford (1992, p. 506)

While few women in contemporary times would make such a clearcut association between menopause and insanity, the association of depressed mood and reduced levels of psychological functioning with hormonal changes remains widespread, although there is little evidence for such a direct link. Instead, the evidence suggests that negative aspects of psychological functioning before and during menopause are more associated with the psychological and social implications of growing older, particularly in the west with its emphasis on youth and physical appearance, than with levels of oestrogen.

In this subsection we have examined the link between sex hormones and behaviour in the case of 'male' hormones, and emotional mood in the case of women (PMT and menopause). It seems clear that there is little evidence for direct links between hormones and psychological functioning. We are all undoubtedly affected by the ways in which our own culture views the link between biology and psychological functioning, and it would seem that it is this, rather than actual biological events that affects us at periods of hormonal change.

In the next subsection we shall examine another possible effect of biological sex differences in humans, the effect of sex hormones particularly prenatal hormones on the brain and central nervous system. The issue under discussion can be put simply: is there any evidence that there are systematic differences between the brains of men and women?

Sex differences and brain function

As mentioned earlier in this chapter there have been some suggestions that sex differences in the brain, and therefore also in the functioning of the central nervous system, affect not only sexual behaviour but also other types of behaviour as well.

Evidence for such speculations emerges from three areas:

1. studies of brain size in humans;
2. studies of brain function in humans;
3. studies of the effect of sex hormones on the brains of animals.

In the nineteenth century a great interest in brain size was demonstrated by many western scientists and social scientists. Needless to say these were almost exclusively male. These investigators concluded that male brains were larger than females and that the brains of Caucasians (those of European origin) were larger than those of non-Caucasians. It is now generally accepted that subjective biases can exert an influence on the conclusions drawn by psychologists and other social scientists, and nowhere is this more clearly demonstrated than in these early studies of brain size (Gould, 1981) which reflected the values of men drawn from the more privileged sectors of the imperial powers. Believing that size of brain was related to cognitive ability and that men's brains were larger than women's (and Caucasian brains larger than black brains) provided a rationale for excluding both women and nonwhites, whether in the colonies, in the European metropolitan capitals or in the burgeoning economy of the USA, from the educational and particularly the higher educational system.

Re-evaluation of such studies of brain size and further research questioned both the correlation of brain size with cognitive ability and the reliability of the cranial measurements on which the comparisons between groups had been based. Interest in this area had waned until very recently when Rushton (1992) resuscitated the debate claiming that his own contemporary investigations have confirmed the nineteenth century findings that the cranial capacity of 'Caucasian-Americans' is greater than that of 'African-Americans' and that the cranial capacity of men is greater than women.

As the well known writer on science, John Maddox (1992) has noted 'Rushton is a controversy in himself' because for some years he has been promoting a particular type of biological determinism which has been severely criticized by a great many psychologists for its unreliable data base and the manner in which he presents his conclusions, which have been largely con-cerned with establishing racial differences in cognitive ability. The study, on which his 1992 conclusions about sex differences in brain size is based, was drawn from data kept by the USA armed forces which record cranial measure-ments (for specifying size of helmets) as well as other more usual data such as height, weight, ethnic group and education, and which indicates that wom-en's brains seem to be 100 cm^3 smaller than men's on average. Rushton accepts that there is no sex difference in intelligence test scores and suggests that this sex difference in brain size can best be understood in the context of evolution-ary pressures for sexual dimorphism which required men to roam from the home base to hunt while women stayed at home (Ankney, 1992). Such pressures, according to Rushton, necessitated male superiority on the spatial skills required for finding their way home and hunting, and in order to ac-commodate such skills their brains became larger than those of women.

In relating his own work to men's reported superiority in spatial skills, Rushton moves into an area of investigation which dominated traditional psy-chological approaches to issues of sex and gender (Hare-Mustin and Maracek, 1990). Such approaches have been concerned with whether there are consist-ent sex differences in cognitive and emotional areas that are displayed amongst all social groups and at all times. Three particular areas, two cognitive and one emotional, have repeatedly been investigated. The cognitive areas concerned are verbal ability, where girls are reported to do better than boys, and spatial abilitity where boys and men are reported to do better than girls and women respectively. (Spatial ability refers to the ability to represent two dimensional and three dimensional configurations in the brain and is thought to underlie tasks like map reading and navigating and academic subjects like geometry.) The emotional area is one which has already been referred to, aggression.

Chapter 5 will explore the extent to which such generalizations about sex differences in verbal and spatial abilities and aggression are justified, and the extent to which such differences can be attributed to physiological differences between the sexes. For the moment, let us anticipate this discussion by indicating that there is little evidence that physiological differences are the major cause of any observed sex differences in either cognitive faculties or aggression.

In carrying out studies of sex differences in brain function in humans, investigators have had to rely largely on indirect means, for example by uti-lizing measures of perceptual function, either vision or hearing, although there have been a few studies of brains at post mortem. In investigating sex differences in the brain function of animals, researchers have been able to make far more direct investigations until recently, when such studies have met with considerable objections from animal rights groups.

These animal studies, largely conducted with rats and mice, have indicated that there are certain structural differences between female and male rodents, for example in the amount of nerve cells in certain areas of a section of the brain called the hypothalmus which appear to be caused by the action of sex hormones. The major focus of interest in this research has been its application to sexual orientation and we will return to this research when essentialist perspectives on homosexuality are considered at the end of this chapter.

The new essentialism – socio-biology

It pays males to be aggressive, hasty, fickle and undiscriminating. In theory it is more profitable for females to be coy, to hold back until they can identify males with the best genes . . . Human beings obey this biological principle faithfully.
E.O. Wilson (1978, p. 125)

Male aggression as we know it today is not simply the product of culture . . . rather it is the result of the decision to hunt large animals which men made a least half a million years ago . . . What prevented early women from taking the male path to violence, our biology, simply put.
(Halliday, 1978)

Socio-biologists are concerned with applying evolutionary theory to 'social conduct' (Siann, 1985) seeking to explain it by relating it to concepts of genetic advantage and biological fitness. While most socio-biologists do acknowledge the role of learning and culture they consider their influence to be very limited, arguing that most human behaviour has its roots in evolutionary mechanisms such as the personal survival of the individual and the reproduction of the group.

They see sex differences as rooted in an evolutionary past in which men were the hunters and woman the primary caretakers of infants and children. Under such circumstances they believe particular and different traits came to be innately determined in males and females. For example, socio-biologists note that female ova are scarcer than male sperm. They argue that this difference has given larger, stronger and more aggressive males an advantage in reproducing because they are more able than their weaker peers to mate with many women hence optimizing their chances of having offspring. Thus, according to socio-biologists, there were evolutionary pressures for men to be adventurous and aggressive and as a result, even today, men are essentially more aggressive, more adventurous and more competitive than females. Such views are based largely on evolutionary theory but they are also buttressed by references to biological research.

As might be expected these views, which downplay the effect of the social environment and culture, have been very critically received by many social scientists (Fausto-Sterling, 1992). They have also attracted a great deal of adverse attention from feminist writers (Birke, 1986). Some of these writers criticize both the methodology and the data base of the socio-biologists, while other feminist writers have responded by accepting their socio-biological model but criticizing their interpretation of it. Thus feminists like Rich (1979) have agreed with the socio-biological position that there are essential and innate differences between men and women, but in their exposition of these differences, these feminists have tended to emphasize other qualities than those identified by Wilson. They have, for example, centred on women's sense of co-operativeness and empathy rather than male aggressiveness.

Other feminists like Alice Rossi (1987) have endorsed an essentialist viewpoint which is based chiefly on studies of interactions between newborn infants and their biological mothers. Rossi believes that these studies reveal that biological mothers possess innate sensitivities to their new-born and that these sensitivities differentiate mothers from fathers and, consequently, indicate at least one area of innate sex differences.

Evaluations of the views of socio-biologists like Wilson have pointed out that the manner in which they draw on biological data to support their overall thesis has led them to overgeneralize. Critics also argue that the socio-biologists reading of evolutionary, biological and anthropological data tends to be very selective (Siann, 1985). Similarly, critics of the feminist essentialist position have tended to focus on the selective manner in which these theorists deploy examples from both biological and anthropological studies, and the extent to which they underplay social and cultural influences (Jaggar, 1983).

Essentialist approaches to homosexuality

In the past two decades a number of researchers have published studies suggesting that sexual orientation is influenced by brain structure and brain processes. The area of the brain which has chiefly been cited as being involved is the hypothalmus. Dorner *et al.* (1975) have suggested that there are consistent differences between the hypothalmuses of male homosexuals and male heterosexuals and that it is these differences that underpin the differences in their sexual orientation. Much the same claim has been made by Simon LeVay (1993) who also argues that the hypothalmuses of male homosexuals show similarity to those of females, and the hypothalmuses of lesbians to those of men. The evidence for these claims is often indirect and is based mainly on studies of animals such as mice and monkeys. For example, researchers have altered the level of hormones which are known to affect hypothalmic function in animals and then observed their sexual behaviour, such as the extent to which male monkeys mounted other male monkeys.

LeVay also cites other evidence to support his contention that homosexuality is at least partially genetically determined. For example, some 'twin' studies show that if one member of an identical twin is homosexual or lesbian there is a higher chance of the other member being gay, than there is if twins are fraternal. Identical twins have the same genetic make-up, or genotypes, while non-identical twins have different genotypes. Consequently if a trait is found to be shared more often by identical, than by fraternal twins, it is often assumed that the trait has a strong genetic component. It could, of course, also be argued that because identical twins are so alike, they get treated alike, and this environmental factor may account for their similarity on the trait in question.

In further support of his thesis that sexuality is influenced by physiological factors, LeVay quotes the finding that many homosexuals and lesbians are aware of their sexual orientation from a very young age. Finally, LeVay notes that the pattern of abilities in male homosexuals, for example their performance at tests of spatial ability, is similar to the pattern of abilities found in women rather than men.

In further support of genetic involvement in homosexuality, some researchers have recently claimed to have identified a particular set of DNA on the X chromosome which is associated with homosexuality (Hamer *et al.*). However, not all homosexual men involved in the study carried this stretch and the researchers concerned regard the set of DNA involved in homosexuality as influential rather than causative (Radford, 1993).

The possibility that homosexuality is influenced by genes has generated a great deal of media interest which has largely been concerned with the possible implications of being able to identify foetuses carrying the DNA sets involved in homosexuality. Simon LeVay is himself homosexual, and there does seem to be strong support for the biological determination of sexuality in some sections of the gay community who have argued that if homosexuality is genetically influenced then practising homosexuals cannot be regarded as in any way morally reprehensible.

The evidence for a genetic involvement in homosexuality is, however, by no means conclusive and many biologists and geneticists regard the hypothesis as speculative. Anne Fausto-Sterling, in particular, has been critical not only of the nature of the studies on the structure and processes of the hypothalmus which LeVay cites, but also of the manner in which researchers arguing for a genetic influence appear to ignore the influence of the social environment. For example, if women and homosexuals show similar patterns of ability this could be ascribed as much to similar interests and life style than to similarities in brain chemistry. Furthermore, if homosexuality was governed chiefly by genetic processes it might be expected that if one member of an identical twin set was homosexual so should be their twin and this is by no means the case for all identical twins studied (LeVay, 1993).

Fausto-Sterling (1992, p. 249) also points out that LeVay frequently writes as if there were clearly defined sexual behaviours associated with each sex, 'ignoring an extensive literature suggesting that both animal and human sexual behaviors are continuous rather than dichotomous'.

However it should be noted that, while LeVay and other proponents of this approach argue for a physiological influence on sexual orientation, they do not claim that it is the only influence.

The nature/nurture issue – what can we conclude?

This section has explored in some detail the evidence for and against biological determinism with respect to sex differences, looking at six areas in turn: abnormalities in sex hormones, abnormalities in chromosomal make-up, the relationship between hormones and behaviour, sex differences in the brain, recent socio-biological and feminist perspectives on biological determinism and biological influences on sexual orientation.

I believe that the empirical studies described in these subsections do not offer strong support for biological determinism. To begin with, as animal studies show, even in sexual behaviour males sometimes behave in a 'female' fashion and vice versa. Second, studies of individuals both with chromosomal and hormonal abnormalities are difficult to evaluate because there is always a complex interaction for the individuals concerned of the manner in which they are reared and the manner in which their particular condition affects their physical appearance. Further there are bound to be individual differences in the manner in which such individuals come to terms with their own gender roles and gender orientations. This is shown particularly in the studies of those individuals with alpha – reductose deficiency (the linked studies in the Dominican Republic, New Guinea and the USA) some of whom apparently live unproblematically as males, some who live unproblematically as females and some who have had difficulties with their gender orientation.

Third, there is no unambiguous evidence linking sex hormones with particular behaviours whether this be male hormones with aggression or female hormones, either premenstrually or at menopause, with particular temperamental states or particular emotional behaviours. Fourth, the evidence for a link between sex differences in abilities and sex differences in the brain is inconsistent, as will be seen in chapter 5. Finally as the rest of the book will amply demonstrate, sex differences in human behaviour are not consistent over time and culture, if we exclude the obvious ones that males produce sperm and that women produce eggs, bear babies and lactate. Thus while the sex we are born with will affect the manner in which we are labelled, whether as female or male, how we develop as a woman or as a man, will owe as much, if not more to 'nurture'.

Notes

1. For example, because of metabolic conditions affecting the manufacture of male hormones or because the cells of the foetal organs may be insensitive to male hormones.
2. For example, because high levels of a hormone called progesterone can break up into substances which act as male hormones.
3. If they have one ovary and one testicle or a single organ containing both kinds of tissue or **pseudohermaphrodites**; if they have one set of testes or gonads but their external genitalia are either not consistent with the gonad or are ambiguous looking.
4. Individuals falling into these categories have two normal X chromosomes, normal ovaries, uterus and fallopian tubes but at birth their external genitalia show varying degrees of similarity to male organs. Now that chromosomal sex can be established easily such individuals are assigned female sex immediately after birth and, with some minor cosmetic surgery and some replacement hormone therapy, follow normal female biological development experiencing puberty and being able to have children. Nevertheless such individuals have been exposed to far greater levels of male hormones than their peers and, as a result, their emotional and social lives have been studied in order to investigate the effect of these male hormones on their gender development and their sexuality. See for example, Erhardt, and Baker (1974).
5. Almost all men between 28 and 32 years of age, born in Copenhagen whose height was within the top 15 per cent of the height distribution for Danish males were investigated. The height criterion was used because both XYY and XXY men tend to be taller than average.
6. There have been three studies which examined the level of aggressive behaviour in girls who had been exposed to high levels of 'male' hormones pre-natally (Money and Ehrhardt, 1972, Money and Schwartz, 1976, and Erhardt and Baker, 1974). In the first study the authors reported no difference between such girls and controls in the level of childhood fighting; in the second the authors concluded that there was no evidence that these girls showed any tendency to manifest levels of overt aggression either in childhood or puberty, and in the third when 17 such girls were compared with their sisters, there was no difference in levels of fighting though the androgenized girls were reported to initiate more fights than their sisters. These studies would not appear to support the claim that high levels of pre-natal male hormones in girls lead to more aggressive behaviour later in life.

Chapter 4

Sugar and Spice; Frogs and Snails

Women's Work
'I've got the children to tend
The clothes to mend
The floor to mop
The food to shop
Then the chicken to fry
The baby to dry
I've got company to feed
. . .
Maya Angelou *And Still I Rise* (1992)

. . . for most American boys, manhood is achieved through a series of informal tests. By not crying or associating with girls, by being strong, tough, good at sports, and willing to fight, boys prove to their peers – and often to their parents, especially fathers – that they are real men.
Myriam Miedzian (1992, p. 87)

D.H. Lawrence on how to bring up children;
(in the case of a girl) Let her learn the domestic arts in their perfection. Let us even artificially set her to spin and weave.
(in the case of boys) First and foremost establish a rule over them, a proud, harsh, manly rule. Make them *know* that every moment they are in the shade of a proud, strong, adult authority. Let them be soldiers. (Lawrence's italics)

In the last two chapters we considered essentialist approaches to sex and gender: approaches that argued that women and men differ in their nature, either because of physiological predispositions or because in their earliest years unconscious processes forge deeply divergent gender pathways. Mainstream psychology has, on the whole, distanced itself from such positions and views of gender within it have developed from a rather different orientation. One in which human beings are seen as shaped not by essential nature but by the environment into which they are born. The stress has been not on nature but on nurture and psychologists, particularly developmental psychologists, have directed their interest and research to the process of **socialization**, a term which is used to cover the influences on the developing child of his or her domestic and cultural environment. From the perspective of socialization theories, men and women are seen to differ largely because of differences in the manner in which their particular society shapes and moulds their behaviour, attitudes and values.

In the first part of this chapter we shall examine the development of views on gender within this perspective following a historical pathway which, not surprisingly, parallels the major changes and developments within mainstream psychology. In the second part of the chapter the emphasis will move away from theoretical approaches and explore some of the empirical research on the developmental trajectories of the two sexes from infancy to adolescence, in order to examine the evidence bearing on the claim that the social environment plays the major role in the production of sex differences.

Theoretical approaches

Behaviourism and social learning

For several decades, the study of gender has used a . . . historically invariant model . . . a kind of static sex-role container into which all biological males and females are forced to fit. This process of fitting into pre-existing roles is called 'socialization'.
Michael Kimmel (1987, p 12)

At home, especially when you are a girl, you are expected to stay at home and do the housework and the boys go out. They seem to go out when they like . . . and I don't think that's really fair.
British schoolgirl speaking in the late eighties, in Wolpe (1988)

For much of this century, particularly in the USA, psychology was dominated by the movement of Behaviourism (Unger, 1990). Behaviourists worked within a perspective that regarded psychology as a science and consequently they placed their major emphasis on the collection and analysis of empirical data. They argued that the only truly 'objective', and thus scientific, data available for psychological analysis were those events that are observable. As a result, they turned their attention to behaviour rather than to feelings or thoughts, claiming that the systematic observation of behaviour would provide the basis for a science of psychology.

Behaviour, they claimed, was almost exclusively dependent on learning and consequently they set out to discover the rules which governed learning. In essence they saw these as reducing to the principle that **behaviour is controlled by its consequences** so that actions which are rewarded (or reinforced) tend to be repeated, and actions which are either not rewarded or which are followed by unpleasant consequences tend not to be repeated. In essence they regarded human behaviour as shaped by the carrot and the stick.

With respect to gender differences, at the simplest level, behaviourists argued these are reducible to the principle that the sexes behave in different ways because boys are rewarded for masculine behaviours and girls for feminine.

In support of these claims, behaviourists pointed to the many instances of parents openly approving and rewarding particular and different behaviours for boys and girl. As for instance when a mother says to her small daughter, 'good little girls help mommys clean up' or a father urges his son to stand up for himself and 'be a man'.

Early behaviourists tended to emphasize the importance of the contingent effect of particular acts. Thus they saw children's behaviour as shaped by direct rewards, praise, punishment or disapproval. Later workers in the tradition, however, like the social learning theorist Albert Bandura (Bandura and Walters, 1963) developed the notions of latent learning from social situations and modelling. They pointed out that a parent does not need to consciously approve or disapprove of particular behaviour or indeed intend to shape different behaviours in boys and girls. The learning process may be latent and far less deliberate because of the child's propensity to copy and imitate the actions of others and to 'model' their own behaviour on the observed behaviour of others. Anyone who has spent some time at all with children will have direct experience of the extent to which children do these things. They copy (or imitate) the actions of others and they model their behaviour on others, as for example when a small child pretends to be driving a car or when a group of children base their play on a popular television series.

However, if we do accept that children 'learn' how to behave by imitation and modelling, we are left with the question of whom they choose for models and why they make such choices. Social learning theorists, basing their claims on laboratory studies, argue that children tend to imitate the actions of, and model themselves on, those whom they perceive to be friendly, warm, attentive, powerful and similar to themselves (Bandura and Huston, 1961, Bandura *et al.* 1963, Mishel and Grusec, 1966). If this is the case then, extending the social learning argument to gender development, social learning theorists have to demonstrate that for boys, men, and for girls, women, encompass the attributes of attractive role models.

Since the attributes of friendliness, warmth, attentiveness and powerfulness are not linked in any systematic manner to gender, in order to account for children modelling themselves on others of the same sex, social learning theorists have had to focus on the attribute of similarity. This they have done in two ways:

1. by claiming that children differentially pay attention to peers of the same sex;
2. by emphasising the bond between children and their same sex parent.

With respect to the first mechanism, Michel, who has been the leading exponent of this approach to gender, puts it this way: 'Boys do not learn about baseball by watching girls and girls do not learn about fashion by watching boys' (Tavris and Wade, 1984). With respect to the second mechanism, social learning theorists have proposed that the relation with the same sex parent is dependent on a process they have called **identification**. The term, identification, refers to a particular form of imitation whereby the child spontaneously copies whole patterns of behaviour without being trained or obtaining direct rewards for doing this.

Research, however, has not in general supported either of these contentions. In the first case, with respect to the influence of their peers, it is clear that, while children tend after the first three years of life to associate largely with their own sex, this does not mean that they are not interested in, and do not observe, the other sex. This can easily be demonstrated by asking a small boy or girl to pretend to be an adult of the other sex. In the second case, with respect to the child – parent axis, it is by no means clear that children identify mainly with the same sex parent. For example many small girls play football or other sports with their fathers rather than their mothers, and some small boys enjoy baking cakes and cooking with their mothers. In any event, placing a major theoretical emphasis on identification with parents as the major source of gender development rests on an assumption that the great majority of children come from intact nuclear families. This is a presumption that might have been made about middle class American children in the middle years of this century but is not one that could generally be taken to hold today, even in a middle class environment.

Apart from these observations of a general nature, it is also worth noting that empirical studies have not provided support for the contention that children identify mainly with the same sex parent. For example, a review of 20 laboratory studies in which children were presented with models of both sexes revealed little consistent tendency for pre-school children to select same – sex models. When shown models who were displaying affection, aggression, toy choices, aesthetic preferences, and other activities, the children's choices were not apparently affected by the sex of those they chose to model (Maccoby and Jacklin, 1974). Further, while some studies do show parent – child similarities on certain dimensions of personality such as values and attitudes, they fail to show that these similarities are related to the sex of the parents (Williams, 1987).

In general, then, it is clear that research has not supported the claim that children automatically model themselves on others of the same sex, whether peers or parents, and this casts doubt on the main mechanism for gender development proposed by social learning theorists.

Social learning theorists have given some consideration to the manner in which some children acquire a homosexual identity, although even the most ardent proponent of social leaning theory would not claim that sexual orientation is acquired only through the processes of reinforcement and modelling. However, it has been suggested by some writers in this tradition that one or two early and positive homosexual experiences can 'fix' a male in lifelong homosexuality. It is proposed that this 'fixing' occurs because if a young boy has had one or more pleasurable homosexual encounters he is likely to fantasize about the experience or experiences while masturbating, thus providing continual reinforcement for this sexual orientation.

Generally, social learning approaches do not tell us a great deal about gender and sexuality because of the assumptions that are made about the relative passivity of the child in the acquisition of gender identity. As we shall see, children do not simply absorb ideas about gender, they think about it as well. Nevertheless it is also clear that in any culture there are both overt and covert forces at work which direct a child's development in such a way that their behaviour is consistent with what is expected by their society of their sex. In the second part of this chapter we will look at a great deal of evidence which does lend support to the claim that very often behaving in a manner consistent with accepted notions of the appropriate behaviour of an individual's sex is more rewarding than the converse.

Cognitive – developmental theory

> Kohlberg's entire theory is couched in male terms. The pronouns are male, the body type discussed is male, even the anecdotal examples are all about male children. Is the theory equally applicable to both sexes?
> Rohrbaugh (1981)

Towards the middle years of this century the dominance of behaviourism within traditional or mainstream psychology came under increasing attack. The reasons for this are complex and manifold[1] but for the purposes of this book, we will focus on three strands. First, it was becoming apparent that the 'objective' measurement of behaviour was less easily achieved than had been thought. To take an example, with particular relevance to gender issues: if it is desired to construct any measure of personality, who chooses the items for the scale? Surely the social class, ethnic origin and gender of those who construct the scale will affect the choice of items? If this is the case, can we talk about 'objective' measurements? Second, behaviourism locates the 'subject' in a passive position. He or she is 'shaped', or 'moulded' by external contingencies with no consideration at all being given to the manner in which he or she actively attempts to make sense of environment. As Tavris and Wade (1984, p. 215) put it behaviourism and social learning view the developing child 'from the outside' without attempting to understand the child's, and later the adult's, own point of view. Third, mainstream psychology in the English speaking world came under the influence of Jean Piaget (1954), the eminent Swiss theorist. Piaget's enormous body of writing about children's cognitive development not only emphasized the child's attempts to actively understand his or her world, but also led to a totally different manner of studying child development emphasizing, in particular, that children's development proceeds in distinct phases.

It was this, third influence, that had an immediate effect on views of gender development. This was because Lawrence Kohlberg (1966), who was to write with considerable influence about gender, commenced the application of Piagetian theory to gender development. From the point of view of this book we need to consider the influence on Kohlberg's theory of gender development of the two elements of Piagetian theory already mentioned. The first is the emphasis on the child's active attempts to 'construct' reality (that is to understand and make sense of the world). The second is the Piagetian claim that the child's cognitive development proceeds in fixed and discrete developmental phases with its further implication that young children think in ways that are qualitatively different from the thinking of older children and adults.

In their consideration of the child's attempts to make sense of gender, in particular, cognitive – developmental psychologists like Kohlberg often make use of the two terms: gender identity and gender typing. The term **gender identity** is taken to refer to the psychological sense of oneself as female or male. The term **gender typing** is taken to refer to the process of developing traits and behaviours that mirror the views of one's society about what is appropriate for a male or female (Unger and Crawford, 1992). According to Kohlberg and his associates, gender identity and gender typing develop in a fixed and relatively immutable way, and, in agreement with Piagetian theory, in discrete stages. The first stage is one achieved between $2\frac{1}{2}$ and 3 years and occurs when the child achieves *gender identity*. At this stage children can identify themselves correctly as a girl or boy and can also correctly identify the sex of others both in real life and from pictures. The second stage occurs when *gender stability* is reached, about age 5. At this stage children know that you stay the same gender throughout life. They do not, for example, make the mistake made by Jimmy in the following exchange:

Johnny (age $4\frac{1}{2}$): I'm going to be an airplane builder when I grow up.
Jimmy (age 4): When I grow up, I'll be a mommy.
Johnny: No you can't be a mommy. You have to be a daddy.
Jimmy: No I'm going to be a mommy.
Johnny: No, you're not a girl, you can't be a mommy.
Jimmy: Yes, I can.
Kohlberg (1966, p. 95)

However, while children at this stage understand that their own sex will not change, according to Kohlberg and associated theorists, their understanding of gender is still very concrete and limited. It does not extend to understanding that changing outward gender attributes, does not change gender. This third stage, according to these theorists, only emerges at around 7 years of age when the stage of *gender constancy* is reached. Gender constancy, the final change, involves the deep understanding that if an adult were to completely change their physical appearance (as in the case of a drag artist), their gender would not change.

It is important to understand that Kohlberg and his associates believe that the child moves through these stages not as the social learning theorists argue because he or she is rewarded and moulded into sex-typed behaviour, but because having acquired gender identity the *child actively selects from the repertoire of social behaviour he or she is exposed to those elements that are appropriate to his or her gender identity*. Further, where social learning theorists see identification with the same sex adults or peers as causing sex typing, Kohlberg argues for the reverse – that is, it is only after the child has achieved gender identity and has started gender typing him or herself, that he or she then identifies with same sex peers and adults.

Kohlberg would not deny that society can reinforce sex-typed behaviour but would claim that this is an additional source of sex typing rather than its prime vehicle. As Unger and Crawford (1992, p. 421) put it:

> The cognitive – developmental perspective does not deny social learning principles; rather it adds to them by offering the intriguing idea that children willingly socialize themselves to be masculine or feminine.

Critiques of Kohlberg's views on gender development have tended to centre on its male bias. As the quote at the beginning of this subsection indicates he approached gender development from the point-of-view of 'male-as-norm' and the limitations this imposes can be seen when we consider the implications for girls.

Kohlberg argues that after achieving a stable gender identity, children then socialize themselves into sex-typed behaviour because they are motivated to be typical girls or boys. His argument then concentrates on the boy pointing out the advantages in terms of power, prestige and ultimate economic advantage of the male role. As indicated earlier, much of his writing is concerned with mapping out how boys continue with their sex-typing into the male role which he clearly regards as superior to the female. Having based the major part of his argument on the boy's acquisition of the male role, he then obviously has more difficulty in explaining why girls should wish to aspire to the female role, since his whole stance is that this role is less rewarding in terms of prestige and competence. In attempting to explain the girl's sex-typing, in terms of his own relative downgrading of the attractions of the female role in comparison to the male role, Kohlberg is forced into some rather contorted arguments. To begin with he points out that many girls go through a 'tomboy' phase, thus proving the superior attraction of male sex-typing. However, he later conceded that not all girls go through this phase and that most who do, emerge from it by middle childhood. Thus he went on to seek out an alternative hypothesis by proposing that girls eventually find the female role more attractive because it is seen often as 'nicer' than the male role.

In addition to the relative weakness of Kohlberg's theory when it is applied to females, his approach has also been criticized by Bem, amongst others, because it fails to ask why it is that sex is the major category by which children come to categorize themselves. As Bem (1983, p. 230) puts it

> . . . the theory fails to explain why sex will have primacy over other potential categories of the self such as race, religion or even eye color . . . most cognitive psychologists do not explicitly ponder the 'why sex' question, nor do they even raise the possibility that other categories could fit the general theory just as well.

Finally, it should be pointed out that research has not supported Kohlberg's claim that children become sex-typed only after achieving an understanding of gender constancy. On the contrary, as Unger and Crawford (1992) point out, empirical studies show that most children show a preference for gender-typed objects and activities by the age of three before gender constancy is normally achieved.

Moving beyond gender-typing

Androgyny

> My personal prescriptions for a liberated sexual identity:
> Let sexual preference be ignored;
> Let sex roles be abolished;
> Let gender move from figure to ground.
> Sandra Bem (1975, p. 223)

The next major development in the psychological study of gender to follow on from the cognitive developmental approach was related to the growing critique of mainstream psychology which was starting to emerge from the growing ranks of women psychologists in the 1970s and 1980s. Spokeswomen such as Mary Parlee (1985) and Carole Gilligan (1982) began to to make explicit the largely male-centered nature of the discipline. They pointed out that theories had largely been constructed from the 'male-as-normative viewpoint' by male psychologists frequently using as subjects samples of students who were predominately male. Concurrently attention was also being drawn to the fact that most psychologists within the western world were also white and middle class (Siann and Ugwuegbu, 1988). These challenges to the latent biases in psychology did not, of course, take place in a social vacuum, but in a period when social movements such as Feminism and Black Consciousness were beginning to make their presence felt throughout the western world.

Pre-eminent amongst the women critics of mainstream psychological approaches to the psychology of gender was Sandra Bem who, with Janet Spence *et al.* (1975), began to explore the relevance to this area of the concept of **androgyny** The word androgyny combines the Greek roots *andro* (male) and *gyn* (female) to refer to a balance of both, and the underlying concept of androgyny as a blending of masculine and feminine attributes has a long history with roots in classical mythology, literature and religion (Unger and Crawford, 1992). Thus to say a person is androgynous suggests that the individual concerned has attributes, physical, psychological or both, that do not reflect the prevalent separate sex-typing of their culture. For example, in the mid 1970s, David Bowie, and in the 1980s, Annie Lennox and Grace Jones, presented physical persona that could be regarded as androgynous.

Bem pioneered a simple questionnaire which she called the Sex Role Inventory (BSRI). According to Bem's original early formulations, scores on this inventory, which is basically a list of attributes on which individuals are required to rate themselves as either high or low, can be grouped into three types of results: a range of scores that fall into the 'male-typed range', a range of scores that fall into the 'female-typed range' and a range which fall into an 'androgynous' range. For example, high male-type scores would include high self-ratings on attributes such as rational, active and dominant; high female-type scores would include high self-ratings on attributes such as caring, pastoral and passive; and high androgynous scores would cover high self-ratings on both male and female sex-type attributes.

In her early work Bem suggested that her reseach and the research of others appeared to show that individuals falling into this third category functioned better and more flexibly than their more conventionally sex-typed peers. Over 100 studies using the BSRI were carried out between 1976 and 1984 and most of these related high androgynous scores to high levels of mental health and, as a result, particularly in the USA, some clinicians even began to discuss how to androgynize their clients and patients (Walsh, 1987).

In the later 1980s, however, methodological criticisms began to emerge both of the content of the BSRI scale and of the manner in which measurements were made. Further doubt began to be thrown on the empirical results linking androgyny with superior adjustment and mental health. For example, Marylee Taylor and Judith Hall (1982) found that certain masculine traits were a better predictor of psychological well-being than androgyny. Further, critics like Bernice Lott started to question whether there are separate and clearly definable masculine and feminine attributes or behaviours. Lott argues that because androgyny scales label some attributes as masculine or feminine this tends to make us give cognitive and linguistic labels to attributes that are simply essentially human rather than typically sex-typed in the masculine direction. Thus a women who describes herself as highly self-reliant, ambitious and analytical increases her masculinity scores on an androgyny scale. But, argues Lott, surely it would be better to regard her simply as high on these attributes rather than masculine:

> Behavior has no gender . . . To label some behaviors as feminine and
> some as masculine, as androgyny researchers do, and then to put the

two artificial pieces back together again . . . is to reinforce verbal hab-
its which undermine the possibility of degendering behavior.
Lott (1981)

Further, Bem herself began to reject the notion that there are independent
variables such as masculinity and femininity and she, with many others, began
to move towards an alternative formulation of the psychology of gender –
gender-schema theory.

Gender-schema theory

Thus if gender-schema theory has a political message, it is not that the
individual should be androgynous. Rather it is . . . that society ought
to temper its insistence on the ubiquitous functional importance of the
gender dichotomy.
Sandra Bem (1987, p. 245)

Gender-schema theory contains some elements of both the cognitive and
the social learning approaches to the developing child. In accordance with
social learning it acknowledges the framework of learning provided by the
social world, and in agreement with many cognitive approaches (Siann and
Ugwuegbu, 1988) it argues that young children construct cognitive 'schemas'
to help them understand and come to terms with both the external world and
their own internal representation of it.

The term, schema, refers to the mental structures children use to encode
and process information. For example, a young child may have a schema
about going to bed which will help her to understand her mother's sentence:
'It's bedtime now'. This schema provides a network of associations which
might embrace, amongst other thoughts, not feeling very enthusiastic about
the prospect of bed but being aware that she is going to comply because she
is a good girl, that she is going to have supper, followed by a bath, a bedtime
story, a cuddle and lights out. Schemas thus also often provide a script which
lays out a set of the likely sequence of behaviours associated with the schema.

To continue with our example, the schema and associated script of bedtime will also provide an organizing framework for the little girl to deal with
other information as on being told, for example, that 'Tommy, next door is
naughty, he always runs away and hides at bedtime'.

Basically schema theory suggests that schemas and scripts provide cognitive tools for thinking about the past, present and future. They are essentially
networks of associations and general knowledge which aid thinking about and
understanding not only the external world but also the internal one. Furthermore they provide a set of flexible cognitive networks into which new experiences or information can be assimilated. Thus a child will not only have
schemas and scripts about referents in the social and physical environment –
for example: bedtime, going to visit the dentist, what a typical boy or girl is

like and what a naughty child is like – she will also have a schema about herself. Something perhaps on the lines of – a small kind of person, who is a girl,
who lives with mummy and is good most of the time and likes ice cream but
prefers staying up to going to bed etc . . .

Applying schema theory to gender, Bem suggests first that sex-typing is
a gender schema that varies from culture to culture. Drawing from learning
theory she proposes that the cultural content of gender schema will undoubtedly be affected, not only by what the society labels as appropriately masculine
or feminine behaviour, but also by the extent to which the culture or subculture
rewards or punishes adherence to such sex-typing. Second, she proposes that
self-schemas, or the manner in which individuals think about themselves, are
permeated to differing degrees by gender schema, both across individuals, and
in the case of any particular individual, across times and social contexts.

In this way any particular individual, growing up in a particular society
will acquire knowledge and feelings both explicit and implicit about the gender typing of their own culture, subculture and domestic environment. This
will give them a readiness to process and organize other schema, including
their own self-schema, with reference to gender schemas. Some individuals
will have fairly rigid gender schemas, closely related to cultural stereotypes
which they will frequently, if not invariably, use as tools in order to organize
and evaluate their own behaviour and to evaluate the behaviour of others.
Such individuals Bem would regard as 'strongly sex-typed'. Other individuals
with less rigid gender schema which they relate less frequently and less strongly
to themselves and others, Bem would regard as 'weakly sex-typed'.

Moving away from this theoretical base to a more prescriptive kind, one
which seeks to move away from sex-typed behaviour, Bem proposed, when
she first wrote about gender schema, that they should play a less important
role in society than they do at present. She also proposed that we should
encourage individuals to view themselves less through the lenses of the gender schema. As we shall see in the next subsection she has currently developed this position towards an even more social and less psychological stance.

Evaluations of gender-schema theory have pointed to the fact that its
approach to the cultural organization of gender is rather apolitical. While it
does take on board the power and relatively universal nature of sex-typing, it
does not acknowledge explicitly that the gender dichotomy has until very
recently spelt out an inferior role for women and a superior role for men in
most societies. It is to this critique of her gender-schema approach that Bem
has most recently turned her attention.

The lenses of gender

My interest has always been in getting rid of gender . . . As soon as I
had done the work on androgyny I thought 'this isn't what I meant
exactly' . . . So I moved onto talking about gender schema . . . and now

I would say that what I was really interested in was the problem of the gender polarizing lens.
Sandra Bem in Kitzinger (1992, pp. 222–4)

In her recent work Bem has expanded and developed her gender-schema approach in two basic ways. First, she has continued to point out the extent to which gender, as a mode for making sense of the world, continues to dominate personal and social life. Second, she has developed her understanding of the social and political implications of this polarization. In short she has expanded on her concern with the extent to which contemporary society continues to use gender as the pre-eminent criterion for segmenting and structuring social life and has moved her focus from the individual to the cultural. She encapsulates her most recent stance in the term **gender polarization**:

Gender polarization is the forging of cultural connections to the male/female distinction so that small if significant differences become large and profound influencing whole areas of people's lives – how they express emotion, how they experience sexual desire. Male/female has become an all-encompassing divide with two, and only two, mutually exclusive scripts, and everyone who diverges from these scripts is problematically deviant.
Sandra Bem in Kitzinger (1992, p. 223)

Bem believes that we should attempt to stem and reverse this process by ceasing to think about 'our maleness and femaleness. Let's stop organizing our lives around gender, including the gender of the people we are attracted to', and start organizing into social movements which, while being originally based on gender categories, seek to overturn such categories:

I think we do need organized social movements that build around being a woman, being black, being lesbian or gay . . . we are going to take this category and transform its meaning and fight for its being privileged or at least not being discriminated against . . . using it for our own politics.
Sandra Bem in Kitzinger (1992, p. 224)

This stance brings her analysis very close to those more structural approaches to gender which will be covered in chapter 6.

Developing differences

There are two sexes. The unpalatable truth must be faced. Your attempts at a merger can only end in heartbreak.
The psychiatrist, Dr Range in Joe Orton's play. *What the Butler Saw* (1986)

The second section of this chapter will briefly review empirical evidence on the differing developmental trajectories of boys and girls as they grow up in contemporary society. In doing this the evidence will be related to the major claim of the theorists whose work we have been considering in this chapter. This claim being that gender differences are largely the result of socialization practices.

Setting the scene

Gender is an invention of human societies, a feat of imagination and industry. This feat is multifaceted. One facet involves laborious efforts to transform male and female children into masculine and feminine adults.

Rachel Hare-Mustin and Jeanne Maracek (1990, p. 4)

Even if we do not agree with the claim that gender categorizations domi-nate our social and mental world, there is no doubt that, in most societies from the moment a child is born, its physiological sex will exert a very powerful influence on the manner in which it is treated, frequently within the family and invariably in the world outside. In the west, as we shall see in chapter 7, gender stereotypes continue to permeate television and cinema, although less blatantly than in the past. Indeed, there have been concerted efforts to reduce gender stereotyping in contemporary children's books,[2] although it is hardly feasible, or indeed desirable, to exert a retroactive censorship on the classics of the past which reflect the far more rigid gender stereotyping of their time. Furthermore, while toy manufacturers no longer produce chemistry sets whose packaging show boys carrying out experiments while girls watch, a Toys 'ЯUs Christmas catalogue (1992–3 pp. 16 and 19), a very large toy supplier in Britain, continues to illustrate tool sets with a boy model and model kitchens with a girl. Moreover, as we shall see, even parents who express the wish to bring their children up in a non-sexist manner continue to treat them, albeit uncon-sciously, in ways that reinforce sex-typed behaviour.

Pregnancy and infancy

In her earlier work Bem claimed that gender is the salient social category in the west and, as we shall see, empirical studies of children's development would certainly lend support to this claim. It is worth noting, however, that the extent to which societies organize social interactions and cognitive categoriza-tions around gender as a pivot has varied over time and place. Anthropologists have shown, for example, that in hunting and gathering societies, both in the past and even in some currently existing, such as among the !Kung of the Kalahari, sex-typing of behaviour and personal attributes is far less rigid than in other cultures (Sanday and Goodenough, 1990). In certain other societies, for example among the Bemba of Central Africa (Nkweto-Simmonds, 1993), little distinction is made between girls and boys in infancy, and traditional names are not gendered and can be used for either boys or girls. It is also worth noting that in contemporary India, even in traditional areas where boy babies continue to be overvalued compared to girls (Hrdy, 1989),[3] to the extent that girl babies are sometimes killed (McGirk, 1993) caste and class provide extremely powerful sources of social categorization and barriers against social interactions between individuals of different castes override gender. Nevertheless, even when gender categorization is least evident, sex-typing and sex-stereotyping tend to favour males rather females.

Unger and Crawford suggest that this inequality can be observed even during pregnancy. First, they claim, in the preference for male babies which has been shown, even as recently as the 1970s and 1980s, in societies as varied as the USA and Korea. Second, in the folklore concerned with predicting the sex of the unborn child which is encapsulated in sayings that tend to symbolize boys positively and girls negatively. For example:

> If a women is placid during pregnancy she will have a boy, but if she is bad tempered or cries a lot, she will have a girl . . .
>
> If her looks improve, she is expecting a boy; if they worsen a girl.
> Unger and Crawford (1992, pp. 231–2)

My own subjective impression is that currently, in western societies, the preference for male babies no longer holds sway and in my own experience, many women express a preference for a girl first. Preferences aside, however, as Bee (1992) points out: 'A newborn's sex is the first thing we ask about'. Furthermore, in most instances, if clothes are bought as presents for the new baby they will be sex-specific because, while there has been an increase in the proportion of unisex baby garments, most babyware departments still segment clothes for even the youngest of babies into those for girls and those for boys. Interestingly the colour coding that we tend to associate with such choices is more recent than might be supposed. According to Marjorie Garber (1993, p. 1) the colour code for baby clothes, which since the 1940s at least has been assumed to be pink for girls and blue for boys, has not always held. In the early years of the twentieth century, boys wore pink, 'a more decided colour' according to the promotional literature of the time, and girls blue which was thought to be 'delicate' and 'dainty'.

Following on from pregnancy and birth, surveys done in the 1960s and 1970s indicated that sex-typing of infants continues. For example, Rubin *et al.* (1974) found that first-time parents of babies rated boy babies higher on attributes such as firm, large, well co-ordinated, and girl babies higher on attributes such as soft, finely-featured and inattentive. These gender distinctions were made even though medical personnel had found no neurological or physical differences between the sexes on the sample concerned. The finding of no sex differences by the medical staff is not surprising as research has indicated no neurological or psychological differences between the sexes either at birth or in early childhood (Bee, 1992).

Despite the fact that there is no evidence to suggest sex differences in psychological attributes during the first years, studies have shown that babies are interacted with in different ways depending on the sex they are thought to be. A number of such studies have used the Baby X technique in which the baby concerned wears unisex clothes and irrespective of his/her sex is presented to some subjects as a girl, and to others as a boy. For example, in 1976 John and Sandra Condry showed men and women a videotape of a 9-month-old infant reacting to a teddy-bear, a jack-in-the-box, a doll and a buzzer, and asked them to rate the infant's pleasure, anger and fear in each situation. The supposed sex of the baby made little difference in the case of the teddy bear and the buzzer but when the baby reacted with agitation and tears to the jack-in-the-box, the baby was more likely to be rated as 'fearful' if presented as a girl, and as 'angry' if presented as a boy. In another Baby X study, even mothers who had earlier said that they believed male and female babies are alike played differently with a baby introduced to them as either 'Beth' or 'Adam'. Mothers playing with 'Beth' tended to hand the infant a doll first, while other mothers playing with 'Adam' handed the baby a train first (Tavris and Wade, 1984).

These and similar studies reflect a general tendency for adults to interact differently with boys and girls, even when the adults concerned are not aware of their implicit gender typing. In most instances the strongest and earliest aspect of this will be parental behaviour. Charles Lewis (1986) has reviewed a large number of studies concerned with parental behaviour with daughters as compared to sons and has concluded that, despite methodological problems with many of the studies, there is evidence that mothers and fathers handle their boys and girls in subtly different ways. For example in one study of the first 3 months of life, parents tended to cuddle opposite-sex children and to offer toys and to stimulate same-sex children (Parke and Sawin, 1980). Other studies suggest that as babies grow older fathers, compared to mothers, are more likely to interact differently with boys and girls. For instance, to engage in more physical interaction games with boys, like throwing them up in the air. Fathers also appear more likely to encourage sex differences than mothers by being more likely to discourage sex-inappropriate play. In an observation study Fagot (1978) showed that fathers encouraged their daughters to stay near them and were especially critical of doll-play in sons.

Some studies, particularly American ones, also suggest that young children themselves tend to interact differently with mothers and fathers, approaching fathers more often for play and approaching the same-sex parent more often in times of stress (Spelke *et al.* 1973). American studies also tend to show that girls are more likely to initiate interaction with adults including parents than boys (Ross and Goldman, 1977). In general, however, it seems that there are clearer differences in parental behaviour towards the sexes, than in boys' and girls' behaviour towards parents of different sexes. Many studies of parent–child interaction support the conclusion that both parents, but particularly fathers, treat their children of different sexes in ways that are consistent with the sex-typing of behaviour.

Studies have also shown that this is characteristic of most adults and that even teachers who explicitly profess not to gender-type do so in subtle ways. Not for example in what they say but in the manner in which they do so (Tavris and Wade, 1984). Such predispositions continue right through the life span because, as we shall see in the next chapter, many of us make attributions about other people based on gender although we are not consciously aware of doing so and even when we explicitly state, and probably believe, that we make no such gender-typed distinctions.

If children are exposed to sex-typing so early on it is not surprising that in the west, at any event, from a very early age children are aware both of their gender identity and of the sex-typing associated with it. It would also seem highly likely that for most children acting in accordance with cultural norms of gender-typing would be likely to produce a gratifying level of praise and encouragement from adults.

Early childhood

As already noted surveys show that most children in the west can identify the sexes of others as well as themselves by the age of $2\frac{1}{2}$ to 3-years and by the latter age there is a marked tendency for children in the west to prefer to play with others of the same sex.[4] Two explanations have been offered for this same sex preference in play. One, to which we will return in the next chapter, is that there are universal and inborn sex differences in the kind of play preferred, with boys preferring higher levels of 'rough and tumble' play.[5] A problem with this explanation is that it is based on what is taken to be a universal preference for same-sex playmates, but while a number of studies in the west do show a high degree of gender segregation in play in pre-school children, studies in the Third World, for example those of Sara Harkness and Charles Super (1985) in Kenya, indicate that gender composition in children's play groups is about equal until about 6 to 9 years and there is no strong same-sex preference in play. A second explanation for gender segregation in play is that in general boys and girls are encouraged to learn to play with different kinds of toys at an early age and then choose friends with the same preferences. Some support for this second explanation comes from studies showing a marked tendency for even very young children to be able to identify sex-appropriate toys and to play with them (Lloyd and Duveen, 1992).

Because most adults continue to follow sex-typing in the choice of toys for young children it is perhaps not surprising that 3 year olds can identify particular toys as being more suitable for girls or boys, but the extent of children's understanding of the sex-typing of behaviour goes far beyond their

Gender, Sex and Sexuality

own social world. For example, Huston (1985) showed that 3 to 4 year olds can even identify the typical occupations of men and women, and by the time children start school they appear to have a considerable knowledge of the sex-typing of behaviour in their own environment.

A number of studies have shown that in these early years there is a developmental sequence in children's application of their knowledge of the sex-typing of behaviour. Typically, at 4 years of age they are aware of the sex-typing of behaviour and toys but are not too worried by trangressions of these codes and categories. However, by between 5 and about 8 they are not only aware of sex-typing but are very condemnatory of anyone who trangresses the codes. In Lloyd and Duveen's words (1992, p. 181) it is at this stage that: 'children are the most conservative social actors in the gender culture of the classroom'. By 9 years of age, however, they are once again far more flexible about such codes.

The following explanation is usually offered for this developmental sequence. Between the ages of about 5 to 8 the child is centrally concerned to discover the rules that govern social behaviour including, of course, those related to gender. Furthermore at this stage they are not only concerned to establish such rules but are also concerned to show others that they adhere to such rules. At this stage they also tend to believe that social rules are moral imperatives. In contrast, at younger ages they are less concerned with seeking and establishing such rules and at older ages, when they are more secure in their social identity, they feel able to treat such social rules with some discretion. This sequence is shown in a study by Damon (1977) who asked children aged between 4 and 9 whether a little boy called George who liked to play with dolls should do so, even though his parents preferred him to play with other toys. Four year olds thought George could play with what he liked. Six year olds thought it was wrong for George to play with dolls. By age 9, however, children differentiated between morality and social custom. For example one boy said: 'Breaking windows you're not supposed to do. And if you play with dolls, well you can, but boys usually don't'.

With respect to sex-typing in the early years of childhood, a finding reported in many, though by no means all studies, is that children agree on male sex-typing in behaviour earlier than they do on female. Furthermore most studies agree that children of both sexes are less concerned about girls behaving in a male sex-typed manner than the reverse and that, on the whole, boys place more emphasis on sex-typing in behaviour than do girls. For example, boys more than girls have been shown to choose as their future occupation, sex-typed careers. These findings tend to be attributed to the relatively greater prestige of males in society at large which children appear to recognize fairly early on. It has been shown that both boys and girls assign more positive attributes to males than to females (Urberg, 1982) and it has also been shown that they assign more value to masculine activities than to feminine ones (Feinman, 1981). These findings are in accordance with the general tendency for both adults and children to be more concerned about boys behaving in a 'sissy' manner than by tomboy girls. As a result, in the very great majority of societies, boys are placed under far greater pressure to conform to sex-typed behaviour than are girls. As Archer (1984) has put it, in society as a whole, there is far more 'rigidity' in the extent to which boy's opposite-sex activities are avoided.

During these years of early childhood it is not surprising then that the social pressures discussed in this section tend to reinforce children's sex-typing of their own behaviour, and that this tendency is stronger for boys than for girls.

Middle childhood

While most studies on gender differences in middle childhood have been done in the west, there have also been a number of cross-cultural studies (Newson and Newson, 1986). In general there is a large measure of consensus that during this period children choose same-sex partners for social interaction and play, and that there are some gender differences in the type of play and social interaction (Smith, 1986) with many studies showing boys continuing higher levels of more rough and tumble play. Usually, however, gender differences in type of play reflect differences in content and themes rather than more basic differences. For example, Lever (1976) showed that both boys and girls played outdoors and played competitively but that boys were more likely to play football and girls rope games and, whereas both played competitively, the competition was more explicit in boys games than in girls.

A great deal of research has been done recently on the manner in which children in the west actively maintain same-sex and avoid other-sex interaction in middle childhood. To begin with there is considerable stigmatization of children, particularly boys, who cross sex boundaries. Related to this is the phenomenon whereby shy and marginal boys may be teased and mocked as being 'sissy' or sometimes in the American setting 'fags' (Unger and Crawford, 1992)[6]. Furthermore boys and girls maintain group boundaries by cross-sex chasing. Such chasing is sometimes explicitly reinforced by remarks like (from girls) 'we don't want any smelly boys with us' or (from boys) remarks like 'girls are such babies'. In the face of such public disapproval of cross-sex interaction it is interesting that privately, at home or in small secure neighbourhoods, cross-gender friendships sometimes continue to flourish.

Such friendships, however, are exceptional and generally in social, home and school situations most children show fairly strong sex-typed behaviour at this period. This is not surprising because research indicates that sex-appropriate behaviour continues to be rewarded and sex-inappropriate behaviour continues to be treated negatively not only as indicated above by peers, but also by parents and teachers (Smith, 1986). As before, this sex-type shaping of behaviour is more marked for boys than girls.

Adolescence

General issues

As children grow older, while girls continue to have more freedom than boys to cross sex-role boundaries it seems that for most girls doing so begins to conflict with a growing sense of the importance of being feminine. For example, interest in outdoor activities and sports decline for both sexes as they grow older but this is more marked for girls (Newson and Newson, 1986) and tolerance of tomboyish behaviour decreases. For very many girls the focus moves towards activities concerned with establishing an attractive physical identity.

As will be discussed in more detail in chapter 7 the pressures on young women to conform to cultural stereotypes of physical attraction have not diminished appreciably in recent years. The contemporary emphasis on the need for all women to be physically presentable is probably related to what has been called the 'superwoman' (Conran, 1991) phenomenon whereby there is pressure on women to excel in all ways. This pressure can be contrasted with cultural expectations in the early years and middle years of this century when there was a marked divergence between the two roles of 'traditional woman' and 'working/new woman'. Because of this a woman who was aspiring to a serious career could afford to pay relatively little attention to the need to also present herself as glamorous. Instead she could present herself as what was termed a 'blue stocking' – a woman not particularly concerned with her appearance. Currently, however, partly because of cultural concerns with image and style, a woman who shows little interest in her appearance is unlikely to succeed in the very competitive labour market or be regarded as interested in relationships with men.

This cultural emphasis on physical appearance is shown by many surveys of adolescents which indicate that adolescents are concerned with their appearance. Young women are more likely than young men to express dissatisfaction with their physical appearance (Offer *et al.* 1988) but this gender imbalance is beginning to be eroded to some extent as advertising agencies have begun to target the male as well as the female market.

Physical appearance, however, is not the only area where surveys have indicated gender differences in the concerns of adolescence. The kind of issues which show gender divergence are illustrated by a recent large-scale survey undertaken in Australia by Glen Evans and Millicent Poole (1991) who surveyed using both interviews and questionnaire, a representative sample of 559 adolescents and young people in further and higher education, in employment and also currently unemployed. Evans and Poole reported that with respect to how they thought about themselves, young women – more than young men – rated themselves as high on attributes concerned with what the authors called 'responsibility' (concern for others, honesty, reliability, trying hard, careful and tidy); on being outgoing; on seeing home life as important and in being prepared to seek help from peers and books. Young women, more often than men, also gave personal development and personal relation-ships as a reason for their most important life concerns whereas young men, more than women, gave jobs and money as reasons for their most important life concerns. In terms of what they wanted from jobs, young women placed more stress on interactions with others and less stress on understanding all aspects of the job whereas young men placed more stress on understanding all aspects of their work and also seemed more concerned with the extent to which work imposed control and structure on their lives.

Similarily in another large-scale survey, this time in the UK, Banks *et al.* (1992) showed gender differences in attitudes to work in that young women were more likely to believe that their future work patterns would be affected by family needs.

These surveys agree with other large-scale studies which indicate that by early adulthood young women have a life perspective that is based more on relationships with others, while young men's perspective tends to focus more on individual achievement.

It must be stressed, however, that these are overall findings relating to the general population and that within particular subgroups such as, for example, the 200 advanced business students surveyed in a study conducted by Beutell and Brenner in the USA, such gender differences may not be observed. Results of this study indicated that, contrary to most previous studies, men reported higher needs than women for security and leisure time while women reported higher needs for achievement and continued growth in skills and knowledge (Unger and Crawford; 1992). In the next chapter gender differences and simi-larities with respect to careers and achievement will be considered in more detail, but at this stage it is important to note that these appear to be diminish-ing (Banks *et al.* 1992).

While surveys indicate that most adolescents are both interested and concerned about their future prospects in the educational and/or employment sphere, their concerns are equally with their social and sexual relationships and it is to these that we will now turn.

Friendships and leisure activities
Generally, research in the past has suggested that during adolescence girls tend to have fewer friends than boys but these friendships tend to be more intimate and confiding (Banks *et al.* 1992). It has also been suggested that both sexes report that their friends are of the same sex as themselves. Recently, gender distinctions with respect to friends have become less marked, both because boys are more prepared than they were in the past to talk confidentially and openly to close friends and also because both sexes show a growing tendency to have friends of both sexes (Beutell and Brenner, 1986).

A number of research studies have focused particularly on the leisure pursuits of young people in Britain and over the years these have also shown a blurring of gender distinctions. Those conducted in the 1970s and early 1980s tended to report a sharply contrasting picture of the social life of the sexes. Young men were presented as being more involved not only in youth clubs and sports but also, particularly in the case of working class youths, as being more strongly influenced by what were termed 'youth subcultures'; a term used to describe an implicitly rebellious posture towards accepted social values, which revolved around street life, alcohol, drugs and strong identification with particular musical styles such as rock and punk (Hebdidge, 1979). Young women on the other hand were presented as not only having fewer but more intense friends than boys, but also as being more home based: involved in a bedroom culture of listening to music at home, talking about boys and pop stars with occasional forays into clubs and discos (McRobbie and Garber, 1976).

More recent studies have shown a blurring and reappraisal of these gender differences. For example, studies have shown that some girls often take more part in leisure activities outside the home than boys (Smith, 1978) while others have reappraised the earlier studies of working class youth and have suggested that the reasons young women were shown to be more home-based than their male peers were less related to interest and inclination than to 'gender subordination'. This term is used by Sue Lees, for instance, with reference to her argument that girls are less likely to be out on the streets than boys because not only is street life more dangerous for girls but also because being out on the streets, unless it is with a boyfriend, lays a girl open to being regarded as a 'slag' (Lees, 1986).

In general most studies of young people in the western world have until recently suggested the earlier involvement of girls in dating and courtship. However, a large-scale recent study in Britain has once again shown a blurring of gender differences in that, by the age of 16, significant proportions of boys as well as girls have a girlfriend or boyfriend. Having a boyfriend or girlfriend tends to reduce the time spent with friendship groups and family. Normally this still seems to happen earlier with girls than boys but, as with most of such gender effects, other variables such as level of education and employment status also play a part (Banks *et al.*, 1992). Indeed, what is striking about recent studies conducted with adolescents is the extent to which social class and education, rather than gender, contribute to differences amongst respondents.

Sexuality and sexual behaviour

I like girls who are good looking, nice personality and not too mouthy
– don't two-time you.
British schoolboy talking in the 1980s, Wood (1984)

(The type of boy to look out for)
If they're kind and they chat alright and they're just kind to you . . .
If he doesn't go around hitting and punching you as some boys do.
British schoolgirl talking in the 1980s, Lees (1986, p. 108)

Most studies of sexual behaviour in adolesence agree on two major propositions. First, that young people begin to be sexually active at earlier ages than in the past and, second, that there are considerable gender differences in attitudes to sexuality though such differences are less marked than they were in the past.

Despite the advent of AIDS and the risk of HIV infection, many adolescents in Britain become sexually active when they are still at school. A recent study surveyed 400 15–21 year olds and found that nearly half of them (45 per cent of the girls and 49 per cent of the boys) had had sexual intercourse by the time they were 16 and 89 per cent, of both sexes, by the time they were 21 (Bowie and Ford, 1989). Despite the lowering in the age when sexual intercourse takes place, there is little evidence to support the notion that promiscuity has increased in that a number of studies have indicated that most young people believe that sexual behaviour should only take place within a loving relationship (Farrell, 1978). Nevertheless there are indications that, in general, young women are both less likely to indulge in casual sex (Spears *et al.* 1991), are much less comfortable with the idea of casual sex and are more inclined to state that they take the dangers of AIDS seriously than are young men (Banks *et al.* 1992).

American studies also suggest that earlier first intercourse for both sexes is associated with smoking, drinking and drug use and that the association between drug use and the early first intercourse is stronger for young women than for young men. McCammon *et al.* (1993) suggest that this may indicate a relationship between unanswered emotional and social needs with early sexual activity, particularly in the case of women.

Sexuality and reputation

> A boy can be called a stud and people like and respect him . . . they can be doing just what they want and if they are called a stud . . . they think it's a compliment . . . It's a sort of status symbol . . .
>
> One thing I noticed there are not many names you can call a boy. . .
>
> You can be called bitch, slag, slut. . .
> British schoolgirls talking in the 1980s, Lees (1986, p. 32)
>
> Guys can go around and screw a lot of girls, and they look macho, but when a girl does it she looks a slut.
> Sixteen-year old American schoolgirl, Coles (1985)

Historically and traditionally in the great majority of societies a double standard of sexual behaviour has prevailed. Sexuality in men, outside the bonds of monogomy, has been condoned and often celebrated; in women it has been condemned and often punished. As we will see in chapter 7, current attitudes to sexual morality and practice indicate that in recent years it has become more permissable for women to express their sexuality, and there is little doubt that young women today are sexually active at earlier ages than in the past. Nevertheless, in early and middle adolescence many girls express concern about their sexual reputation and, while the double standard is no longer as powerful as it was in the case of adult sexuality, in adolescence gender differences in the extent to which sexuality can be overtly displayed persist. Thus, according to Sue Lees (1986), it is somehow wrong and horrible for a young girl to invite sexual activity but somehow natural for a boy to encourage her.

However, while overt displays of male heterosexuality may be encouraged, any behaviour in young men that suggests homosexuality will be roundly condemned and boys who are are too friendly with girls or who are seen as feminine run the risk of being 'called poofters and sissies' and being 'constantly likened to girls' (Spender, 1982). Consequently, the preservation of sexual reputation in adolescence may be problematic for boys as well as girls and, for both sexes, such concerns may be made more problematic and more pressing if the individual concerned is not heterosexual.

Reviewing gender development in adolescence it seems clear that in many ways gender differences are diminishing. For example, attitudes to work and careers are probably influenced as much by social class as by gender, and leisure pursuits are far less affected by gender than in the past. Young men as well as young women are also now being bombarded with messages from the media that stress the importance of physical appearance, as we shall see in the next chapter. Furthermore sexual behaviour, for example the age at which a steady boyfriend/girlfriend is acquired, is also more similar for the sexes than it was in the past. In addition adolescents, unlike children of younger ages, very often explicitly dispute the sex-typing of careers and leisure activities.

It might be argued then that the social environment no longer plays such a powerful role in shaping sex-typed behaviour and attitudes during adolescence, and that as a result it can no longer be claimed that sex differences are largely due to socialization. However, I believe this view to be mistaken. This is because, while explicitly the emphasis in schools and in many, but not of course all, homes may be that both males and females can choose the careers and behave in the manner that suits them as individuals, implicit messages may continue to support gender schema that are very different. Noticeably, for example, in the context of sexuality where as we have seen the double standard continues to play an important part in the way adolescents think about their world.

Developmental trajectories: what can we conclude?

In the beginning of this chapter theoretical approaches to gender that stress the role of nurture rather than nature and that emphasise the role of socialization processes were outlined. Following that a large number of empirical studies were reviewed which indicate the extent to which variables in the social environment, particularly the attitudes and behaviour of adults, continue to exert pressure for the sex-typing of behaviour in children as they grow up. The discussion also indicated the extent to which children and young people themselves police their own behaviour at different times and to different extents in conformity with the external pressures.

Consequently, gender differences are affected by a number of the processes discussed in the first part of this chapter. There is no doubt that social learning does contribute in terms of the differential rewards offered to sex-typed versus non sex-typed behaviour, particularly when boys are young, and with respect to sexuality as girls grow older. It also seems clear that children acquire gender identity very early and that as a consequence most children actively, particularly when they are young, seek approbation by behaving in accordance with the sex-typing they see around them. However, the evidence now suggests that as children move into adolescence the sex typing of behaviour, interests and values becomes less salient and variables such as social class, education and employment status become more influential. Nevertheless, as the next chapters will continue to demonstrate, there is little doubt that as a result of social learning, acquiring gender identity and living in a highly sex-typed society, no matter how we might seek to modify those lenses, most of us continue to observe both ourselves and others through gender-polarized lenses, though there may be a great deal of variation in the extent to which we do so (Lott, 1990).

Notes

1. For a critique of the behavioural approach with particular reference to gender, see Hare-Mustin and Maracek (1990).
2. Details of moves to reduce stereotyping in children's fictions can be obtained from The Book Trust, 45 East Hill, London SW18 2QZ.
3. Further, with the advent of new technology that enables the sex of unborn babies to be identified, there have been a number of reports in the press, of the abortion of girl babies. Reports have also been made of medical practioners opening clinics devoted to guaranteeing the conception of boy rather than girl babies.
4. Trevarthen (1993) indicates that his studies show same sex preference at earlier stages than this in that babies prefer to look at films and photographs of same sex babies.
5. Rough and tumble play is a term used in both animal and human studies to describe very physical and boisterous play.
6. As Unger and Crawford (1992) point out, young children may not be completely aware of the adult meaning of this term.

Chapter 5

Poles Apart? Abilities, Attributes and Social Behaviour

When I attended Eton in the 1970s boys had their pubic hair sprayed silver, were thrown into hot baths or stripped naked and smeared with potions whose recipes do not bear repetition. Over the next few decades, these boys will go on to become Cabinet ministers, generals, bishops, bankers and pillars of the establishment . . .
David Thomas (1993, p. 53)

We must start with the realization that, as much as women want to be good scientists or engineers, they want first and foremost to be womanly companions of men and to be mothers.
Bruno Bettelheim (1984)

The content of the last chapter was concerned in the main with what has been called traditional or mainstream psychological approaches to the study of sex and gender with the discussion focusing on theoretical approaches and developmental studies. In this chapter the stress continues to fall on mainstream approaches, exploring what has been perhaps the major preoccupation of traditional approaches to sex and gender. This is the study of sex differences in abilities, attributes and social behaviour.

As noted in chapter 1, the vision of male and female as different and opposite not only permeates western culture but also transcends it because it has characterized most known cultures. Related to the vision of the sexes as different is the notion that, as a result of this opposition, males and females have mutually exclusive attributes and qualities. In delineating the poles of this opposition there is some degree of consistency across most cultures. Most notably in terms of the activities that have been characteristic of the sexes. In general, women have tended the children and engaged in small scale agricultural work remaining inextricably linked to domesticity. Men, on the other hand, have been less tethered to the domestic hearth. Usually, if a society's economy included hunting large game, men have been the primary hunters; if the economy utilized mining and the processing of hard metals, men have been the miners and metal workers, and traditionally men have fought the wars (D'Andrade, 1966). Not surprisingly, then, the sexes have been ascribed those attributes that most contribute to these activities; women the attributes of

compassion and passivity, men the attributes of aggressiveness, activity and curiosity (Williams and Best, 1990).

However, even if in the past men fought the wars, there have certainly been female military tacticians such as Boadicea and Elizabeth I. In this century we have also seen women fighting: in the Wars of Independence in countries like Zimbabwe and Mozambique, in Israel and even in World War II when women fought as soldiers in the USSR. In this century, too, women like Golda Meir, Indira Gandhi and Margaret Thatcher have demonstrated that women can lead as effectively as men. Indeed the fact that women can rule as effectively, and sometimes as despotically, as men had already been demonstrated long before this century by monarchs such as Catherine the First of Russia.

Furthermore, women like Anita Roddick of The Body Shop have shown that in the contemporary world of finance women can initiate and control large financial concerns. In non-western settings, for example in west Africa, there is a long tradition of powerful, wealthy and successful women traders and entrepreneurs.

Such exceptions to women's traditional roles have tended to occur when there have been loopholes in men's power. For example, when a woman succeeded to the throne or inherited the symbolic mantle of a male relative, as in the case of Nehru's daughter, Indira Gandhi. Similarly the emergence of women traders in west Africa can be seen as linked to periods of transition in the history of slavery and colonialism when women were able to seize the initiative as the structure of the economy shifted.[1]

I would argue that these exceptions point to a proposition that will be developed further both in this and the next chapter. This is that male and female differences in behaviour are as much linked to power imbalances between the sexes as to psychological differences between them. In general, this proposition has not been considered by mainstream psychologists who have until very recently attributed sex differences in behaviour to fundamental differences in the abilities and attributes of the sexes. This chapter documents this mainstream psychological tradition focusing in turn on the following areas: physical, cognitive and social behaviour. In this discussion we will be returning to some areas that were briefly discussed in chapter 3 when we looked at socio-biological approaches to sex and gender.

In this chapter the term 'sex differences' will be used rather than 'gender differences' because the great majority of the studies referred to were carried out within the mainstream psychological tradition of categorizing in terms of sex rather than gender.

Physical differences between the sexes

The arms of the men are almost as free of heavy muscle as those of the women, yet the potentiality for the development of heavy muscle is there; when Balinese work as dock-coolies . . . their muscles develop and harden. But in their own villages they prefer to carry rather than to lift, and to summon many hands to every task . . . If we knew no other people than the Balinese we would never guess that men were so made that they could develop heavy muscles.
Margaret Mead, writing about Balinese men quoted by (Fausto-Sterling, 1992, p. 217)

Strength and size

Throughout the life span there are differences between the sexes in physical growth and development. At birth boys tend to be bigger and throughout childhood they tend to be both taller and heavier than girls. At about 11 years of age, however, the direction of the differences change, because the growth spurt which is characteristic of puberty occurs about two years earlier for girls than for boys. As a result, for a year or two, around 12 to 13, girls are on average taller and heavier than boys. These differences in size aside, there are minimal body differences between the sexes before puberty, except of course for differences in the genitalia.

Boys are, however, more likely to suffer greater morbidity, that is to suffer more from illnesses, and indeed to die than girls and this tendency for males to die at a younger age than females occurs throughout the life span. It is generally agreed that there are two major causes for these differences in morbidity and mortality. First, men are more likely to take risks and as a result are more likely to die in accidents or fights, from smoking and from alcoholism. Second, their lower resistance, in general, to disease can be ascribed to genetic differences linked to the nature of the X chromosome, of which women have two and men one.[2]

While the life expectancy of men is lower than that of women, they are in general physically stronger and as a result men tend to outdo women in almost all sports and athletic events. The one athletic event that women do excel in is marathon swimming where women's greater body fat provides superior buoyancy and protection against the cold. While there is no doubt that these sex differences in attainment in sport are ascribable largely to sex differences in both strength and in physique, there are also indications that culture may also play a part. For example, in what was East Germany, where training and coaching methods differed less for the sexes than anywhere else in the world, the size of sex differences in sports like swimming was considerably smaller than in the rest of the world (Fausto-Sterling, 1992).

Rough and tumble play

'William! you've been playing that dreadful game again!' said Mrs. Brown despairingly. William, his suit covered with dust, his tie under one ear, his face begrimed and his knee cut, looked at her in righteous indignation.
'I haven't . . .'
From *Just-William* by Richmal Crompton (1992)

In the last chapter it was noted that in many parts of the world, particularly in early and middle childhood, children tend to play in same-sex groups. It has been suggested that the chief reason for this is that there are innate sex differences in play patterns. In particular, it has been claimed that boys are innately more disposed to rough and tumble play than girls. The term 'rough and tumble' is seldom tightly defined but in general it is used to describe energetic and boisterous play.

Evidence for this conclusion is somewhat tenuous. The first strand of such evidence derives from studies of the play patterns of other species, particularly primates. Some of these studies have indicated that the level of activity in young primates is influenced by androgens, the male hormone. It is also worth noting, however, that other studies of primate behaviour have shown that the level of rough and tumble play is affected by the social composition of the group as well as by the sex of the young animal. For example, Goldfoot and Neff (1978) investigated the level of rough and tumble play in juvenile female rhesus monkeys living in five member groups. This form of play is rare among females living in all-female groups. However the researchers found that it was considerably commoner in females in one-male, four-female groups and lower again in females living in two-male, three-female groups. The researchers suggest that this is because males initiate the activity and select male partners for it. If no male partner is available they engage a female in such play. Thus it can be seen that sex differences in rough and tumble behaviour is not entirely controlled by biological variables even in the case of non-human species.

The second strand of evidence relates to studies of children. Studies of sex differences show no consistent sex differences in activity in infancy but some observational studies have claimed that in early childhood boys show higher levels of rough and tumble play than girls (Smith, 1978). The problem here is that because the term rough and tumble is very imprecise, different studies use different indices for labelling play patterns as rough and tumble. In general, in early childhood, as in infancy, there are no consistent sex differences in activity level but boys are more likely than girls to wrestle and play fight (Tavris and Wade, 1984). It is not clear, however, that such sex differences are innate because, as we have already seen in the previous chapter, adults particularly fathers interact differently with boys and girls. It is equally feasible that if boys do show a greater propensity for rough play, this may be due to the fact that, as infants, boys are likely to have experienced rougher handling in play than girls.

Cognitive differences

If we wish a woman to fulfil her task of motherhood fully, she cannot possess a masculine brain. If the feminine abilities were developed to the same degree as those of a male, woman's maternal organs would suffer and we would have a repulsive and useless hybrid. P.J. Moebious, 1907, in *Concerning the Physiological Intellectual Feebleness of Women*, (Starr, 1991, p. 195)

While in recent years there has been something of a backlash to feminism, it would be a brave individual who would challenge the right of girls to equality in education during the school years. Yet, the acceptance of that right is really only comparatively recent. In the nineteenth century it was widely held that education for females would inevitably lead to unpleasant physical and mental consequences. This viewpoint is encapsulated by the quote at the beginning of this subsection.

Nineteenth century views on sex differences were heavily influenced by Darwinian theory with its focus on the differences between species and groups (Hyde, 1990). Attention was focused particularly on brain size which was regarded as being linked to intelligence. The further corollary was that as women's heads and brains are smaller than men's, women must be less intelligent than men. As already indicated in chapter 3, studies documenting such differences were seriously flawed and by the beginning of the twentieth century were seldom quoted.

It was at this period that the mental testing movement began to take off. Founders of this movement like Alfred Binet in France (Binet and Simon, 1912) and Lewis Terman in the USA (1916) were not particularly concerned with sex differences and it was only in the 1930s and the 1940s that attention returned to sex differences in mental abilities. This was caused in part by the fact that views on the nature of intelligence had changed. Early theorists such as Terman had believed that intelligence could be measured and expressed as a single figure IQ – intelligence quotient – score, but researchers working in the 30s and 40s such as Thurstone (1938) regarded intelligence as multifactorial, i.e. having a number of different components. When such researchers began testing large groups of subjects on their multifactorial tests, they also began to look for sex differences in the resulting scores and by the mid-60s literally thousands of studies documenting sex differences on mental tests had been published.

In 1974 Eleanor Maccoby and Carole Nagy Jacklin published a monumental review and assessment of studies which had investigated sex differences. With respect to sex differences on mental tests they concluded that these had been established in three areas: females show greater verbal ability and males greater ability at mathematics and at tasks requiring spatial ability. As already indicated in chapter 3, spatial ability has been defined as the ability to represent two dimensional and three dimensional configurations in the brain.

While Maccoby and Jacklin's book was a pioneering attempt to codify and assess sex differences, it has been substantially criticized (Block, 1976). These critiques have focused mainly on the criteria they used to decide whether the percentage of studies indicating a particular difference was sufficiently large to conclude that there was an established sex difference. Following on such criticisms a new statistical technique was applied to reviews of studies of sex differences. This technique is known as **meta-analysis** and it has radically altered the assessment of sex differences within mainstream psychology.

In the *first* stage of a meta-analysis, studies concerning the area are collected. In the *second* stage, a statistical analysis is then computed on each study which compares the difference between the sexes to the difference within each sex group. This improves on past methods because past methods only established whether there was a gender difference whereas this new method indicates how large the difference between the sexes is in real terms. In other words it recognizes that each sex is not homogeneous and it compares the variability between males and females with the extent to which males differ from each other and females differ from each other. In the *third* stage the statistics derived from the individual studies are aggregated and in the *fourth* stage the statistic derived from this aggregation is assessed with reference to one or more defined criteria. Although the criteria chosen do differ, they are clearly designated and usually allow us to draw a conclusion as to whether the effect of the variable under investigation (in this case gender) is more, less or equally powerful than the effect of other variables such as social class or attitudes. A further conclusion may be made as to whether differences between men and women are greater, equal or less than differences within samples of women and men.[3]

Verbal abilities

> Girls begin to talk and to stand on their feet sooner than boys because
> weeds always grow up more quickly than good crops.
> Martin Luther, in *Table Talk*, 1533 (Starr, 1991, p. 36)

A widely prevalent view holds that women talk more than men. There is
no evidence to support this stereotype nor the linked one that women gossip
more than men (Tavris and Wade, 1984). There are, however, indications that
women and men do differ in the ways they use language in social situations
and we shall return to these differences later. This section is concerned, however, not with the social use of language but with the studies that have attempted to measure sex differences in verbal ability.

Studies which have attempted to assess such differences have focused on
a wide variety of indices including measures of articulation, spelling, punc-
tuation, sentence completion, vocabulary size, ability to name objects, sentence
complexity and fluency. They have also attempted to assess differences on
more sophisticated criteria like reading comprehension, creative writing and
the use of language in logical reasoning.

In their 1974 review of such studies Maccoby and Jacklin summarized the
results of 85 studies and concluded that in very early childhood girls' abilities
mature somewhat more quickly than boys. They also concluded that following
infancy boys and girls are then similar in verbal ability until about 11 years of
age when girls move ahead of boys.

This view of sex differences in verbal ability has held until very recently
and has been accompanied by a general acceptance that at all ages boys are
more liable than girls to experience severe reading difficulties (Unger and
Crawford, 1992).

Recently, however, Janet Hyde and Marcia Linn (1988) performed a meta-
analysis on gender differences in verbal abilities. In this study 165 studies were
evaluated and it was concluded that the resulting statistic of female superiority was so small as to indicate no meaningful sex differences in verbal
abilities. This conclusion is now generally accepted and as Plomin and Foch
have noted about children in general: 'If all we know about a child is the
child's sex, we know very little about the child's verbal ability' (Fausto-Sterling,
1992, p. 30).

It should be remembered, however, that the finding that more boys than
girls experience severe verbal problems has not been contested. Two causes
have been suggested for this finding. First, as has already been indicated, in
general more boys than girls are likely to suffer from pathological conditions
and thus boys are more likely than girls to stutter or be diagnosed as dyslexic.
Both of these conditions may affect verbal performance.[4] It has also been
suggested that in primary schools, teachers are likely to find boys' social behaviour less acceptable than girls' and this may affect the extent to which boys
are moved out of mainstream classrooms and into remedial situations.

Mathematical ability

As a mathematics teacher with over 25 years in dealing with female pupils and female mathematics teachers, I do have direct evidence . . . mathematics is the water in which all intellectual creativity must mix or survive. Females, by their very nature, are oleaginous (oily) creatures in this regard. Or . . . as the song says, 'Girls just wanna have fun'.
American high school teacher, 1984 (Fausto-Sterling, 1992, p. 14)

In their 1974 survey of gender differences, Maccoby and Jacklin reported male superiority in mathematical abilities. Male superiority was also confirmed in a meta-analysis performed by Hyde in 1981 (Mullen, 1993) although as Hyde (1990) later concluded this superiority was 'not as large as the prominence of such findings in reviews and textbooks would indicate'. Subsequent meta-analyses, however, have indicated little support for male superiority in mathematics.

In addition to meta-analyses, which include all studies including some very small-scale ones, there is another powerful source of data in this area. This derives from the research which has been conducted on sex differences in performance at standardized mathematical tests during the school years.

Turning first to the recent American research, this has indicated that girls' mathematics performance outstrips boys at primary school ages; that there are usually no sex differences in mathematical skills during the intermediate years of schooling; but that by the end of high school males have the advantage.[5]

British research has until recently shown somewhat similar findings, indicating no evidence for male superiority until the latter years at secondary schools. However, within the past 15 years the difference between male and female performance in secondary school mathematics has decreased and boys now only do marginally better than girls at mathematics at GCSE.[6] These recent results certainly do not point to an innate superiority for males in this area. Nevertheless, the stereotype that females are fundamentally less able than males at mathematics persists.[7] Belief in this stereotype has been fuelled by recent research on sex differences in the brain. This research has focused particularly on the effects of reported sex differences in the brain on an ability that is commonly regarded as underlying many mathematical tasks – spatial ability.

Spatial abilities

In the area of sex differences in abilities this aspect of cognitive functioning has received more attention than any other with most reviews concluding that 'males have superior spatial ability'. Although this term 'spatial ability' has been used earlier in this book for the sake of convenience, it is clear that in fact it is inaccurate to talk about 'spatial ability' in the singular because there is little doubt that there is no *one* clearcut and easily identifiable ability underlying the manner in which we perceive and mentally manipulate our visual images (Hyde, 1990).

The initial aim of this section is to differentiate between different spatial abilities and to indicate the extent to which sex differences in such abilities have been established. Following on from this the evidence will be examined that sex differences in these areas are caused by innate physiological differences between the sexes. Finally consideration will be given to the effect of environmental factors on sex differences in this area.

Literally hundred of tasks have been used to test spatial abilities. Not surprisingly, then, there is a degree of controversy surrounding the manner in which such tests can be grouped (Unger and Crawford, 1992). Some commentators even question whether the notion of spatial abilities is a useful psychological concept (Caplan *et al.* 1985, pp. 786–799). Most reviewers, however, retain the tripartite demarcation of spatial abilities suggested by Linn and Petersen (1985) in their meta-analysis of sex differences in this area – spatial perception, mental rotation and spatial visualization.

Spatial perception tasks require the test-taker to extract aspects of spatial information without being influenced by its perceptual context. One particular set of spatial tasks was developed by Witkin *et al.* (1962). Performance at these tasks was taken by Witkin to be a measure of field independence. Witkin claimed that people who score highly on tests of field independence are more analytical, more active and less conforming than people who obtain low scores. Despite the fact that most studies show no sex differences on this task, and despite the lack of evidence linking performance at this task to other attributes such as analytical reasoning, (Siann and Ugwuebu, 1988) Witkin and his associates built up an elaborate theory of sex differences based on the belief that women are usually less field independent than men and that they are as a result less analytical, more passive and more conformist than men. While Witkin's approach received general credence in the past, in recent years its influence has declined considerably.

Generally gender differences are not shown on some tests of spatial perception such as Witkin's tasks, but sex differences have been shown on other tasks of spatial perception such as the water-level task,[8] as well as on some, but not all, tests of the second and third aspects of spatial ability demarcated by Linn and Petersen (1985), mental rotation and spatial visualization. There is considerable variation, however, both in the size of these gender differences and in the ages at which they appear. Gender differences are also less likely to appear in complex tasks of spatial visualization. It is also important to note that in the spatial tests which are administered on a nationwide basis in the USA, as part of college entrance requirements for example, differences between the sexes are diminishing appreciably, showing a 59 per cent decline over 40 years (Feingold, 1988).

The fact that gender differences on tasks of spatial abilities are diminishing suggests that these differences are not innate, nevertheless a considerable body of opinion exists which argues for innate causation. Let us briefly sum up these opposing positions starting with the claim that the differences are innate.

Innate sex differences in spatial abilities

Perhaps the most eminent exponent of innate sex differences in spatial ability is Doreen Kimura (1992) who has argued in a recent review that 'different patterns of ability between men and women most probably reflect different hormonal influences on their developing brain'. Much of the research she cites in support of this contention is indirect. This indirect evidence is from two sources: studies performed on rats and studies performed with homosexuals in which she cites evidence of differences reported on male homosexual brains compared to male heterosexual brains at autopsy. She then links this brain difference to studies that show male homosexuals perform worse at some spatial tests than male heterosexuals arguing that both women and male homosexuals perform worse at spatial tests than male heterosexuals because of similarity in their brain structure. She argues that this link between brain physiology, sexuality and test performance is 'exciting' in that it suggests that male homosexuals not only differ from heterosexuals because aspects of their brain function are different but also that this difference in brain function affects cognitive abilities. She does concede, however, that interests, experience and other motivational factors may also account for the differences in test performance between hetero- and homosexual males.

Other studies which she cites are more direct. These are of two types. The first type are concerned with linking the measurement of the levels of androgen (male hormone) in heterosexual males and females with their performance on spatial tests. The results of such studies are, however, inconsistent (Shute, 1983). In one, for example, more masculine women, as measured by androgen level, performed better at tests of spatial ability (in line with her hypothesis) but in the case of men the opposite was found, i.e. more masculine men performed worse than less masculine men (which was not in line with her hypothesis).

The second set of direct studies are those concerned with the hemispheric lateralization of the brain. It has been argued that men's brains are more highly lateralized than women's and that the more lateralized the brain, the better the person will be at spatial tasks. Thus providing a biological base for sex differences in spatial abilities. However, the studies on which these contentions are based are poorly documented, based on small numbers and inconsistent (Caplan *et al.* 1985).

The evidence, cited by Kimura and summarized above, does not lead me to believe that there is, as yet, convincing evidence that the documented sex differences in spatial ability are caused by innate sex differences in the brain. Nevertheless the fact that there is *as yet* no convincing evidence for such innate causation does not imply that it can be ruled out. However, even if such innate causation were to be convincingly demonstrated, meta-analyses indicate that such causation would account for only a small amount of the variation in performance in tests of spatial abilities (Fausto-Sterling, 1992).

Socio-cultural effects on sex differences
In contrast to the contention that the observed sex differences in spatial tests are due to innate sex differences in the brain, is the contention that socio-cultural factors are likely to be implicated in these sex differences in spatial abilities. There is in fact a large body of research which appears to support this latter contention. To begin with the toys that children are given tend to be sex-typed and boys are more frequently given toys which provide training in spatial skills such as construction kits than are girls (Unger and Crawford, 1992). Boys are also allowed more freedom in their movements than girls and a number of studies indicate that ability to follow maps and visualize unfamiliar environments when constructing maps is related to the extent to which children are given opportunities to move around and learn about their neighbourhoods (Matthews, 1987).

The content of spatial ability tasks may also play a part in the genesis of sex differences because many spatial tests consist of items that are stereotypically masculine in nature. For example, steering speedboats and the mental manipulation of the kind of geometric shapes associated with woodwork (Siann and Ugwuegbu, 1988). A number of studies have shown a relationship between item type and gender. In one such study Crawford *et al.* (1989) showed that women scored better at memorizing the kind of spatial tasks required when the tasks were connected with making a shirt whereas men scored better when the same tasks were connected with making a workbench.

There are also a number of studies which link sex differences on spatial ability with other motivational factors. For instance some studies indicate that women whose self concepts are less sex-typed as stereotypically feminine score better on spatial tests than women with more stereotypically feminine sex-typed self concepts (Krasnoff *et al.* 1989, Signorella *et al.* 1989). In concordance with such findings my own research showed that in a sample of Scottish secondary schoolgirls, those who were keener to pursue careers throughout their lifetime performed better at spatial tasks than those who predicted that they would give up work when their children were small (Siann, 1977).

If, as suggested above, motivational factors and experience can affect performance at spatial tasks, it is not surprising to find that training in spatial skills improves the performance at spatial tasks for both sexes — in some cases in such a way as to wipe out boys' previous superiority at the tasks (Conner and Serbin, 1985). There is no doubt, then, that there is a great deal of evidence pointing to the effect of socio-cultural influences on sex differences in spatial ability. This effect can also be seen in the variability in which sex differences in spatial abilities are reported across cultures. For example, a number of studies have shown no gender differences in spatial abilities in some Third World societies (Siann, 1977). Furthermore, in some east European societies *more* women are admitted into engineering faculties than men and engineering is regarded as a profession or vocation in which spatial abilities play a most important role (Durndell, 1992).

Nevertheless, it cannot be gainsaid that sex differences in spatial abilities are the most consistently reported sex differences in ability and because of this consistency sex differences in both spatial and mathematical abilities continue to receive a great deal of attention in the media. A central focus of the research concerns the causation of such differences and the interest almost invariably centres on studies which implicate biology rather than social factors as the major causal factor. Feminist commentators have frequently pointed to the fact that such studies are often used to justify the low numbers of women in professions such as engineering and the higher levels in computing. They argue further that this orientation towards the possible biological causation of cognitive differences moves attention away from continuing gender inequalities in educational and vocational provision. It is to these areas that we shall now move asking whether education, vocational guidance and management practice serve to intensify sex differences in achievement.

Education, careers and employment

Education

Educating a woman is like pouring honey over a fine Swiss watch. It stops working.
The American novelist, Kurt Vonnegut (Starr, 1991, p. 200)

That many, if not most, teachers treat boys and girls differently is beyond dispute. In the early years teachers have been shown to implicitly reinforce sex-typed behaviour. For example Serbin and O'Leary (1975) showed in an observational study that the kind of attention boys got promotes their self-reliance while interaction with girls promotes dependent behaviour. Many studies at the primary school level confirm their finding that in general girls receive praise and encouragement for behaving well socially while boys are more likely to be admonished for rowdy behaviour. If, as has been suggested, children seek attention, it is not surprising then that the sex-typing of girls as relatively docile and passive and boys as active and more disruptive continues.

Teachers are often not aware that they are continuing to reward sex-typed behaviour and many would explicitly prefer not to. Nevertheless as children grow older implicit differences in the way teachers treat the sexes continue. Valerie Walkerdine has focused particularly on the operation of these processes. She argues first of all that during their training teachers learn about the active enquiring nature of childhood. She then claims that teachers see boys as naturally active and enquiring with the type of developing mind that leads naturally to high academic performance. Girls on the other hand, particularly well-behaved girls, are seen by teachers as passive, conforming and helpful, and in some sense as sub-teachers assisting the teacher in regulating the class-room climate rather than as natural academic high-fliers.

These implict beliefs lead teachers, according to Walkerdine, to treat children with similar levels of performance in maths differently depending on which of the three following groups they fall into:

1. girls who conform to the stereotype just described, i.e. they are passive and conforming;
2. girls who do not conform to the stereotype, i.e. they are challenging;
3. boys.

In order to support this proposition she cites the kind of comments made by teachers about three kinds of high maths achievers falling into categories 1–3:

1. Quiet. Gets on very well, sits down and gets on with it. Very rarely makes mistakes. Good handwriting. Technically, she's very good and creatively she has the ideas . . . she's not outstanding, no . . . but always does her best . . . her behaviour is impeccable . . .
2. She's very good, she's very able. She's a madam, that's unfortunate . . . she won't take any advice really . . . and she's got this unfortunate attitude that's rather domineering.
3. I would say he's the brightest child in the class . . . He can be very rude . . . But he has a very good ability, very interested in everything, . . . an all-round ability with lots of potential . . .

Walkerdine believes that it is these implicit attitudes and beliefs held by many teachers that make it more rewarding for girls to continue to play the role of conforming, helpful, passive sub-teacher in the classroom, even if once they are outside the classroom they revert to less controlled behaviour. In the terminology to be explored in the next chapter, Walkerdine claims that girls continually have to 'position' themselves differently according to society's expectations. For example, as passive conformers with teachers, but as outgoing, sexy and extrovert outside the schoolroom with boys. Boys on the other hand, according to Walkerdine, are less under pressure to play different kinds of roles in school and outside (Walkerdine, 1986).

Career choice and career guidance

We could make an epic catalogue of male achievements, from paved roads, indoor plumbing, and washing machines to eyeglasses,

antibiotics and disposable diapers . . . When I cross the George Washington bridge or any of America's great bridges, I think: *men* have done
this. Construction is a sublime male poetry . . . If civilization had been
left in female hands, we would still be living in grass huts.
Camille Paglia (1993, pp. 37–8, authors italics)

    While studies such as the one just described by Walkerdine illustrate that
subtle processes are at play which continue to reinforce sex-typed behaviours
in schools, (Baker and Davies, 1989) there is no doubt that many teachers
explicitly reject sex-role stereotyping. Nevertheless, studies concerned with
encouraging more girls to enter professions such as engineering and computing show that many young women report that some teachers and vocational
advisers advise girls against studying subjects such as science, engineering and
computing, endorsing no doubt some of the views expressed in the quote by
Camille Paglia at the beginning of this subsection (Kelly, 1987). It should be
noted, in passing, that Paglia is a an American professor of the humanities
whose views on sexual differences have received considerable media attention partly because of their perceived anti-feminist bias. Yet other studies show
that even when teachers and vocational advisers provide girls with encouragement to pursue such careers, girls themselves report that they are put off by
what they report as the male dominated climates of university and college
departments of engineering and computing (Durndell *et al.* 1990). It is important to note, however, that while women on some engineering courses continue
to feel marginalized (Tytler, 1993, pp. 6–7), iniatives such as WISE (Women
Into Science and Engineering) (Healey, 1993) receive considerable support
from professional engineering bodies such as the The Engineering Council.
    It is not only in areas like computing and engineering, however, that there
is a sexual imbalance in aspirations to higher education. For while more women
are now entering many professions which were previously largely male preserves such as medicine, dentistry, veterinary medicine, law, accountancy and
architecture, a sexual imbalance continues in applications to both Oxford and
Cambridge with headteachers reporting that girls continue be more fearful
than boys of being turned down (The Engineering Council, 1993). Even when
girls achieve places at Oxbridge, however, their confidence compared to boys
is likely to be further undermined by the extremely small minority of women
in academic positions, particularly at the senior level, where Oxbridge continues to appoint fewer women to professorships than other British universities
(Tytler, 1993).
    Stereotypes about careers do not of course apply only to girls and women.
Many boys have in the past experienced very negative reactions from both
parents and teachers if they have indicated an intention to enter vocations or
professions which have traditionally been seen as the prerogative of women
– for example, hairdressing, teaching, nursing and social work. Nevertheless,
once they do enter such professions they are more likely to reach the upper
echelons than are their female peers. For example, although 80 per cent of

teachers in the UK are female, men are four times as likely to become heads of secondary schools (Roberts, 1992). This bias is in conformity with the top levels of the employment market where success continues to favour males disproportionately. This gender inequality which women experience is sometimes referred to as the glass ceiling.

Employment

(How) I have been feeling for the past ten years as a woman in the workplace: angry, pissed off, chagrined, subjugated, ignored, put down, left out, devalued, and insulted.
American woman writing to a magazine in 1992 (Roberts, 1992, p. 190)

The image of man the hunter is a noble one . . . Yet, of course, the reality of commuter life is the very opposite of that. . . . The structure of industrial life for men requires obedience, submission, often accepting insults.
David Cohen (1990, p. 102)

Although more British women are now in employment than ever before, this employment continues to be largely part-time and, even when women's qualifications are equal to men's, they frequently continue to be paid at lower rates and to attain less responsible positions (Roberts, 1992). In the past, such relative disadvantage could have been ascribed to explicit processes of discrimination, but discrimnatory practices are now no longer legal and other mechanisms must be responsible for sex differences in employment.

In the early 1970s, Martina Horner (1972) suggested that the chief reason underpinning women's underachievement in the labour market was a tendency in women to fear success, arguing that they did so because they believed that success in employment necessarily entailed social rejection. This hypothesis became one of the most extensively studied psychological theories about women's behaviour in the 1970s and early 1980s, possibly because it resonated with current media images of women, for example, that women suffer from a Cinderella complex (Dowling, 1981) which leaves them with a fear of independence.

Horner's theory has, however, been heavily criticized both by feminists who argued that it led to a blaming-the-victim approach and also on methodological grounds because other researchers, attempting to replicate her work, showed no consistent sex differences on her measures of fear of success (Tresemer, 1977).

Nevertheless to many the idea that most women fear success and undermine their own attempts to achieve success by a degree of ambivalence seems intuitively correct (Unger and Crawford, 1992). Studies such as the one conducted by Rosalind Coward in Britain recently (1993) do suggest that some highly educated women believe that if a woman concentrates intensively on her career her personal relationships, particularly in the family setting, will inevitably suffer.

Many other women, whether or not they are highly educated, take issue with this and contend that the fact that women achieve less in career terms than men is due, not to their own ambivalence, but to structural differences in the lives of men and women. They point particularly to the implications for women of taking time off from their careers to have babies and stay at home with young children, and to the well documented disadvantages this brings for their careers in comparison to men.

Such disadvantages apply not only to women in the labour market, but also are equally of relevance to other areas as well. Recently the novelist Candida McWilliam has argued that female writers are handicapped in comparison to their male peers because for female writers: 'with the birth of each child you lose two novels' and as an instance of the kind of pressures imposed by the full-time care of young children she describes an instance where her young son 'came into the room and put a box on my head. I asked him what he was doing and he said, "Trying to stop you thinking"' (Coles, 1993).

It is clearly not open to doubt that without adequate child care facilities women rather than men continue to be disadvantaged in their careers. However it is not only in terms of such obvious disadvantages that women are impeded, there are rather less obvious processes which impede their advancement. One such process has been labelled 'selective interpretation'. This term refers to a process which occurs when people perceive identical behaviour in different manners. With respect to sex, selective interpretation can be said to occur when judgements differ depending whether a particular action is thought to be made by a man or a woman. Selective interpretation, with respect to sex, has been shown, for example, in academic contexts with the operation of what has been called the 'Goldberg' effect.

The Goldberg effect is named after Goldberg (1968) who found that women rated academic articles attributed to male authors more positively than when the same articles were attributed to women authors. Subsequent attempts to replicate Goldberg's findings have not been consistent but it is generally accepted that one of the factors people of both sexes utilize when making judgements about written material is the sex of the author. It is also accepted that many people do tend to give higher ratings to male rather than female authors particularly when the content of the article is in a stereotypically male domain (Gallivan, 1991).

The selective interpretation illustrated by the Goldberg effect is an example of what has been called 'attributional bias'. This occurs when people make use of cognitive rules-of-thumb to assist and speed up their thinking. One such bias is of course sex-role stereotyping and even those of us who would hope otherwise frequently find, to our chagrin, that we utilize gender schema unwittingly. For example when someone comes back from a hospital appointment with a consultant, we might ask: 'What did he say?', making a stereotyped assumption about the sex of a senior clinician.

Furthermore, for many of us attributional bias extends beyond suppositions about the likely sex of the person in a particular occupational role. It can be observed as well in the manner in which we make judgements about the behaviour of people within occupational roles. This is particularly true of those in management roles. Research indicates, for example, that women who exert power over men in the work situation are far more likely to be negatively judged than either men with power over other men or women with power over other women (Unger and Crawford, 1992). In one study, experienced managers rated men who were portrayed as influential in a corporate setting as significantly more powerful, as higher in position, and as warmer than women in identical situations. Additionally when men exercised expertize they were seen as particularly powerful and active while when women did so they were seen as far colder than the men (Wiley and Eskilson, 1982).

Many women in senior management complain of this bias and they often feel very isolated as well, partly because there are few role models and partly because there are few other women on the same grade in whom they can confide. Some women in senior occupational roles also complain of being made to feel the token woman. Rosebeth Moss Kanter (1977) has written extensively of women in such positions who feel that they are more invisible and isolated than men and that they are likely to be defined in stereotypically feminine terms. In addition, as is the case with members of other minority groups, (for example black people in senior management positions) they are likely to be seen by others, and frequently by themselves as well, as representing the interests of their group rather than of themselves.

Not all token women operate in management positions of course. Tokenism is also found on the shop floor and when women work in such positions they often feel uncomfortable because of the male culture of such groups. Some studies which have documented such situations indicate that the men in such groups may sense this and may make explicit attempts to censor both their language and the content of their conversation. In a study of the kitchen staff in exclusive restaurants in Minnesota, where the chefs had traditionally been men, one of the chefs interviewed reported about the changed situation when a woman chef was appointed as follows:

> . . . the behavior that goes on in the kitchen. Sexism and crude jokes
> . . . It's amazing how when you get a woman in the kitchen the attitude changes entirely. Everyone clams up a little bit and they are careful about what they say.
> Fine (1987)

However, while women may experience negative aspects of employment, such as the glass ceiling, tokenism and lower rates of pay in the labour market, the situation for many men in the labour market is currently far from rosy. To begin with, as the recession has bitten, large numbers of full-time jobs have been replaced by part-time jobs. For various reasons these are more likely to be filled by women than men and, as a result, the rise in unemployment has been accompanied by a tendency for men at all levels to be made redundant and to be replaced by part-time employees who are more likely to be women than men (Hartnett and Bradley, 1986). Research has indicated that unemployment has very serious pyschological repercussions for men largely because for most people the major component of the male sex-role is that of breadwinner. Men are also more likely than women to be dependent on workmates for social interaction. Furthermore, if a woman becomes unemployed, the alternative identity of partner/wife/mother is generally more acceptable to her than the alternative identity of partner/husband/father to an unemployed man (Hartnett and Bradley, 1986).

Even in employment, however, the majority of employed men experience particular psychological pressures that are less likely to be experienced by women who have not, in general, been subjected to the belief that failure in the labour market implies failure as a person. David Cohen (1990, p. 6) writing about this puts it this way: 'Man. . . . sees his job as the pivot of his identity. He will, therefore sacrifice his all to work'.

The implications of such a belief were encapsulated in the 1940s and 1950s by Arthur Miller's (1989) *Death of a Salesman* but the tradition lives on as can be seen, for example, in the plays and films of the contemporary American writer and director David Mamet (1984) which document the despair and disintegration of personality in men who perceive themselves as failures in the pursuit of material and occupational success.

If men and women appear to experience work and unemployment somewhat differently can this be traced to different sets of social motives and social behaviour? This is the question we will be considering in the next section.

Social and emotional differences

To be a woman or a man, then, is first and foremost to inhabit particular positions in the social landscape.
Alastair White (1989, p. 20)

The developmental psychologist, Colwyn Trevarthen (1992), contends that there are innate motivational differences between males and females such that at birth they are predisposed to develop rather different sets of motives and emotions. This is not a view that has received endorsement from most developmental psychologists who believe that from birth and well into the first few years of life there are remarkably few social and emotional differences between girls and boys (Bee, 1992).

Despite these early indications of minimal sex differences in early childhood, there are indications that from about 4 years of age consistent sex differences are shown in some aspects of social behaviour. In the sections below these differences are reviewed and discussed with reference to some of the concepts that have already been presented – 'essential' sex differences, socialization practices, gender concepts and power imbalances between the sexes.

Although some sex differences in social behaviour are reasonably consistent, it should always be remembered that they are not large and meta-analyses of such differences indicate that the category of sex accounts for as little as five to ten per cent of the overall variability in the social behaviours discussed below (Eagly, 1987).

Easing things along

Why can't a woman be more like a man?
. . . .
Men are so pleasant, so easy to please
Whenever you're with them you're always at ease.
Professor Higgins in *My Fair Lady* (Lerner)

The worthy professor was obviously overstating the case for his sex because a number of studies, largely it must be admitted conducted in laboratories, have shown that in general, women tend to agree more than men, to conform more to majority opinion and to be more amenable to persuasion (Eagly and Wood, 1991, pp. 306–15). This tendency for females to be more likely to contribute to smooth social relationships in groups can be seen at relatively early ages. In one study 92, children of both sexes, aged between 7 and 9 years, were observed attempting to join two other children who were playing a board game. They did not know the children playing the board game well and in some cases the children playing were both girls, in other cases they were both boys. The results showed that female 'guests' were less obtrusive in their approaches than male 'guests' and female 'hosts' were more attentive than male 'hosts' (Borja-Alvarez *et al.* 1991).

There is some evidence, however, that cultural and contextual factors may modify these sex differences. For example, Adams (1980) showed that in a sample of black American people the sex differences in persuasion were reversed, with black men in a group situation being more easily influenced than black women. Other studies of conformity have shown that altering the context (for example, if responses are made in private rather than in public) alters conformity levels for men, but not for women, in that men are less likely to be influenced by others if they respond in private than if they are required to make their responses public. Unger and Crawford (1992) interpret this in terms of the greater pressure on men, compared to women, to preserve a public image of independence and of being able to withstand the influence of others.

Social interactions in general

As already indicated, there is some indication that women (in the west at any rate) are more prepared than men to facilitate social interaction. In doing this, they appear to be aided by a greater propensity to communicate non-verbally. In social situations women smile and laugh more than men (Eagly and Wood, 1991), use their faces and bodies more expressively, touch people more and move closer to them. Women also report showing more empathy with others although when empathy is measured, not by self report but by measuring variables like physiological changes, sex differences decrease (Eisenberg and Lennon, 1983).

However, sex differences in social interactions are by no means invariant. This can be seen if we look at what is called 'dominance' behaviour. This refers to the kind of non-verbal signals that are normally transmitted by people who feel themselves to be in control of social situations. They tend, for example, to take up more personal space, to point more and to interrupt more. In general when men and women have equal power, as when they are peers in the same profession, men show dominant behaviour. But in situations where women have more power than men, for instance a woman lecturer with male students, women show dominant behaviour (Unger and Crawford, 1992).

Verbal communication

A talkative female is one who talks about as often as a man. When females are seen to talk about HALF AS MUCH AS MALES, they are judged as dominating talk.
Dale Spender (1978, p. 19)

Differences in the way men and women talk have received a great deal of media attention, particularly following a recent book by Deborah Tannen, called *You Just Don't Understand* (1991). In this book she argued that while both men and women need intimacy and independence, women tend to focus on the first and men on the second and that these differences lead the sexes to ascribe different underlying meanings to the same utterances. She illustrates this theme by instances such as the following where a woman, trying to initiate a free-wheeling discussion with her partner, may ask: 'What do you think?'. He may interpret this as if he was being asked to decide and tell her what to do rather than help her to explore alternatives. In this way her desire to use the situation to augment their intimacy as a couple, and his desire to demonstrate his autonomy and dominance, may lead to an impasse in the conversation.

Tanner provides only anecdotal support for her argument and draws her examples from a very restricted social range. It could be argued that her book merely illustrates a truism which is that particular groups may have particular conversational styles. It also seems inherently unlikely that, even if men and women do have different conversational styles, by the time they reach adulthood they would not have learnt to decode the implicit meanings in the opposite sex's conversations.

Her book, however, follows on an academic tradition which has argued that there are consistent sex differences not only in verbal behaviour but also in the attributions that attach to these differences. Dale Spender, for example, argues that women force their voices into higher registers than they need to, interrupt less than men and use more 'tags' (such as, didn't you? isn't it?) at the end of their sentences than men. In this way, she argues, women present themselves as more tentative and less powerful than men. Furthermore, Spender claims that in a television chat show if a woman and man talk exactly the same amount, the woman will be perceived as dominating the conversation (Graddol and Swann, 1989).

In conformity with Spender's chat show example, it has also been suggested that irrespective of sex differences in speech, women often experience a double bind when they reach positions of prominence or power. If they speak in a firm and direct manner they may be perceived as bossy whereas a man speaking in an identical manner will be perceived as acting in a style appropriate to his position. In addition, women in power may be evaluated differently by male and female subordinates. Indeed, Unger and Crawford (1992) cite a study showing that men pay more attention to women who speak tentatively than to women who speak assertively but that other women pay more attention to women who speak assertively.

The studies cited above have been concerned with gender issues in verbal communication, but language in itself also carries implicit messages about gender and, in English at any rate, words for women and men are rarely parallel. Consider how the following words reflect the difference in men and women's traditional social roles:

Governor and governess
Master and mistress

In the first case, the word *governor* retains an aura of power – as in the governor of a colony or a governor of a school – while the word *governess* refers to a woman who holds a fairly menial position. In the second case, while the words *master* and *mistress* can both be used to refer to people in authority, *mistress* also has an additional and less socially desirable meaning. Similarly, while the word *queen* – as in a reference to a homosexual – has a derogotary use, the word *king* does not.

Group behaviour

The experimental studies described in the last section cover social and verbal behaviour in general but a number of more specialized studies have been conducted looking at sex differences in small groups usually in laboratory settings. Some of these studies in groups behaviour indicate that women appear to concentrate more on facilitating social interaction than men do, while men appear to concentrate more on the task in hand. Further studies of gender differences in leadership style in such groups indicate that women, on the whole, are more inclined than men to adopt a democratic and participatory style particularly in mixed sex-groups (Eagly and Wood, 1991). It has been suggested that these sex differences in group behaviour are due to differences in the psychological characteristics of women and men in that, usually, women are more interested in people and men in issues.

Reinterpreting the findings of such studies, it could be equally well argued that gender related differences in group behaviour are attributable less to psychological characteristics than to two social processes. First, the fact that women often have less power and status than men and that as a result they need to be more accommodating. Second, the fact that, as has been suggested occurs with verbal behaviour, different attributions are made about the sexes even when their behaviour is the same. Thus a women who acts assertively in a group is likely to be regarded as dominating, whereas a man acting in the same manner is likely to be regarded as authoritative. Consequently women learn to police their behaviour in groups to avoid social stigmatization.

Helping behaviour

If women are more likely to smooth social processes, are they also more likely to be helpful? Sex differences in helpfulness have received a great deal of attention and, because helpfulness has been interpreted very inconsistently, reviewing the studies is a very complex task (Salminen and Glad, 1992). In general it has been found, not surprisingly, that men are more likely than women to help when the helping can be construed as either chivalrous or heroic and some studies show that men are more likely to help an attractive female (Eagly and Wood, 1991).

Although many studies concerned with helping focus on sex differences, an additional focus can assist in interpreting their results. If, for example, the studies incorporate clues about the social status of the participants in the study, it is shown that both men and women are less likely to assist women who are higher in social status than themselves, than they are to help women who are equal or lower in social status to themselves. But neither sex show any differences in helping behaviour to men of different social statuses. In a similar manner, in the USA white men are less likely to help black men higher in social status to themselves than they are to help black men of lower social status (Unger and Crawford, 1992). These results can be interpreted as follows. First, people are often more prepared to offer help to those lower in status than themselves than they are to help those higher in status. Second, in general, where there no other indications of social status or power most people operate with what we have called the attributional bias that men have more status than women, and whites more social status or power than blacks. If, however, the situation indicates that in this context the women or blacks involved are high in status then this contextual social status will cancel out the more usual status differentiations of white higher than black; men higher than women.

Competition and aggression

A number of psychological studies have shown that in many situations women are more supportive to each other than men (Lott, 1990) and it is a commonly held stereotype that men are more competitive than women. What happens, however, when women move into situations where mutuality and conciliation are not in their own interests? For example into situations that encourage competitiveness, separateness and self-interest? Studies of women in such contexts suggest that in these circumstances women very often show much the same behavioural attributes stereotypically associated with men. Thus Keller and Moglen (1987) have shown that female academics show similar levels of competitiveness to men. Furthermore, the contemporary political scene has indicated that women politicians once they attain power are no less likely than men to compete ruthlessly with their political peers.

Competitiveness is often linked to aggressiveness as stereotypically masculine. There are, however, problems in defining what is meant by aggressiveness (Siann, 1985). If it is taken to refer only to behaviour involving physical violence, then there is no doubt that there are very consistent sex differences in aggressive behaviour. If, however, aggression is defined in such a way as to include verbal behaviours such as sarcasm and verbal abuse then sex differences are by no means consistent. Indeed some laboratory studies that have utilized measures of aggression like the propensity to give other subjects electric shocks have shown that there are no consistent sex differences in this propensity (Frodi *et al.* 1977).

If, however, we move away from verbal aggression and away from laboratory studies, it is incontestable that men in all known societies show higher levels of physical violence than women (Miedzian, 1992) although there are some indications that sex differences in this area are lessening. First, because there is a growing tendency for women to fight as soldiers and second, because more women are becoming involved in violent crimes (Siann, 1985).

In interpreting these sex differences in violent behaviour there is, as indicated in chapter 3, strong support particularly from socio-biologists for the claim that men are naturally more aggressive than women although the evidence for this claim is by no means conclusive. An equally plausible explanation for the observed sex differences can be offered by the argument that sex differences in aggression are largely due to socialization practices and in particular the emphasis on the masculine mystique with its focus on toughness, dominance and the repression of compassion and empathy.

Accounting for sex differences in social behaviour

What are little girls made of?
Sugar and spice and all things nice.
What are little boys made of?
Frogs and snails and puppy-dogs' tails.
(Anon)

Essentialist perspectives on sex differences in psychological attributes

Chapters 2 and 3 of this book examined essentialist viewpoints which claimed that there are deep and unchangeable differences in the nature of the two sexes. In the case of the socio-biologists because of innate sex differences which are based in evolutionary processes, and in the case of psychoanalytic perspectives because of the psychodynamics of infancy and early childhood. These viewpoints will now be related to the discussion just completed of sex differences in social behaviour starting with the psychodynamic viewpoint.

The psychodynamic viewpoint

> Male society . . . overlooks the fact that women's development is pro-
> ceeding but on another basis. One central feature is that women stay
> with, build on, and develop in a context of connections with others.
> Jean Baker Miller (1986, p. 83)

In many ways the foremost proponent of this perspective with reference to social behaviour is Carole Gilligan (1982). She based her approach on a reinterpretation of some studies on moral development that had been made by Lawrence Kohlberg (1981). Kohlberg had presented a large number of subjects with a series of hypothetical moral dilemmas and then on the basis of these subjects' responses proposed that there were five invariant stages in moral development culminating in a last, and most sophisticated, stage where moral decisions were made with reference to absolute moral principles. Kohlberg and his associates also suggested that their research showed sex differences in moral development because they claimed that fewer females than males reached the final two stages of moral development – stages four and five. Not surprisingly these findings were contested by female psychologists, particularly Gilligan, who pointed out: first, that there was an inherent bias in the theory in that Kohlberg had based his stages on initial studies of the manner in which adolescent males, but not females, thought about the moral dilemmas; second, she pointed out that there was further implicit bias in the manner in which Kohlberg ordered the stages. This was because in constructing the order, Kohlberg had rated stage three which is concerned with defining morality in terms of the care for others, not hurting others and having a responsibility for others with whom one is connected, below stages four and five which are concerned less with the practical implications for other people and more with abstract principles. In ordering the stages like this, Gilligan claimed, Kohlberg was biased towards a male model of moral development.

Following on from these criticisms of Kohlberg's theory of moral development, Gilligan outlined an alternative theory. She proposed that moral development does proceed differently for the two sexes and as a result women and girls speak *In A Different Voice* – the title of her book – from men and boys about issues of morality. She located these sex differences in morality in sex differences in the experiences of infancy and early childhood. Basing her analysis on the work of Nancy Chodorow (see pp. 33–4) Gilligan suggested that, where mothers are the primary caretakers of very young children, female infants are treated in ways which contribute to feelings of connectedness and identification with the mother, while male infants are encouraged to feel separate from the mother. Society then continues to reinforce such differences and as a result women grow up with an orientation towards social values, relatedness, intimacy and caring for others, and boys with an orientation towards separation from others and interest in objects and issues rather than people.

A number of feminist psychologists have supported Gilligan and have claimed that it is these early experiences in infancy and their subsequent reinforcement that lie at the base of the kind of differences in social behaviour discussed above. Many, such as Jean Baker Miller (1986) go further and argue that these differences give women greater strengths than men, for example greater sensitivity and greater compassion, and that women should emphasize and build on such sex differences. Writing in this vein, Sara Ruddick (1987) has proposed that women's psychological predispositions to be peacemakers, facilitators, moderators, caregivers and sympathizers enable them to serve as peacemakers and collaborators in the public as well as the private arena.

However, as Bernice Lott (1990) has pointed out there are other implications of this essentialist position that may not necessarily be constructive. To begin with the essentialist proposition that there are womanly and manly attributes which are very firmly rooted in the unconscious can lead to a position that suggests that women and men will remain locked into different ways of behaving in social situations and that there are in fact different, and to some extent, impenetrable spheres of personal development for the two sexes. Furthermore, this position gives the impression that change in the area of sex differences in social behaviour can only be achieved with great difficulty because, of necessity, it involves trying to undo deeply embedded psychological attributes.

The socio-biological position

> It pays males to be aggressive, hasty, fickle and indiscriminating. . . . . It
> is more profitable for females to be coy . . .
> E.O. Wilson (1978, p. 125)

As was indicated in chapter 2, socio-biologists also believe that there are identifiable and different psychological attributes characteristic of the two sexes. However, unlike psychoanalysts they locate these differences not in infancy but in evolutionary history. Consequently socio-biologists would argue that the consistencies in social behaviour summarized and discussed above are relatively immutable because they are due to essential and innate differences in the psychological natures of the two sexes. They see women's greater social sensitivity and interests as deriving from their evolutionary role as the caretakers of children and men's greater propensity to be involved with non-domestic issues with their evolutionary role as hunters.

Empirical support for the essentialist position on social behaviour
In terms of empirical support for essentialist positions on gender differences in social behaviour, the fact that sex differences in social behaviour tend to be consistently in one direction (women more socially responsive in their orientation than men, and men less concerned with the personal implications of their behaviour than women) does tie in with essentialist approaches. On the other hand, as was demonstrated in the description of the empirical findings, these sex differences can be modified by changing the context and by changing the status of participants. This suggests that the sex differences are not as essential as theorists such as Gilligan on the one hand, or Wilson on the other, might suggest.

Socialization perspectives on sex differences in social behaviour

(Sex role theory) is concerned with explaining the manner in which psychological differences between the sexes is structured and maintained by the process of socialization.
Hargreaves and Colley (1986, p. x)

As we saw in chapter 4, sex role theorists argue that if there is any consistency in sex differences in social behaviour these can be attributed to socialization practices. They claim that each society stereotypes particular sorts of behaviour as sex-typed in the male or female direction. Once children have acquired their gender identity they proceed to monitor their behaviour in conformity with these stereotypes. This sex-typing of behaviour is further reinforced by the rewards which society provides for sex-appropriate behaviour.
     This approach to sex differences in social behaviour can, and sometimes is, construed as suggesting that there are stable sex differences in psychological attributes. In other words that because of experience, stereotypes and beliefs men and women reliably behave in different ways. However, as the discussion above has indicated, changes in the social context often alter sex differences in social behaviour. When gender role is salient, sex differences tend to occur. At other times, when gender roles are less salient, sex differences

are less often observed. For example, Jerome Adams (1984) has shown that in co-educational intakes at military training establishments in the USA, where attempts have been made to eradicate differences in the way female and male cadets are treated, sex ceases to be a predictor of differences in social behaviour. This and similar studies suggest that when sex differences in social behaviour are observed, they are not due to immutable and stable sex differences in psychological attributes, but are instead fragile, related to social context and consequently easily modifiable.

Empirical support for socialization approaches to sex differences in social behaviour
In this and the previous chapter a great deal of evidence has been presented supporting the contention that society rewards behaviour that is appropriately sex-typed. Evidence was also reviewed which showed that the majority of children themselves monitor their behaviour both consciously and unconsciously so as to fit in with cultural stereotypes about sex roles. There is, indeed, little doubt that sex differences in social behaviour frequently result from conformity to gender expectations and gender related experiences. However, there are wide inconsistencies in studies of sex differences in social behaviour and these differences are very sensitive to social context.

Structuralist perspectives in sex differences in social behaviour

As indicated in the discussion of Sandra Bem's recent work (pp. 74–5) the chief problem with attributing sex differences in attributes and social behaviour to socialization is that it does not come to terms with the inequalities that have held until very recently between the sex roles of men and women. It takes no account, for example, of the pervasiveness within society of the following view that was recently expressed in a book about fatherhood:

> In western culture – and much more emphatically in other cultures –
> the father of the family is still the embodiment of power and authority
> in the eyes of children. Of course, the status of women has markedly
> improved, and your mother may be a managing director, a professor,
> a judge or perhaps a Cabinet Minister. Probably, however, a few more
> generations must pass before equality of men and women is reflected
> in psychological consciousness, notably the consciousness of children.
> Jones (1993)

In the next chapter we will look at what was called in chapter 1, structuralist approaches to sex and gender. These perspectives locate sex and gender differences in a social framework which takes into account the power inequalities that have until very recently pervaded the social and cultural world of men and women.

Notes

1. For a discussion of the associated issues see Ottenberg (1959).
2. Some conditions are linked to X chromosome transmission which means that females are less likely to suffer from them because even if one of their X chromosomes carries the condition the other may not. This affords females relatively greater protection from such conditions, compared to their male peers who, because they only have one X chromosome, have no such protection. In other cases men are disadvantaged compared to women because the X chromosome also carries genes for the production of immunity agents and women have two of these compared to the one in men. See Williams (1987).
3. See Fausto-Sterling (1992) and Mullen, 1993 for a fuller description of the technique.
4. Geschwind (1982) proposed a complex set of associations between left-handedness, certain disorders of the immune system and some developmental disabilities such as stuttering and dyslexia, and differences in levels of testosterone. Linked to this set of associations he also proposed that mathematical genius is associated with the effect of testosterone on the maturing brain and thus to males. His work, however, has been severely criticised on methodological grounds. See also Bleier (1988).
5. Unger and Crawford (1992) noted that men also tend to do better than women at mathematics in tertiary education. In many instances, however, such differences in achievement, particularly in the USA, can be largely attributed to the fact that males tend to take more demanding maths options at school. See also Fausto-Sterling (1992.)
6. GCSE figures published by Department of Education in June, 1993. For a discussion of sex differences in mathematics at the tertiary level, see Cohen and Fraser (1992).
7. There is in fact very little evidence to suggest any connection between sex differences in mathematical abilities such as mathematical reasoning and physiological sex differences, such as sex hormones. For example, when Kimura and her associates investigated the link between testosterone (the male hormone) and mathematical reasoning, they found that men with lower levels of testosterone performed better i.e. the more 'masculine' the hormone level, the lower the performance at the maths test (Kimura, 1992, pp, 81–87).
8. In the water-level task, test-takers are asked to make judgements about the level water would take in a tilted beaker.

Chapter 6

Structuralism, Feminism and Post-feminism

In passing I would like to say that the first time Adam had a chance, he laid the blame on woman.
Nancy Astor, speaking at the beginning of the 20th century (1993, p. 101)

There is not a war in the world, no, nor an injustice, but you women are answerable for it.
John Ruskin in *Sesame and Lilies* (Starr, 1991, p. 79)

In the first chapter of this book, it was suggested that there are three major approaches to sex and gender – essentialist, socialization and structuralist approaches. Subsequent chapters have dealt with the first two of these – chapters 2 and 3 with essentialist and chapters 4 and 5 with socialization approaches. The present chapter will concentrate on the third approach, beginning with anthropological perspectives. Following on from this we will consider the impact of feminist thought on the psychological study of sex and gender and finally we will look at the adult lives of males and females from a structuralist and post-feminist perspective.

Structural approaches to the social sciences are concerned with illuminating the deep structures that have been conceptualized as underlying not only social behaviour but also the manner in which we think about the social world. As noted in chapter 1, a number of theorists have suggested that a major feature of such conceptualizations is a tendency for them to be organized around networks of opposites, e.g. male – female and masculine – feminine. While the male – female or sexual bipolarity is, in a sense given, in that all societies dichotomize infants at birth into boy or girl, the second polarity is not. This is because although there may be certain similarities across most societies there are also cultural differences in the manner in which the attributes of masculine and feminine are prescribed. Structuralist approaches suggest that it is such prescriptions that provide the basis of gender.

In this sense, as Hare-Mustin and Maracek (1990, p. 3) put it, 'gender is an invention of human societies, a feat of imagination and industry'. They also suggest, as noted in chapter 1, that this invention, or as they sometimes term it 'construction', is reproduced in three ways:

1. in the manner in which infants are gradually transformed into men or women;
2. in the manner in which the social world is organized into men's and women's spheres;
3. in the manner in which we think and talk about the terms male and female.

The preceding chapters of this book have provided some support for these claims about the role of cultural variables in the genesis of gender and additional and rather more direct evidence is offered by examining anthropological studies of sex and gender. It is to these that we now turn.

Anthropological perspectives on sex and gender

Sociology is the study of the clad, anthropology is the study of the unclad.

Informal rule of thumb for confused students of the social sciences, *circa* 1970.

Although the English word 'anthropology' is considerably older, the idea of anthropology as a general science of human beings was essentially a creation of the nineteenth century and, as such, its roots in Darwinism can easily be traced (Bullock and Stalleybrass, 1982). Essentially it was concerned with understanding contemporary western societies by examining their roots in more 'primitive' societies. Consequently western anthropologists journeyed from Europe and the USA to what we now term the Third World and attempted to gain a deep understanding of particular groups of people by living amongst them.

The work of these early anthropologists is almost always profoundly ethnocentric, that is, heavily influenced by the implicit values of European culture. Furthermore, until women began to be more involved in the field, it also suffered from a male bias (Tavris and Wade, 1984, p. 4) in that male anthropologists understandably emphasized the roles and viewpoints of men in the cultures they were studying. Moreover, although issues of what we now term gender were never centrally examined, early anthropologists reported that male domination over females was universally observed.

More recently this assumption has been questioned. For example, Annette Weiner (1976) reanalysed the famous early twentieth century studies of Bronislaw Malinowski (1962) amongst the Trobianders and concluded that female Trobianders exercised considerable power in their own right. Furthermore in a study already mentioned in this book, Marie Lepowsky (1990) reported that in a culture she studied in New Guinea, there is no tradition of male dominance. Even more provocatively, some anthropologists have recently argued that as apparently basic a category as male/female may simply be a human invention rather than a universal biological distinction. In support of this they point to the extent to which societies vary in the manner in which they distinguish between males and females (Tavris and Wade, 1984).

Thus while in some societies, for example, many, but by no means all Muslim cultures, gender categories are very rigidly applied (Siann and Ugwuegbu, 1988), in others, such as amongst the Balinese, gender categories are very flexible (Atkinson, 1982). Even more dramatically in some societies such as the Hua of New Guinea, gender categories are not immutable. Older women can become in social terms, men; and older men, after ritual imitation of menstruation and childbirth, can become, in terms of their social role, women (Meigs, 1976).

Additionally, in some cultures there were, and are, institutionalized ways for people to change gender without, as in contemporary western culture, altering their physiology such as in operations performed on transsexuals. For example, some native American cultures have a custom known as 'berdache' where a man can play the social role of a woman in all major aspects of life (Whitehead, 1981). Similarly, amongst some central African people, a woman with enough wealth can buy the status of a man (O'Brien, 1977).

These instances from anthropological studies lead to a reappraisal of two commonly held beliefs about gender in the west. First, that it is the major and most important way to classify people. Second, that gender is immutable unless it is modified by surgery. Anthropological studies can, however, also broaden our understanding of gender issues in other ways: with reference to status inequalities between the sexes; with reference to sexual rituals; with reference to social control and with reference to sex and temperament. Let us now examine each of these briefly.

Status inequalities between the sexes

Although there are notable exceptions, in most societies men have dominated over women. It is clear, however, that there are marked differences in the extent of this dominance. A number of anthropological studies have investigated the variables that affect the extent of male dominance. Tavris and Wade (1984) conclude that these indicate that sexual inequalities in dominance are often influenced by the economic and social pressures in the society concerned. The links, of course, are very complex because the influence of external pressures, such as wars or colonialism, can affect customs which can then affect the economic balance between the sexes. For example, as men were drawn into towns when east African and central Africa became colonized by the European powers, the exploitation of women's agricultural labour increased (Nkweto-Simmonds, 1987).

One of the major aspects of economic pressures is of course the production of food. A number of studies have investigated the extent to which this is associated with women's status. Peggy Sanday (1981) studied 12 societies in which female status ranged widely. She utilized four indicators of women's status:

1. material control – whether women distributed food outside the family;
2. demand for female produce – whether there is a demand for the food women produce outside the family;
3. political participation – whether women influence political decisions;
4. group strength – whether women belong to women's groups which can advance their interests.

Using these four measures to get an index of status, she related this index to the percentage of food produced by women. She found that there was not a direct relationship. Instead she reported that women were more likely to have high status, not in societies where they actually produced the highest percentage of food, but in those where there was a relatively equal division of labour between the sexes.

Thus an example of a society where women's status was high is that of the Iroquois. In this North American society men prepared the fields and women planted and harvested the crops. The tribe also fished and hunted with both men and women fishing while hunting was carried out mainly, but not exclusively, by men. In this society there was a relatively equal production of food and this was accompanied by a relatively equal sexual balance in participation in the making of political decisions.

Other studies have also emphasized that it is not only the amount of food that is produced that is important in contributing to the status of women, but also that women's status is related to the extent to which this food is prized by the society. For example, when it is high in protein it tends to be valued in comparison to other foods (Tavris and Wade, 1984).

The extent to which men dominate over women is, however, not only related to food production, it is also related to the extent to which men and women in any particular culture work together. It has been shown that the mutual interdependence of the sexes in the work situation is associated with relatively lower levels of male dominance (Johnson and Johnson, 1975). Low levels of male dominance have also been observed in societies where the systems of beliefs about gender stress that males and females are complimentary, rather than different to each other (Sanday and Goodenough, 1990). In a similar manner, male dominance tends to be lower in societies where both sexes value nurturing and co-operation in social life.

In general, in societies where there is economic interdependence between the sexes, where co-operation between the sexes is high and where mutuality is stressed, gender inequalities in status tend to be low and male dominance tends to be minimal. Women in such societies are consequently likely to be autonomous economically and as a result, as in the Vanatinai society studied by Lepowsky, women as well as men occupy public and prestige -generating roles. The existence of such societies indicates that as Lepowsky (1990, p. 214) puts it:

... that the subjugation of women by men is not a human universal and is not inevitable, and that sex role patterns and gender ideology are closely related to overall social systems of power and prestige.[1]

Anthropological studies such as the one referred to above serve to reinforce a structural approach to gender because they show that gender issues are associated with social processes and social forces as well as with the socialization of sex-typed behaviour.

Sexual rituals

Many societies prescribe sexual rituals. For example in connection with childbirth, menarche (onset of menstruation) and menstruation. There are wide variations in these rituals. With respect to menarche, many societies confine girls to particular areas at the time menstruation is expected to begin and during this period they are taught by older women about the sexual mores of their society (Siann and Ugwuegbu, 1988). In contrast, in most contemporary western societies, there is no public acknowledgement at all of this important event in a young girl's life. On the contrary, both the girls concerned and their families are very reluctant to talk about it and Unger and Crawford (1992) report that the great majority of young girls do not discuss the onset of menstruation with anyone except their mothers.

The way menstruating women are treated also varies a great deal. Some societies make no prescriptions at all about this while many others, including some western societies until very recently, have believed that menstruating women pollute and contaminate, and consequently have restricted the actions and behaviour of women during menstruation. Some societies, such as orthodox Jews, do not allow sexual intercourse during, and for some days after, menstruation.

Rituals concerned with childbirth also show wide variation across societies. In very many societies, especially until recently western societies, husbands or sexual partners have been almost totally excluded from childbirth. In other societies husbands have traditionally been involved in both the course of the pregnancy and in childbirth. Anthropological studies show this involvement to vary a great deal from societies where men may restrict their eating of certain foods during the pregnancy to societies where men are involved in what has ben called 'couvade'. Couvade is the word used to refer to a deliberate imitation of pregnancy. The extent of this imitation varies a great deal but in one society, reported on by Paige and Paige (1981), the husband also takes to his bed or hammock, writhes and moans and finally 'gives birth' in conjunction with his wife.

One of the most extreme sexual rituals is circumcision. Where this is practiced in western societies, this is confined to males and tends to be carried out at birth. In non-western societies this is often carried out in later childhood or in early adolescence and may be extended to females as well as to males.

Female circumcision is a practice which has been very widely practised in parts of Africa and Asia. It varies from relatively minor clitoral incisions to the almost total removal of the clitoris. In some cases infibulation, sewing up part of the genital area, is also practised. In many instances female circumcision is followed by considerable medical pathologies such as infections, haemorrhages and chronic pelvic infections. Not surprisingly, then, female circumcision is a very controversial issue and there is considerable pressure both in western countries, where some immigrant groups still practice it, as well as in Africa and Asia to prohibit it entirely. Nevertheless, there is some indication that women from communities which practice female circumcision do not always themselves wish to see the custom banned (Epelboin and Epelboin, 1979).

If we are interested in issues of gender, we may ask what purposes these rituals serve. Not surprisingly, psychoanalysts locate these rituals and taboos in unconscious motivation. For example, they may relate male circumcision to castration anxiety and father – son rivalry, and menstruation taboos to men's fears of rampant female sexuality. Looking at the taboos from an anthropological perspective Paige and Paige (1981) have suggested that rituals are used to convince and persuade others of one's intentions. In the case of circumcision they argue that when parents allows members of their own groups to circumcise their sons – and more controversially and rarely their daughters – they are demonstrating to their own group and to outsiders, that they are loyal to their own group. In the case of couvade, the father is emphasizing to other members of his group that he is the father of the child his wife is about to bear. In the case of ceremonies associated with menarche, it is being demonstrated that the girls concerned are now of marriageable age.

Other explanations of sexual rituals are more pragmatic. It has been argued that rituals concerned with when sexual intercourse can take place serve to control population growth. For example, the Jewish practice of confining intercourse to the middle and latter end of the menstrual cycle when women are more likely to conceive is likely to increase the population, as of course is the Catholic taboo on most methods of birth control. On the other hand, some societies with limited resources help to lower the birth rate by only allowing heterosexual intercourse at particular times.

It is most likely, of course, that these explanations are not mutually exclusive and that sexual rituals and taboos serve many interacting purposes, including one additional purpose: the social control of women.

Social control

Women were probably the first slaves, and while elite women had considerable power in early states, they were subject to men of their class. Women not only did not 'progress' but have been increasingly disempowered, degraded and subjugated.
Marilyn French (1992, p. 1)

History is replete with instances of the social control of women by men, ranging from the manner in which women were denied the suffrage and the power to control their own financial resources until very recently in the west, to the manner in which girls and young women could be bought and sold as concubines in China until the 1950s.

This social inequality has been tempered of course by time, social class and circumstance. Indeed, as already demonstrated, both historical and anthropological sources have shown periods and societies when such inequalities are, or were, absent or relatively slight. Furthermore, as Marilyn French concedes in the quote above, elite women in all hierarchical societies have had more power and status than men from lowlier classes. Nevertheless, the fact that men have dominated over women in most societies is undeniable and such inequalities obviously have also contributed to sexual rituals and taboos.

Female circumcision, for example, has served to control women's sexuality and the taboos surrounding menstruation have served to remind women that, in comparison to men, their sexuality and physical nature is repellent. As Norman Mailer in *The Prisoner of Sex*, 1971, puts it: '. . . that unmentionable womb, that spongy pool, that time machine with a curse, dam for an ongoing river of blood' (quoted in Starr, 1991, p. 45) echoes a theme in western thought going back through the centuries. For example, Hesiod's recommendation in *Work and Days*, circa 800 BC, to men in the ninth century: 'Never wash in water that a woman has used . . . for there is a dismal forfeit that will contaminate (the male body) (quoted in Starr, 1991, p. 49).

Women have also been subjected frequently to physical constraints on their movements as well as on the manner in which they dress. Sometimes this has been very explicit. For example, in the social rituals of Victorian England where upper class young women could not meet with men outside their immediate family if they were not accompanied by a chaperone. At other times the restraint has been, or is indeed still, imposed on them less by custom than by social conditions. For example, the restraint imposed by the fact that in many western cities an unaccompanied woman may place herself in great physical danger.

Westerners sometimes regard the practice of purdah as the most extreme example of such social control. Purdah is the term used to refer to the rituals of seclusion imposed on many eastern women, particularly those living in Islamic cultures. These include aspects of their dress such as the wearing of the veil, or chador (an all-enveloping cloak); the restriction on social mixing with men other than members of the immediate family and as a result, in some cases, their attendance at single sex schools and, very exceptionally, single sex universities.

While many western commentators, including some feminists, have regarded purdah as the epitome of men's social control over women, large numbers of Islamic scholars, including the distinguished woman writer Rana Kabbani (1986), dispute this conclusion.

In the first place they argue that the practice needs to be seen in the context of the honour which all families wish to preserve. Family honour, known as 'izzet' in most Muslim cultures, rests on the behaviour of individual members of the extended family and requires piety, responsibility and conformity with recognized social and religious customs. For women, chastity and sexual purity are essential and purdah is seen as protecting their honour (Mernissi, 1971).[2] The manner in which purdah is interpreted varies a great deal and while in the past purdah involved the almost total seclusion of women in the home, (Mahfouz, 1991)[3] this is certainly not the case today. For example, in a recent interview contemporary Iranian feminists (Siann and Knox, 1992) claimed that the practice of purdah, far from precluding women from taking an important role in social and political life, actually facilitates this by freeing women from the need to play the dual roles imposed on the western working woman – competent worker and desirable/ feminine woman. In short, they argued, purdah eliminates the need for a woman to be a sex-object. They also stressed the advantages purdah confers in terms of guaranteeing the personal safety of women, noting that their chadors acted as a protection against the baser instincts of men and enabled them to walk down the streets of cities on a basis of equality with men.

It has also been pointed out that even when, in the past, women were confined to their home by the operation of purdah, this was by no means always a negative experience. Lila Abu-Lughod (1983), for example, who lived with Bedouin women, described how much autonomy they had within the domestic setting and the positive, supportive atmosphere of a female world with a shared experience of humour, affection and warmth (Jeffery, 1976).

In the light of studies such as those described above, Tavris and Wade (1984) argue that western interpretations of purdah have tended to be highly ethnocentric in conformity with a general tendency to regard non-western modes of male – female interaction as inferior to western. It would be more appropriate they claim to see purdah as an example of the monitoring of female chastity that has, in the past, characterized very many societies. Such monitoring of chastity serves the dual purpose of protecting young women from unwanted pregnancies and ensures that when they marry, they marry men who are members of their own social class or clan.

Thus purdah should not be seen as a bizarre and repellent eastern custom but should instead be related to practices such as the chaperonage of young women in Victorian Britain. It is worth noting too, that even in the middle years of this century restrictions on the leisure activities of unmarried daughters were very commonly practised in certain Catholic societies, for example in the rural villages of countries like Greece, Spain, Portugal and Italy.

In concluding this section on social control I would argue that the discussion illuminates once again the manner in which cultural variables modify the balance of gender relationships. A related issue is the manner in which cultural variables affect the perceived psychological attributes of men and women, and it is at this that we shall now look.

Culture gender and temperament

Throughout history, the more complex activities have been defined and re-defined, now as male, now as female, now as neither, sometimes as drawing equally on the the the gifts of both sexes, sometimes as drawing differentially on both sexes.
Margaret Mead (1971, p. 336)

Margaret Mead is perhaps the anthropologist best known to the general public, particularly in the USA. She was born in 1901 and from the early 1930s until the 70s played an important role in the formation of American attitudes to issues concerned with gender and sexual morality. Her field work as an anthropologist was carried out mainly in Samoa and New Guinea and it was her stay in New Guinea that laid the basis for her seminal work on the manner in which culture shapes the personalities of women and men.

In the book she wrote about this, *Sex and Temperament in Three Primitive Societies* (1938), she examined three very contrasting societies. In the *Arapesh* tribe both sexes exhibited nurturant and maternal behaviour and both looked after the children. Children were betrothed in childhood and small boys learned to assist with the feeding and care of their small wives-to-be. Members of both sexes learned to be co-operative, unaggressive and concerned with the needs and rights of others. The model personality was much the same for both sexes and was similar to the model of female behaviour in America at that time. The second tribe she described, the *Mundugumor*, also exhibited little difference in the model attributes of females and males but these attributes differed considerably from those approved by the Arapesh. Both sexes were expected to be ruthless, aggressive and strongly sexual and there was little emphasis on nurturant or caring behaviour even in relation to very small children. The society appeared to value the kinds of traits in both sexes that were traditionally associated with the extreme kinds of masculine behaviour in the USA.

The third society she described, the *Tchambuli*, unlike the other two did show marked variations in the model behaviour expected of males and females. This sex-typing, however, contrasted markedly with the sex-typing of behaviour then prevalent in the USA. Amongst the Tchambuli, women took charge of all business and domestic affairs. They worked in large groups and the socialization of small girls was directed towards competence and responsibility. Men, on the other hand, spent most of their time, not working but in their ceremonial houses, carving, painting, gossiping and exhibiting considerable rivalry with each other. Little boys were absorbed into this way of life from an early age.

It was from consideration of these three societies that Mead developed her ideas concerned with the effect of culture on temperament. She argued that societies reinforce and censure particular attributes which are not neces-sarily, as in the case of the Arapesh and Mundugumor, related to the sex of the individual. But if these attributes are related to sex, the attributes considered appropriate to each sex can vary with culture. This was the case with the comparisons she drew between the Tchambuli and American culture. What is important is the influence of culture on the social behaviour expected of individuals of both sexes. As Mead (1935, p. 280) put it:

> Standardized personality differences between the sexes are of this order, cultural creations, to which each generation, male and female, is trained to conform.

Mead's conclusion that culture selects and shapes sex-typed behaviour has been confirmed by other anthropological studies which have demonstrated that the psychological attributes associated with the two sexes does show variation across cultures (Sanday and Goodenough, 1990). Despite recent re-appraisals and reanalysis of some of her work, (Freeman, 1983) notably her studies of adolescence in Samoa, Mead's work on sex and temperament re-mains very influential and has had particular impact on feminism. It is to this topic that we now turn.

Feminism

> Feminism is a:
> socialist, anti-family movement that encourages women to leave their husbands, kill their children, practise witchcraft, destroy capitalism and become lesbians.
> The American evangelist, Pat Robertson (1992)

> The thing women have got to learn is that nobody gives you power, you just take it.
> Roseanne Barr (1993, p. 161)

As Corinne Squires (1989, p. 1) has noted, 'Feminism and Psychology are important for each other.' Nineteenth and early twentieth century feminists often cited psychological studies which pointed to the role of social learning in shaping sex-typed behaviour. Additionally, from the opposing perspective of psychoanalysis, a number of early psychoanalysts, mostly but not always women, endorsed feminist demands. This interaction will be discussed in this section and we will look first at the influence of feminism on the study of gender. Following on from that we will examine what have been called 'back-lash' effects – that is the manner in which some men and women have con-strued feminism as having a negative effect on the psychological development of their own sex. Finally the chapter will end by focusing on some of the ways in which structural approaches to gender and feminist thought has impacted on the adult lives of women and men.

Feminism and gender

As Rosemary Tong (1992) has noted, feminism, like most broadly based philosophical perspectives, accommodates a number of diverse approaches. Not all of these approaches deal directly with the issues of gender with which this book is concerned. Consequently this discussion will be confined only to those approaches which have contributed to the psychological understanding of gender issues: the existential, the psychoanalytic, the radical, the constructivist and the post-modern.

Existentialist approaches

> Now, what peculiarly signalizes the situation of woman is that she – a free and autonomous being like all human creatures – nevertheless finds herself living in a world where men compel her to assume the status of the Other.
> Simone de Beauvoir (1984, p. 29)

Jean-Paul Sartre with his companion and lover Simone de Beauvoir (Tong, 1992)[4] had a powerful and in many ways dominant influence on French intellectual thought in the middle years of this century. Both were heavily influenced by philosophers such as Hegel and Heidegger and both worked within a philosophical tradition which has become known as existentialism.

Existentialists argue that human beings are self-creating in that we are not naturally endowed with particular psychological characteristics but acquire these characteristics by the kind of choices we make in life. In this manner we 'create' what we become. While Sartre and his predecessors within this tradition elaborated this approach within the framework of typically masculine choices, de Beauvoir illuminated the implications of the existential approach for women.

In her extremely influential book, *The Second Sex*, she argued that men centre on themselves as 'Self' and consequently regard women as 'Other'. She believed that men's conception of women's 'otherness' centred on their perception that women lack certain qualities. Thus women's difference from men is seen by men not as an alternative and positive difference but as an imperfection. In thus making women the negated self, de Beauvoir argued, the situation is created whereby regarding Women as Other, man perceives her as a threat to Self and as such needs to subordinate her to him. More importantly for women's psychological development, de Beauvoir proposed that women are not only regarded as 'other' (and inferior to men) by men, but internalize this point of view and come to accept the position of men as essential and of women as inessential (McCall, 1979).

She went on to suggest that there are three basic propositions which reinforce this asymmetry between the sexes. First, that in all societies this binary opposition with men dominant over women has existed and continues to exist. Second, she suggested that the division associates masculinity with culture and feminity with nature and, thirdly, she linked the first two propositions by suggesting that males dominate women as culture dominates nature.

Given her gloomy diagnosis of women's position, what steps did de Beauvoir believe that women could take to escape their destiny? First, she suggested that they should demand the right to work as equal to men. Second, she encouraged them to follow in the tradition of earlier women intellectuals and writers such as Virginia Woolf and probe the human condition in their thoughts and writing. Finally, she recommended that women should work with men towards the transformation of society and the economic independence of women.

De Beauvoir's influence has been very great. It was felt, for example, in anthropology where her conception of the universal duality male dominant/female subordinate, tallied with the anthropological views referred to in the earlier sections of this chapter. Her contribution to twentieth century French literature is also indisputable, but pre-eminently she contributed to feminist thought by her insistence that women should strive for economic independence and intellectual parity with men.

In conclusion, and with particular relevance to the issues central to this book, she forced women to look critically at the manner in which they have tended to internalize their 'otherness' and to collude with the belief, held until very recently by the very great majority of men, that somehow at some fundamental level women are not only different to men but, particularly in areas of the intellect, inferior. It is the persistence of this belief that leads to instances of what was referred to in the last chapter as the Goldberg effect where women, as well as men, rate journal articles more highly if they believe them to be written by a man rather than by a woman.

Psychoanalytic approaches

> . . . to free herself from what is holding her back, a woman must do more than fight for her rights as a citizen; she must also probe the depths of her psyche in order to exorcise the original primal father from it. Only then will she have the space to think herself anew and become who she has the power to be.
> Rosemary Tong (1992, p. 172)

Psychoanalysis has never been overtly anti-feminist in that there were a number of women psychoanalysists from the beginning of its development. However, as was evident from the discussion in chapter 2 of this book, early psychoanalysts tended to develop their discussion from a description of the period of early childhood, which they called the Oedipal stage, in which they gave far more emphasis to the experience of boys than they did to the experience of girls.

Many feminists working within a psychoanalytic perspective have, not surprisingly, focused on this aspect of psychoanalysis. Some, like Juliet Mitchell (1974), have accepted the importance of this stage, arguing that it is the vehicle by which patriarchy, or male dominance, is perpetuated. Nevertheless, while accepting its centrality in psychological development, Mitchell has argued it must be destroyed. Other feminist psychoanalysts, like Sherry Ortner (1975), have contested Mitchell's position proposing that rather than attempting to destroy the Oedipal stage, it should be transformed by instituting a system of dual parenting which would change the dynamics of the classical Oedipal stage.

However, a more powerful reinterpretation of the psychoanalytic tradition has come from feminists working within the psychoanalytic tradition who focus less on Freud's psychosexual stages, such as the Oedipal stage, and more on the psychoanalytic view of the role of infancy and early childhood in perpetuating subtle and pervasive gender differences. Theorists falling into this tradition like Chodorow (see chapter 2) and Gilligan (see chapter 5) have argued that it is in the earliest years that gender differences are forged. For it is at this period that girls develop a greater need than boys to love and be loved and to be accommodating to the needs of others; while boys learn that it important to distance yourself from others and to concentrate on achievement in the world outside the family. Consequently such theorists, endorsing Ortner's recommendation, though from a rather different perspective, argue that feminists and psychoanalysts alike must strive for dual parenting. The presence of both sexes ensuring that boys as well as girls come to value feelings of nurturance and girls as well as boys come to value the need for autonomy.

Radical approaches

> I have come to believe . . . that female biology – the diffuse, intense sensuality radiating out from the clitoris, breast, uterus, vagina; the lunar cycles of menstruation; the gestation and fruition of life which can take place in the female body – has far more radical implications than we have yet come to appreciate.
> Adrienne Rich, quoted by Lynne Segal (1987, p. 9)

All feminists no matter what their orientation explicitly challenge the manner in which a world dominated by men has not only subordinated women but has also created a framework in which men's achievements are valued more than women's. Consequently all feminists would endorse the position that men, whether wittingly or unwittingly, frequently act against the interests of women. From this stance, feminists criticize what they call patriarchy – a world dominated by, and run in the interests of, men. Most feminists trace the development of patriarchy to cultural and social processes and argue that it is the role of feminists to oppose these processes. A minority, however, operating sometimes from an essentialist position locate the source of partriarchy and its oppression of women in differences in the very nature of men and women. They argue, for instance, that women differ fundamentally from men in what Adrienne Rich has called the 'cosmic essence of womanhood'. They believe that this essence, combined with women's capacity for motherhood, enables women to lead lives which are more in tune with the natural world than are the lives led by men.

Consequently some radical feminists recommend that instead of trying to minimize gender differences, women should instead establish a new and very different approach to femininity by reversing patriarchal dualities. Totally rejecting any move towards androgyny, women should glory in their difference from men (Tong, 1992) and value the qualities men have traditionally criticized in women such as passion, fertility and irrationality.

Perhaps the most extreme proponent of this perspective is Mary Daly who writes of men's rule as 'poisoning', 'polluting' and 'contaminating' and pleads passionately that women replace it with their own 'elemental' purity. They must embark on a spiritual odyssey into 'woman's space'. In order to do this women must totally transform the language of gender and the manner in which men have labelled women in the past:

> Breaking the bonds/bars of phallocracy requires breaking through the radiant power of words, so that by releasing words, we can release our Selves. Lusty women long for radiant words, to free their flow, their currents . . . The race of Lusty Women, then, has deep connections with the Race of Radiant Words.
> Daly (1984, p. 4)

Words like witch/crone/hag should be reclaimed from their negative connotations and women should confer on them fundamentally new and positive meanings, revelling in a flight from the oppression of men and creating a new 'Race of Lusty Women'. From this position Daly promotes 'Lusty Women's' separation both from a male-centred world and from those women who have been unable to free themselves from this world: the 'Painted Birds' (stereotypically feminine women), the 'token feminists' and the 'fembots' (female robots or professional women).

Daly's radical feminism is not widely subscribed to but it has been influential in two ways. The first is one which she would no doubt endorse: it has helped to create a climate where women can transform their status as 'other' from a negative lack to a positive difference. It has also been influential in a completely different way. This is in fostering a particular stereotype of feminists which has created a degree of antagonism towards feminism in both women and men. This issue will be explored in the discussion on the backlash to feminism in the later part of this chapter.

Social constructionist approaches

> For constructivists, values and attitudes determine what are taken to be facts.
>
> Rachel Hare-Mustin and Jeanne Maracek (1990, p. 23)

Social constructionist is a term that is used by American theorists (Unger and Crawford, 1992) who write about the psychology of gender from an overtly feminist perspective. This perspective suggests that gender operates at individual, interpersonal and cultural levels to structure people's lives. Thus in Sandra Bem's phrase (see chapter 4) most of us, for most of our lives, view the world through 'gender polarizing lenses' making judgements and attributions about ourselves and others that are coloured by their gender, our own gender and the kind of behaviour we regard as appropriate for each gender.

This approach to psychology also challenges one of the key assumptions of mainstream or traditional approaches to psychology in that it contests the traditional contention that psychologists can operate from a value-free and objective stance. On the contrary, social constructionists argue that traditional approaches are neither value-free nor objective. This is because these approaches have been dominated by the presumptions, and frequently the biases, of middle class, white males. As evidence for these assertions they point to the work of psychologists like Lawrence Kohlberg (see chapters 4 and 5) whose theories were built on studies conducted with groups of subjects which were almost exclusively male.

Social constructionists also point to the fact that in western society, until very recently, males have dominated over females. This has given males a power base from which they have tended to overvalue male achievements and undervalue female achievements. For example, they point to the fact that while it has been frequently reported that women score higher than men on many tests of verbal ability and men score higher than women on many tests of mathematical ability, media attention is focused on the areas in which men do better than women, rather than the reverse.

Because social constructionists argue that it is the dominant groups whose power and assumptions shape our social world, they also take into account that male dominance and power over females is frequently overlaid and made complicated by social class and ethnic differences.

Evidence supporting social constructionist approaches can be found in those studies reviewed in the last chapter which indicated that identical behaviour carried out by men and women is frequently rated and appraised in different ways. As for example when a female manager is perceived as bossy but a male manager behaving identically is perceives as authoritative.

Post-modern approaches

> The more multiple the acknowledged parts of the person are, the more capable they will be of identifying with many different positions

... women are likely to incorporate greater multiplicity than men ...
Wendy Hollway (1989, p. 129)

Recently a number of feminist psychologists, influenced by the French thinker, Foucault (1979), have written about gender issues from what has been called a post-modernist, or sometimes post-structuralist (Hollway, 1989), perspective. In general the post-modernist movement in the social sciences, in conformity with social constructionist approaches, disclaims the search for enduring, absolute and universal truths. Instead its protaganists argue that it is impossible to escape the bias of our own personal and cultural positions (Morawski, 1990).

The post-modernist position, however, goes further than social constructionist approaches. This is because post-modernists not only argue that it is difficult, if not impossible, to agree about the objective nature of the outside world, but they also maintain that our experience of our internal world is also at its core, fragmentary and shifting.

In essence they deny that we have any stable and coherent internal 'self', instead they argue we continually change and 'position' ourselves. For example, a woman scientist may position herself as a caring mother in conversations with a group of other young mothers but as an ambitious scientist in conversation with a group of young scientists. However, this positioning is not only actively carried out, but it is also in a sense forced on her by the different social dynamics. Other people treat you differently depending on the social role you are perceived to be playing. In addition, according to Hollway, we do not actively position ourselves all the time. In many instances our positioning is unconscious and may only reveal itself when we take up different positions in our discussions and interactions with others.

A young man may, of course, also position himself differently at different times. For example, as a loyal fan of a fooball club on a night out after a Cup Final on the one hand, and as a responsible young father when applying for a bank loan, on the other. However, if he is white and middle class, because his social and gender groups are those dominant in society, he has to shift his position less. In general, according to those arguing for a post-modernist approach, multiplicity is less characteristic of dominant groups than of those with lesser social power. So, for example, multiplicity of positioning is more characteristic of black groups than white. Amina Mama puts it this way:

> The capacity to occupy many social positions is true of many, if not all, black people who have lived in the west, in ways that are not necessarily so for white people who have lived in Third World countries because of the historical status of expatriate communities as colonizers.
> (Hollway, 1989, p. 130)

Like the feminists working from anthropological and social constructionist approaches, post-modern feminists emphasize the manner in which power and status imbalances between the sexes create sex differences in behaviour.[5]

Psychological aspects of the feminist backlash

Many new breeds of woman are upon the earth: there are female body builders whose pectorals are as hard as any man's, there are women marathon runners . . . there are women administrators with as much power as any man; there are women paying alimony and women being paid palimoney . . .
Germaine Greer, 21st Anniversary edition, (1991, p. 9)

It is undeniable that the opportunities open to women have expanded in the past 20 years. Women prime ministers are no longer uncommon. Women have attained high positions in military establishments, for example in the USA army, and the the last two American ambassadors to the United Nations have been women. In many countries more women have been appointed as judges although this level of the legal profession has tended to remain very much a male preserve, perhaps because judges are, on the whole, older than most other professional groups. The sexual ratio in entry to professions, such as medicine, law, dentistry, veterinary medicine, is far more balanced and indeed in most cases has reached parity. The role of women in the media has also changed in that there are a now a large number of women commentators, reporters and analysts, and they are no longer confined to women's issues but comment on financial, political and military issues.

This is not to deny that there are obstinate and obdurate pockets of resistance to sexual equality, notable in the church and, in Britain, in the selection of women as parliamentary candidates. Furthermore, as discussed in chapter 5, there tend to be relatively few women in senior positions in management or in academic life, particularly in the more prestigious universities. Nevertheless, that the position of women in the occupational field and in public life has changed dramatically is not open to serious arguement.

The extent to which other aspects of sexual inequality have changed is more controversial. A number of feminist authors have argued that there has been little movement in areas such as violence against women and in the provision of child care facilities for women. Some feminist authors have also maintained that there has been a backlash against the advances that women have made in the occupational and social fields.

Backlash (1) – the undeclared war against women

The backlash decade produced one long, painful and unremitting campaign to thwart women's progress.
Susan Faludi (1992, p. 492)

. . . men-as-a-caste – elite and working class men – continue to seek ways to defeat feminism by rescinding or gnawing away at its victories (legal abortion), confining women to lower employment levels (putting

a 'glass ceiling' over professional women) or founding movements aimed at returning them to fully subordinate status ('fundamentalism').
Marilyn French (1992, p. 5)

Susan Faludi has argued that after the strides made by women in the 1960s and 1970s, the 80s were a decade in which forces antagonistic to the rights of women gathered strength and attempted to reverse the gains that women had made. In support of this claim she mustered large numbers of media reports which have been concerned with the apparently ominous aspects of women's progress.

She quoted media reports which focused on the unhappiness with their personal life reported by some women at the peak of their careers, or which highlighted the ambivalences felt by working mothers. She referred also to Hollywood films such as *Fatal Attraction* in which a career woman is shown to be flawed, unhappy, neurotic and malign in contrast with the benign and favourable portrait of a wife and mother. She suggests that these instances all point to a backlash phenomenon which seeks to 'refeminise' women so that women once again become eager to marry and to devote themselves to the welfare of their children and husbands. She does not suggest that the forces of the backlash are conspiring to stop women working. On the contrary she suggests that working women are seen as positive provided their motivation to work is largely to bolster the family income thereby increasing domestic consumption.

In a similar vein, Marilyn French has suggested that modern cultures, at least since the invention of agriculture, have been engaged in a systematic war against women and that the strides that have been claimed for women in the last decades are illusory. Instead, French claimed, women have continued to be heavily discriminated against, notably in the area of violence against the person. She reported that in the USA nearly 2 000 000 men batter their partners and about four women a day die as a result of male abuse.

Both French and Faludi cite the violence against abortion clinics which they argue has contributed to the lowering of inhibitions against killing women. Both refer to the case of Marc Lepine, the 25 year old engineer, who shot 14 young women at the University of Montreal in 1989 claiming in his defence that the women were 'all a bunch of fucking feminists' (Doody, 1992).

Yet both Faludi and French have had to come to terms with the fact that even if the backlash effect is masterminded by men, phenomena they cite as part of the backlash involve women as well as men. For example, the graduates and successful women interviewed by Rosalind Coward (1993) who are ambivalent about their pursuit of careers and the women who, even if provoked to do so by men, demonstrate at the gates of abortion clinics. Thus, if there has been a swing away from overt campaigning for the rights of women it has to be related to the manner in which women as well as men view issues connected with feminism. Consequently in the next section we will review the evidence concerned with women's attitudes to feminists and feminism.

Jobs for the Girls

Backlash (2) – women's views on feminism

Q. 'What flashes into your mind in response to the word feminist?'

A. 'Short hair, hairy legs, my old lecturer who was a lesbian.'

'A rather opinionated bossy woman who likes to get into arguments and calls 90 per cent of men male chauvinist pigs and always feels that the world is male dominated.'

'A woman trying to be a man. Insecure with her sexuality, so she turns it against men – a man-hater.'

'An annoying pain who dresses like a man and moans about pathetic petty little problems.'

'A woman with glasses, curly hair and a moustache wearing green wellies and riding clothes.'

'Usually a woman who can't get a man.'

'A feminist is a woman who insanely believes in female rights. Some may even go as far as saying that God is a woman.'

'Middle class woman standing "ranting and raving"–about relevant issues but in an over dramatic way.'

'Someone concerned with the need to free women from the subordination imposed upon them by society.'

'Getting the best of both worlds for me really – usually females fighting to compete in a man's world.'

Female first year students studying at Scottish universities in 1993 (Beloff *et al.* 1993).

In a recent study conducted at three Scottish Universities, I and my colleagues canvassed the views of over 1000 first year undergraduates on feminists and feminism. There were roughly equal numbers of males (505) and

Clever - have to be more astute than the opposition
Have to be tactful and able to compromise

Drawing by female undergraduate in a survey of attitudes to feminists, Beloff *et al.*, 1993.

females (556) and the majority were social science students although a sizable minority were studying engineering and science.

Although the majority of women, 63 per cent, said that they were either very or quite sympathetic to feminism, and only 5 per cent said that they were not at all sympathetic to feminism, their views on feminists were less positive. Of the 95 per cent of women who made extended comments about feminists, just over half made negative comments while significantly fewer made positive ones (38 per cent).

The overall impression gained from this survey was that only a minority of the women in the sample identified with feminists and many actively wished to distance themselves from them. These findings reinforced the picture which had been built up by asking about this informally. It was also buttressed by the number of times women were heard to say 'I'm not a feminist but . . .'

I believe that this 'but' is important. Most women appear to value the advances made in the area of women's rights. They will, if pressed, acknowledge that these advances were achieved as the result of the efforts of feminists in the past. Most also feel strongly about any discrimination they experience from men, at any level, and most will take action against such discrimination. Relatively few, however, identify with feminists because they regard feminists as women who 'go over the top' or in the words of one female respondent 'women who should calm down a bit'.

Comments made by the women respondents about feminists were also frequently related to their appearance. These comments tended to reflect a view that I have come across frequently in conversations with women of all ages, which characterizes feminists as sexually unattractive to men. Furthermore in responses to the survey there was frequently a sense that admitting to being a feminist would mark one out as essentially unfeminine. This descriptor is one which I believe most women regard as essentially uncomplimentary although I have to admit that I have nothing but anecdotal evidence for this belief.

Quite obviously the comments made in the paragraph above apply in the main to heterosexual women, although I have also met a small number of lesbians who also appear to wish to distance themselves from feminists.[6]

Turning to the subject of feminism rather than feminists, women appear to me, both from this survey and in my own experience, to have a kind of pick and mix attitude to feminism. In general they are aware that the term 'feminism' covers a very broad range of perspectives. They are also, in the main, very favourably disposed to anything they see as contributing to the advance of women. Consequently large numbers of our respondents indicated that there are aspects of feminism that they support. But the proviso was frequently made that they would not want to do this in an extreme manner. These views resonate with those of very many women with whom I have discussed issues relating to feminism and it seems particularly characteristic of younger women.

Christine Griffith (1989), writing about a study she conducted with a group of young working class women in their last years at school and as they entered the job market, has indicated rather similar findings. She reported that while her respondents were sympathetic to many of the demands of feminism they frequently made the disclaimer that 'I'm not a women's libber'. As in the university survey reported on above, this disclaimer appeared to be related to the notion that collective female resistance is negative, unattractive and unfeminine.

There is no doubt that such stereotypes are fostered by the media but there is also little doubt that the stance taken by radical feminists, such as Mary Daly (1984) and Andrea Dworkin (1980), who do a great deal to court publicity, also contributes to the impression many women have of feminists as 'hating men/excessive/pushy/overly pushy/dominating/opinionated/righteous/narrow minded' to quote some of the comments made by female undergraduates in our survey.

Both surveys also indicate, I believe, a continuing ambivalence felt by very many women. This is that while they wholeheartedly endorse equal rights for women at work, in the home and in society at large, at some very deep level, they fear that too campaigning an attitude to women's rights is somehow related to a loss of femininity. Such ambivalences were referred to in chapter 5 and we will return to the issue in the concluding sections of this chapter.

Backlash (3) – men respond to feminists.

Q. 'What flashes into your mind in response to the word feminist?'
A. 'Dyke, short hair, whingeing, self defence, chip on shoulder.'

'Usually unreasonable, vulgar, lesbian 60s.'
'Big, fat, dresses like a man, looks like a man, acts like a man and
    hates men, single.'
'A plain looking woman with spectacles, lots of books on her library
    shelf and a propensity for argument . . .'
'Women with too much attitude.'
'A woman who is pushy, sometimes aggressive in advancing women's
    place in society. She is normally unattractive . . . men find it hard
    to get on with her perhaps because she frightens them.'
'Fine up to a point. Any feminist who goes over the top is just going
    to get ignored.'
'Over the top women. Don't get me wrong, I agree with equal rights.'
Male first year students studying at Scottish universities in 1993 (Beloff *et al.* 1993)

As noted above, Susan Faludi has asserted that there is currently a powerful backlash, initiated by men, against feminism. Her contention is certainly
supported by a number of books published in the past decade. These fall into
two types: those written by men who appear repelled and threatened by the
advance of women; and those written by men who have reappraised gender
positions. Before discussing these books, however, I would like to turn to the
responses made by the male undergraduates in the survey described above.

In general, as with the women, men were more favourably disposed
towards feminism than towards feminists. Almost 90 per cent of men made
extended comments about feminists and 56 per cent of these were negative.
On the other hand, 39 per cent said that they were very or quite sympathetic
towards feminism and only 16 per cent said they were not at all sympathetic
to feminism.

Their views on feminists, however, as revealed by the extended comments and drawings they made, were considerably less favourable. They often
paralleled the remarks made by the women respondents and large numbers of
men also commented that feminists are 'over the top' or in the words of the
quote at the beginning of this section have 'too much attitude'. There were
also a great many very unflattering references to the personal attributes and
frequently to the appearance of feminists. Like the women respondents, many
male respondents appeared to perceive feminists as unattractive, unfeminine
and antagonistic to men. It should be remembered, however, that these negative
views of feminists were not in general accompanied by a rejection of feminism
because only 16 per cent of the men indicated that they were not at all sympathetic to feminism.

Those men, however, who declared themselves unsympathetic to feminism, tended to display a very deepseated antagonism to feminists. For example,
the three men who made the following comments:

'Man-hating, politically correct, brash, rude, ugly, masculine'
'A hypocrite-silly cow that thinks about no 1. No sex please – I am a
    feminist.'

137

Drawings by male undergraduates in a survey of attitudes to feminists, Beloff *et al.*, 1993.

Lesbian
sergeant major type
too fat or too skinny

boring lesbo

too fat

Drawing by male undergraduates in a survey of attitudes to feminists, Beloff *et al.,* 1993.

'A feminist is an ignorant woman who doesn't have a clue what she is standing for, and *just can't face the fact that masculinity is the master race*' (my italics).

Such masculine antagonism and distaste for feminists has also been reflected in two recent books, *No More Sex Wars* and *Not Guilty: In defence of Modern Man* (Thomas, 1993). In the first of these the journalist Neil Lyndon (1992a) claims that the assumptions feminists make are:

.... false in logic, false in their assessments of social change and its consequences, false in the deductions and conclusions to which they lead.
Lyndon (1992b)

Lyndon bases these claims on his interpretation of recent changes in the areas of sexual equality. For, while he accepts that women were discriminated against in the past and that there was a necessity for this to be redressed, he takes issue with feminist interpretations of both the inequalities and the changes. To begin with he challenges the notion of patriarchy and the fact that until recently there have been massive sexual imbalances in power. Second, he

139

claims that the changes in women's lives that have taken place over the last hundred years are due to social processes, such as equal rights legislation and the advent of reliable contraception, rather than to the efforts of feminists. Third, he argues that women are now in the ascendent and legislation, for example with respect to child custody, favours women. Finally he contests the notion that women suffer from male violence to any appreciable extent arguing that women grossly misrepresent the extent to which they are the victims of male violence. On the contrary he claims that large numbers of men are attacked by their wives and partners but that this is under-reported because:

> so completely has the public absorbed the battered-woman image that
> it has become genuinely difficult to set out the facts.
> Lyndon, (1992c)

Lyndon's extremely critical approach towards feminism and feminists is echoed by David Thomas (1993, p. 1) who argues that women simply cannot be worse off than men because:

> . . . if men are so much better off than women, how come so many
> more of them kill themselves.

Like Lyndon he sees contemporary western society as 'obsessed with women to the point of mass neurosis' (Thomas, 1993, p. 2) and like Lyndon he believes that sexual equality legislation and recent social changes following on from such legislation have now disadvantaged men. But behind both books, it seems to me, is the lament of the last quotation I have given from our survey – women no longer accept that 'masculinity is the master race'.

I believe that both these books and some of the responses to our survey indicate that for a minority of men the victories won recently by women are extremely threatening and that such men do reflect the backlash to feminism about which Faludi and French write. Unlike Faludi and French, however, I do not believe that this backlash is organized, or indeed, very powerful. But I am convinced that, for a minority of men, women's equality in the home, at work and in social life does represent a very great psychological threat to which they react with fear and on occasion with violence. We will return to this issue in the next chapter.

Quite another backlash effect has been shown by a number of men who have responded to the change in women's power and status by arguing for a redefinition of masculinity. This has taken two forms. The first was the advent of the 'new' man and the second was the advent of the 'wild' man.

Backlash (4) – redefining masculinity – new men and wild men

> Men are changing – not perhaps with the bang of transformation, but
> also not simply with a whispered hint of a slight nudge in a new

direction. New role models for men have not replaced older ones, but have grown alongside them, creating a dynamic tension between ambitious breadwinner and compassionate father. . . . .
Michael Kimmel (1987, p. 9)

In the 1970s and 1980s a number of men, in direct response to feminism, formed themselves into consciousness raising groups. In these groups they attempted to come to terms with the premise held by feminist women that 'the personal is political' and they also attempted to make changes in their own attitude and behaviour that would meet the changing needs of women. Paralleling these responses at the personal level, a number of academics, most but by no means all male, set out to study changing approaches to gender in men (Cohen, 1990).

Most of these men took on board the basic premise of feminism that most societies have been patriarchal in that their power structures have privileged men rather than women. In seeking to redress this at the personal level they set out to review their own responses to women. It was out of such groups that the profile of the 'new man' was delineated – caring, compassionate and committed to equality with his wife or partner in the home and his female colleagues at work. Masculinity was no longer to be equated with dominance and men, as well as women, were to be prepared to talk openly about their feelings. Furthermore, sexual relations between the sexes were to reflect equal respect and concern for the differing sexual needs of men and women (Hearn and Morgan, 1990, Chapman and Rutherford, 1988).

Such a redefinition of masculinity began to be reflected by departments of men's studies, designed to run in parallel to the burgeoning departments of women's studies and to forge and investigate new models for modern men. Sociologists, in particular, began to analyse the extent to which power inequalities between the sexes had in the past constrained the way women and men could interact with each other and they also began to seek ways to reverse such inequalities.

There is no doubt that some of the changes proposed in the men's groups of the 1970s and 1980s have occurred. Men do more housework and spend more time with children than they did previously, though they still do considerably less of both than women (Kimmel, 1987). Men are also more prepared to talk about their feelings and emotions than they were in the past, as is very clearly seen in the number of men who do so in the media.

Furthermore, although as we shall see in the next chapter there is no evidence that rapes and sexual assaults on women are declining, most men no longer openly harass women sexually. Moreover they are far less likely than they were to talk in a sexist way – in the company of women at least.

I believe that these changes do reflect a genuine alteration in the notion of masculinity. As Kimmel notes in the quote in the beginning of this section, new role models for men have come into being. Nowhere is this more apparent than in the area of fatherhood. It is now almost universally accepted that childen's loving relationships should be with men as well as women as is evidenced by the condemnation, and frequently stigmatization, of one-parent families by many politicians and in certain sections of the media. Thus, even those men who most contest the advance of feminism, for example Lyndon and Thomas, place a very central emphasis on the rights of men as well as women to nurture and care for their children.

The emergence of new role models for men which brought masculinity closer to what had previously been considered to be more typical of femininity was soon met with resistance. In particular, in the USA, a new form of essentialism emerged. A number of men's groups were formed concerned that the new direction in defining masculinity epitomized by the new man, betrayed the true nature of masculinity. Robert Bly (1993), probably the most prominent member of such groups, put it this way:

> We are living at an important and fruitful moment now, for it is clear to men that the images of adult manhood given by the popular culture are worn out: men can no longer depend on them.

Bly, who has been very influenced by the psychoanalyst Carl Jung (see chapter 2) argues that men and women differ in their nature but that western society has blurred this difference. He believes that men need to make strong social bonds with other men and that this is particularly important for fathers and sons. These bonds are best forged, according to Bly, in conditions which bring the men and boys concerned close to nature so that boys can get into contact with what he calls their 'wild men':

> When a man gets in touch with the Wild Man, a true strength may be added. He's able to shout and say what he wants in a way the sixties-seventies man is not able to . . . (but) the ability of a male to shout and be fierce does not imply domination . . .
> Bly (1993, pp. 26–7)

Bly also claims that women themselves reject the wimpish nature of new men and secretly long for the return of wild men. His concept of the return to the essential nature of masculinity, is epitomized by the figure representing masculinity in a European folk tale, *Iron John*. Thus 'Iron John' provides the title for his book.

I believe that Bly's writing and his organization of retreats where men can reclaim and reshape their masculinity reflects a response to the challenge posed to many men by the growing domestic and social power of women. Like many of the male respondents to our survey and like Neil Lyndon and David Thomas, Bly gives the impression that as women continue to move into areas which have previously been exclusively male, their sense of their own personal masculinity is powerfully challenged.

Adult lives

There is no doubt that feminist and structuralist approaches to gender are now being absorbed into areas of psychology where previously more traditional or mainstream perspectives dominated.[7] This is particularly noticeable in two areas: sexuality and family life.

Sexuality in adult life

Heterosexual relationships

If love is the answer, could you please rephrase the question.
Lily Tomlin (1993, p. 49)

In the first chapter of this book sexuality was reviewed from a historical perspective and we noted that it is now generally conceded that women are no less sexual than men in that their interest in, and response to, sexuality is as intense as men's. However, as was shown in chapter 4, young women are still keenly aware of the double standard which permits and encourages young men to experiment sexually but disapproves of young women who act in a similar manner.

Nevertheless, the evidence is that young women commence sexual relationships at much the same age as young men and that increasing numbers of women as well as men have adulterous relationships after marriage. There is also evidence that women rather than men tend to initiate divorce proceedings. Furthermore, throughout the western world, while greater proportions of the population marry than in the past, people are marrying later and young people of both sexes are far more prepared to live together in stable relationships and have children without getting married (Unger and Crawford, 1992). There is little doubt, however, that despite this shift in behaviour some gender differences in attitudes to sexuality at all ages continue to operate.

Young women are both less likely to engage in casual sex than young men and are less comfortable with the idea of casual sex. They are also more likely to state that they take the danger of contracting Aids more seriously than are young men.

Rhoda Unger and Mary Crawford argue that, despite the changes brought about by feminism and women's changing position in society in general, gender differences in sexuality continue to be pivoted on deeply internalized scripts of male dominance and female passivity. They note that the strategies spelled out for the sexes continue to differ. For young men the message continues to stress having sex, for young women the stress is on avoiding it. Thus American studies show that the first time couples date, it is mostly men who seek to initiate sexual relationships while women are more likely to strive not to 'turn men on'. As dating continues the pattern does too. One study of

American students showed that while men complained of not having inter-course often enough, of having too few partners and of not having enough oral sex, women expressed dissatisfaction because of lack of foreplay, painful intercourse and because of experiencing feelings of fear and guilt (Darling and Davidson, 1986).

It is not only studies of students, however, which continue to show the persistence of the concept of male dominance in sexuality, men's greater pro-pensity for sexual dominance is shown in other studies as well. For example, Blumstein and Schwartz (1983) surveyed married, cohabiting, gay and lesbian couples and found that in all types of relationships men continued to stress the need for dominance. Women, on the other hand, stressed the need not for submission but a reluctance to dominate and a need for closer emotional relationships.

While studies such as these appear to support the notion that men con-tinue to be more likely to associate sexuality with sexual performance and women to associate it with emotions, this does not preclude the fact that both men and women are frequently very ambivalent about these aspects of sexuality. For, while women may condemn casual sex, as they move out of adolescence they become less preoccupied about their sexual reputations and, as Gad Horowitz and Michael Kaufman (1987) point out, for many men there is now a large degree of conflict about sexuality. While many social messages spell out that heterosexual masculinity is associated with power over women, in the sense that men are projected as the dominant partner, there are other messages concerned with the need to avoid the exploitation of women.

Sexuality for older heterosexual women continues to be permeated with ambivalences. To begin with most women continue to be exposed to the message that for women, satisfying and stable emotional relationships are all important. Furthermore, fiction directed at young women continues to stress the importance of romance. But there are other messages too. For example, role models like Madonna present an active and initiating version of female sexuality.

In order to illustrate the nature of such ambivalences let us look at two hypothetical relationships which are both built on a number of real life case studies. In the first instance consider Sally, aged 24, and Peter, aged 25, who have been living together for three years. Both are recent graduates with similar degrees and come from similar backgrounds and both have similar careers. When it comes to discussing issues concerned with interpersonal re-lationships, whether social, emotional or sexual, they agree that women as much as men can take the initiative. They also believe in sharing household chores, shopping and cooking and they have a joint bank account.

Sally applies for and gets a new job which brings with it a very large increase in salary. Peter professes not to mind that Sally now earns almost one and a half times his salary. On the strength of Sally's rise they decide to buy a car. Sally tells her best friend that she is going to take a back seat in the choice of the car because 'Peter is feeling pretty threatened by my new job, so I'm being very careful not to make him feel inadequate'. I would suggest that were the positions reversed Peter would not express the same inhibitions.

I believe that Sally and Peter epitomize two continuing tendencies in heterosexual relationships. First, the sense that many women have that men's egos are very easily threatened by their partner's achievements and second, that in most heterosexual relationships women work more actively than men to preserve the emotional equilibrium.

The second couple, Liz and David are older and have children in their early twenties. David is at the peak of a reasonably successful career while Liz has a part-time job which she feels does not really stretch her. Liz discovers that David is having an intense relationship with a younger woman. David is very upset by Liz's discovery of his affair and regrets hurting her by his behaviour. Liz is deeply upset at her discovery and is particularly resentful that David is being unfaithful at a time when she feels her own sexual desirability is declining. She wants, however, to preserve their marriage, provided he ends the relationship and that it remains a secret from the rest of the world. This is not, she confides to her friends, because of any great love she still feels for him but because the fate of a single woman in her fifties is one she wishes to avoid and because she believes that society still looks down on a woman who 'can't keep a man'. Should they split up she cannot see herself meeting a single man her own age and she will not entertain the idea of a relationship with a younger man. David, on the other hand, cannot understand her attitude and claims that she is struggling to preserve their marriage less out of love for him than out of a desire to retain the status of a married woman.

The differing perspectives of David and Liz illustrate three further themes in heterosexual relationships. First, the normality and social acceptability of sexual relationships between older men and younger women compared with the reverse. Second, the lingering feeling many heterosexual women have that a single woman inevitably is an object of pity or derision because she is seen as lacking in sufficient femininity to hold a man. Finally, many women, particularly older women, still define their identity in terms of being a wife or partner.

In conclusion, I would reiterate that while sexual inequalities in education and employment are being eroded, and that while sexual differences in attitudes, values and behaviour are diminishing in general, when it comes to issues concerned with sexuality, gender differences in attitudes, values and behaviour remain.

Homosexual and lesbian relationships

> I was aware of my sexuality at age nine, which makes a nonsense of an age of consent of 21 and of the ideas of CONVERSION, PERVERSION and the CORRUPTION of youth.
> Derek Jarman (1993, p. 144)

In chapter 3 we looked at a perspective on homosexuality and lesbianism which argued that sexuality is largely innately determined. At that stage I indicated that the belief that homosexuality is somehow inborn is one that is increasingly being held by many members of the gay and lesbian community.

It is not, of course, the only perspective. It was argued, for example, in the last century and even by some psychiatrists during this century that homosexuality was a pathological condition which could be cured by medical means, by for instance the administration of hormones (Ruse, 1988). As we have seen, other perspectives on homosexuality traced its origins to individual experience. Psychoanalysts argued that sexual orientation is forged during infancy and early childhood by psychodynamic forces in the nuclear family, while social learning theorists claimed that sexual orientation owes a great deal to the manner in which sex-typed behaviour is shaped and reinforced by socialization for those particular individuals who become homosexual or lesbian.

All these differing perspectives tend to regard sexuality as very central to the core of self. They all make the assumption that whether one is heterosexual, bisexual or homosexual, one's sexuality is not easily influenced by social context or transient conditions. On the contrary it is seen as an essential part of identity. There is, however, another perspective on homosexuality which owes its origins largely to anthropological studies which takes issue with these assumptions. This perspective (Caplan, 1987) suggests that the manner in which sexuality is perceived is constrained by cultural practices and values.

According to this viewpoint, while in the west we tend to regard sexuality as a core component of self, in certain other cultures sexual behaviour, in terms of hetero or homosexuality, is not regarded as central to personal identity. In certain societies, for example, during male initiation rites, all males take part in homosexual activities although in adult life there appears to be few, if any, homosexual relationships (Caplan, 1987). In other societies, for example, amongst certain Muslim groups in east Africa, gender and sexuality appear not to be strongly linked in people's minds. A young woman on her own, a state which is not regarded as acceptable for young women, can move in with a richer, older person who may be either male or female and have sexual relations with them. She can later have sexual relations with a person of a different sex to her protector. Thus the younger woman's gender is not seen as necessarily predicting, or limiting, her sexual behaviour (Shepherd, 1987).

Anthropological studies of sexuality such as the ones cited have had very little influence on homosexual and lesbian groups in the west. Feminism has, however. Feminists, of all persuasions, together with gay activists have exerted considerable political pressure since the 1960s to change public perceptions of homosexuality and lesbianism. This has resulted in a general acceptance by most members of the public that homosexuals and lesbians are not deviant in any pathological sense, and has also resulted in changes in legislation decriminalizing sexuality (for example between adult consenting males) which had previously been prescribed. Certain inequalities remain however. For instance in the UK, the age of consent for homosexuals is defined as 21, whereas for heterosexuals it is 16.

Despite these changes, sexuality for homosexuals and lesbians remains far more fraught with difficulties than it does for heterosexuals. This is particularly the case during puberty and adolescence when the social context for young people is usually regarded by teachers, parents and peers as unproblematically heterosexual. This means that 'coming out' during these years offers few role models and, as a result, although very many homosexuals and lesbians report that they were aware of their sexuality from a relatively early age, (Ruse, 1988) few come to terms with it until their late adolescence or early twenties.

Later in life homosexuals and lesbians continue to experience considerable discrimination at many levels, and many members of the general public continue to show high levels of prejudice against them. A tendency which has certainly not been lessened by the erroneous labelling of AIDS as a gay disease.

Marriage, partners and family life

Ah, how good it is to come home to your wife when she *believes* in you and submits to your purpose that is beyond her. Then how wonderful this nightfall is. How rich you feel, tired with all the burden of a day in your veins, turning home.
D.H. Lawrence (1971, p. 193, his italics)

She rose to his requirements, dropped
The playthings of her life
To take the honourable work
Of woman and of wife.
Emily Dickison, *The Wife* (1900)

Sometimes I wonder if men and women really suit each other. Perhaps they should live next door and just visit now and then.
Katherine Hepburn (1993, p. 49)

It is not likely that even Neil Lindsay or David Thomas, in their flight from feminism, would endorse the kind of sentiments encapsulated in the first two quotations above because views on marriage and parenthood have changed enormously over the last hundred years.

In particular since the 1960s, and certainly influenced by the feminist movement, notions of marriage and parenthood have been permeated by an acceptance of a number of propositions about gender roles which would have been regarded as totally unacceptable in the past.

To begin with, parenthood is no longer seen as necessarily linked to marriage, partly because of the rise of single parent families and partly because a significant number of couples living in stable relationships do not marry. It is now also generally accepted that mothers of even very young children are likely to work, not only part-time but also full-time. It has been accepted that mothers, as well as fathers, have the right to pursue fulfilling and satisfying careers, although the organization of child care still falls disproportionately on mothers. Finally, fathers have become far more actively involved in parenthood (Niven, 1992, White and Woollett, 1992) even if, as we have seen in chapter 4, fathers and mothers continue to play somewhat different roles.

There is no doubt that these changes owe a great deal to more flexible notions of gender, and that feminism as well as more structural approaches to gender have contributed to these changes. It should not be forgotten, how-ever, that changes in the economy, such as greater male unemployment and more part-time jobs for mothers, have also played their part in the relative blurring of gender roles in the family. Furthermore, the rise in unemployment amongst young males, particularly amongst those with few educational qualifications, has meant that it has become far harder for such men to play the traditional role of breadwinner and, consequently, more and more young women are bringing up children in one parent families.

Conclusions

In this chapter we have surveyed the effects of our understanding of gender relationships, of structural approaches to gender and of feminism. Together with the rise of the gay movement they have contributed to radical changes in the way in which men and women live their lives, think about gender issues and relate to each other. In general, they have been associated with a blurring of gender roles and an equalization in gender opportunities but, particularly in the area of sexuality, gender differences in values and behaviour remain.

Notes

1. It should be pointed out that the Vanatinai are a matrilineal society (i.e. lineage is related to the mother not the father) and that this often also contributes to the status of women.
2. Mernissi (1971) argues that while purdah has the expressed purpose of protecting women's honour, there are dual traditions in Islamic thought concerning whether this is threatened more by women's latent but strong sexuality or by men's inability to control their sexuality.
3. Mahfouz (1991) describes the manner in which purdah affected the lives of Egyptian women at the beginning of this century.
4. Although many people believe that Sartre was de Beauvoir's lifelong mentor and lover, it has become increasingly clear that although they were lovers early on, in later life their physical relationship ended. Although de Beauvoir had originally been Sartre's student she later became his intellectual companion and sometimes his teacher.

.

5. As Celia Kitzinger (1991, pp. 111–30) has pointed out, it is only very recently that psychology has taken the concept of power on board.
6. We were not able to make any assumptions about the sexuality of the respondents to our survey, but it seems very likely that the very great majority of negative responses about feminists were made by heterosexual rather than lesbian women.
7. See for example the series Psychology published by Sage and the journal *Feminism & Psychology*.

Chapter 7

Fatal Attractions

It is significant that there is a difference between the sexes in the type of phantasy which will appeal to each. The idea of being seized and borne off by a ruthless male who will wreak his sexual will upon his helpless victim has a universal appeal to the female sex. It is the existence of this phantasy which accounts for the wide popularity of such figures as *The Sheikh*, Rhett Butler, or even King Kong.
Anthony Storr (1970, p. 91)

American girls are like horses, very independent. They have never been controlled by anybody. But if you can break them in, they are very grateful, *as all women are.*
Michael Caine, 1974, – my italics – (Storr, 1970, p. 130)

In this last chapter issues relating to sexual antagonism, in particular, sexual assaults, rape and date or 'acquaintance' rape and finally violence will be considered. These issues cannot, of course, be considered out of their social and cultural context. Such contexts are perhaps best observed by looking at gender images and stereotypes, both historic and contemporary, and it is to these that we now turn.

Stereotypes and images

Stereotypes serve as the agents of social messages about the appropriate roles and behaviours of women and men.
Rhoda Unger and Mary Crawford (1992, p. 125)

Stereotyping and counter-stereotyping

Psychological approaches to the study of sex differences have traditionally placed a heavy emphasis on the role of stereotypes (Unger and Crawford, 1992). Stereotyping is said to occur when a group is portrayed in such a way that all members of the group are regarded as having the same set of

150

characteristics, attitudes or conditions of life (Durkin, 1986). Quite clearly stereotyping in the area of gender is linked to what has been referred to in this book as sex-typing.

As noted in chapter 4, many psychologists, particularly those from behaviourist or social learning backgrounds, have argued that one of the major reinforcers of sex-typed behaviour is the extent to which the media depict males and females in a sex-typed manner (Liebert and Sprafkin, 1988). The major avenues for this sex typing have been films, television and tabloid newspapers. Most of the research on this topic, however, has been carried out on television coverage, largely because the majority of the population, particularly young children, spend more time watching television, and more recently videos, than listening to the radio, going to the cinema or reading.

The extent to which American television in the past showed men and women in a sex-typed manner has been documented in very great detail. For example, studies in the late 1970s and early 1980s reported that three-quarters of all leading characters on prime-time television were male; men were also more likely than women to be shown to exercise creativity, solve problems, give orders and help or save others. Furthermore, men were also more likely than women to be shown to be rewarded for such actions (Sternglanz and Serbin, 1974). Women, on the other hand, tended to be portrayed as deferential, passive and compliant (Tavris and Wade, 1984).

Women were also more likely than men to be shown as victims, but were less likely to be victimized if they played conventional roles, for example if they were married. Women were almost always portrayed as housewives and, if they were shown as working, were unlikely to be in professional, interesting or challenging occupations (Unger and Crawford, 1992). Commercials, in particular, sex-typed women as the consumers of beauty products and products for the home while advertisements for cars, insurance and banking services were almost always directed at men. When there were authoritative voice-overs in commercials, for instance by medical experts, the voices were usually male. Moreover, while women presenters were invariably young and conventionally attractive many men presenters were older and not necessarily conventionally goodlooking.

Similar sex-stereotyping has been shown until recently on British television. Women were outnumbered by men, shown in a narrower range of occupational roles and tended to be shown as more emotional and as less dominant than men. Furthermore, as in America, they were more likely to be portrayed in commercials as consumers of beauty and household products and less likely to do authoritative voice-overs (Gunter, 1986).

In recent years there have been dramatic changes in such sex-typing. Women are frequently portrayed in professional roles, as detectives, as experts and women now present hard news programmes and documentaries, and appear as experts in a wide range of fields from astronomy to financial forecasting. Furthermore, there has been a movement, particularly in programmes directed at younger people, towards counter-stereotyping, that is the presentation of images of men and women that run directly counter to traditional sex-typing (Durkin, 1986).

Despite these changes certain biases remain, particularly in the area of commercials. For example, a study of prime-time adverts on ITV in 1990 showed that men continued to outnumber women, continued to be more likely to do voice-overs, and were more likely to be seen as in paid employment. Moreover even though men as well as women were portrayed as doing housework, men were more likely to be shown as doing it for friends while women tended to be shown doing housework in their traditional role within the family. Gender differences were also shown in the physical appearance of the sexes in that more women than men were shown to fall into the 21–30-year-old age group and youth, good looks, blonde hair and ideal body type were more characteristic of the women appearing in the commercials than of the men (Cumberbatch, 1990).

However, while there is no doubt that sex-stereotyping did, and to some still does, characterize a great deal of media portrayals of the sexes, it is by no means a foregone conclusion that such stereotyping necessarily contributes to sex differences. As Tavris and Wade (1984) point out perceptions of sex roles are not simply shaped by any one source. So that, while children watch a great deal of television, it is highly unlikely that television alone can account for the sex-typing of behaviour because children are presented with a wide range of other sources of information about the social world at home, at school and at play. Furthermore, the notion that behaviour is shaped by the media, places the consumer in a very inactive role and the media in the role of what has sometimes been called the 'hypodermic syringe' (Howitt, 1982). The analogy here is that the media simply inject information and attitudes into a passive consumer with the flow of influence in one direction only, from the media to the viewer, reader or listener.

Empirical evidence, however, suggests that the hypodermic syringe is not a particularly useful analogy. To begin with, a number of studies show that people do not simply absorb what is presented to them in an inert fashion. Instead it appears they are more likely to pay attention to, and be influenced by, those media messages which resonate with and reflect their own views and that they tend to reject messages which conflict with their own understanding of the world (Cumberbatch and Howitt, 1989). Furthermore, the media are generally regarded by the public with a degree of cynicism so that even very young viewers tend to view TV with scepticism particularly when it comes to, what is perhaps still the heaviest purveyer of sexual stereotypes, commercials (Cullingford, 1984). Thus the notion of the viewer as passive does not seem appropriate. Neither does the uni-directional nature of the hypodermic syringe analogy. This is because what is sold in newsagents, heard on the radio and shown on TV is increasingly driven by market forces and audience ratings. Thus consumers affect what is presented to them as well as the reverse process and the direction of influence proceeds in both directions.

Images and cultural representations

> Confronted by images, our impulse is to understand rather than to
> find things incomprehensible. In a familiar culture it is not the difficulty
> of finding and making meanings which is most striking but the way
> in which these meanings depend on assumptions shared between the
> producer of the image and the context in which the image appears at
> least as much as on the image itself.
> Richard Allen (1992, p. 22)

While psychologists have tended to give stereotypes a central role in
discussing the manner in which messages about sex differences are conveyed,
analysts writing in the area of cultural theory have placed more emphasis on
the notion of cultural representation and images. From this orientation the
media is seen as interacting with, and representing, notions of femininity and
masculinity which are already embedded within the culture. Furthermore, as
the quote by Allen at the beginning of this subsection indicates, cultural theorists point out that images are never perceived in isolation; it is the context that
helps fix the message. For example, Allen cites five pictures of female soldiers
he viewed at the beginning of the Gulf war. In the first, women soldiers were
seen boarding a plane on a television newscast; in the second, a newspaper
pictured a woman soldier sitting cradling a rifle; in the third, also in a newspaper, a woman soldier on guard duty was shown gazing across a desert; in
the fourth, a woman soldier was interviewed on television about her family
and in the fifth, the child of the woman last mentioned was seen on television
in its grandparents' house watching its mother on the screen and saying 'that's
my mummy'.

Allen writes that all five pictures started from the same point – 'a desire
to picture a woman soldier'. However, while the first placed women soldiers
in a factual context, the second two 'sexualized' them because the photos
occupied almost full pages, were close-ups and were shown in papers which
usually showed pin-up pictures of women in that position. The final two
identified the woman soldier primarily in her role in the family.

In this way, Allen argues, media representations frame and focus images
in a manner which reflects the viewpoint of the journalist or producer. However, while such framing may reflect the journalist's or producer's intention, it
may be rejected by the viewer, who may sometimes actively, and at other
times less consciously, reinterpret an image. For example, a woman viewing
the third picture, the woman soldier gazing across the desert, may focus long-
ingly on the solitude not the incipient sexuality perceived by Allen.

Allen's analysis focuses on what would at first glance appear to be a
counter-stereotypical image – women at war. But he shows that, in essence at
least, four of the pictures are framed within a very ancient dichotomy – woman
as madonna (mother) and woman as whore (the sexualized photos). Although
it should be borne in mind that such a framing may not be interpreted in this
manner by the viewer.

Images and themes

The madonna and the whore

> For every glowing portait of submissive women enshrined in domes-
> ticity, there exists an equally important negative image that embodies
> the sacrilegious fiendishness of what William Blake called the 'The
> Female Will'.
> Sandra Gilbert and Susan Gubar (1979, p. 28)

Both feminist and cultural theorists frequently point out that, until very recently, and largely as a result of the patriarchal nature of most societies, the arts have tended to focus far more on men's portrayal of women than the reverse. Particularly in visual arts where women have been the focus of the male artist's, and commonly the male viewer's, gaze (Berger, 1990).

It has often been suggested that male portrayals of women have frequently pivoted around a dichotomy where at one pole woman is worshipped as pure, virginal (when unmarried) and chaste (when married), while at the other pole she is seen as a dangerous seductress. This dichotomy is often seen at its most extreme in fundamentalist religious thought. For example, within the Judaeo-Christian tradition, not only did Eve betray Adam, but according to the ancient Hebrew tradition, so did her predecessor Lilith who was the first woman God made. While God made Adam of dust, Lilith was made of filth and sediment. When Adam tried to impose his will on her, she challenged him and accordingly was banished and in revenge became a spirit of evil who seduced men from their wives and populated the world with furious demons (Tavris and Wade, 1984, Unger and Crawford, 1992).

Both Lilith and to a lesser extent, Eve, represent the dangers and seductiveness of female sexuality and they stand in marked contrast to the purity of the virgin Mary and the chastity of other biblical figures like the faithful Ruth of the old Testament. These biblical oppositions prefigured a dichotomous view of femininity that has been markedly persistent. Jane Ussher (1991, p. 86), for example, has pointed out that in the nineteenth century, in particular, the 'juxtaposed images of woman as angel and as a castrating sexual monster' permeated western thought. Contrast these two images:

> . . . the strange woman, she the flower, the sword
> Red from spilt blood, a mortal flower to men,
> Adorable, detestable.
> Swinburne, 1865 (Starr, 1991, p. 61)

> . . . the rose-lipt girls are sleeping
> In fields where roses fade.
> Housman, *The Shropshire Lad* (1896)

Images like these induced not only men but also women themselves to regard eroticism in women as dangerous, unnatural and incipiently evil, and to idealize submissiveness and sexual innocence. The fate of women who openly rejected this straitjacket was isolation, ostracization and, as in a number of fictional portrayals of such women–Tolstoi's, Anna Karenina and Thomas Hardy's, Tess – a violent and untimely death.

Such images are not only to be found in the past but they also continue to be found in mainstream fiction and films even at the end of the twentieth century (Smith, 1993). For example, in the contrast in the film *Fatal Attraction* between the conventional and virtuous wife and the assertive and sexually rapacious mistress and the violent death met by the sexually predatory figure played by Diane Keaton in *Waiting for Mr Goodbar.*

It has frequently been suggested that the source of this dualistic image of women is to be found in men's fear that the sexual woman is potentially the castrating she-devil. Consequently men need to continually monitor and keep in check sexual initiative and independence in women and to remind them of the fate that potentially awaits them if they step too far out of line. It has also been argued that it is this fear, allied to men's envy of women's reproductive powers, that fuels the misogyny which is characteristic of the portrayal of women by many, but by no means all, men both in the past and, to a lesser extent, in the present.

The beauty myth

> We are in the midst of a violent backlash to feminism that uses images
> of female beauty as a political weapon against women's advancement:
> the beauty myth.
> Naomi Wolf (1990, p. 2)

The ideal woman is not only traditionally chaste and sexually submissive she is, of course, also beautiful and desirable. And if she is not born beautiful, according to Naomi Wolf in *The Beauty Myth*, she is nowadays expected to remedy this deficiency to the best of her abilities.

While many feminists have written critically about the emphasis placed on women's appearance in contemporary culture few have had so powerful an impact as has Naomi Wolf. She argues that while beauty in the past was merely associated with desirable qualities in women, female beauty in present times has become an imperative. This has come about in the following way according to Wolf. In the past women were kept in their place by confining them to the domestic sphere. Following the limited success of the woman's movement, however, men threatened by women as rivals in the workplace and deprived of women's constant ministration to masculine needs in the home:

> reimposed on to liberated women's faces and bodies all the limita-
> tions, taboos and punishments of the repressive laws, religious
> injunctions and reproductive enslavements that no longer carried suf-
> ficient force.
> Wolf (1990, pp. 5–6)

According to Wolf, even successful and potentially powerful women have internalized the message that unless they are sexually desirable, beautiful and youthful in appearance they are worthless. Consequently in the grip of a destructive obsession, women diet, spend large amounts of money on clothes, hairstyles and cosmetics and are ravaged by self loathing when they fail to match up to the lithe, desirable and unflawed images perpetually presented in the media by models and film stars. Wolf argues that this quest to conform to media images results in a uniformity of aspiration – women 'lack the choice' (Wolf, 1990, p. 228) to aim for anything other than the current media ideal.

There is no doubt that Wolf is correct in her documentation of the extent to which the lives of a majority of women in the west, particularly in their younger years, are dominated by a desire to present themselves as attractive and desirable. Most younger, and a large number of older, women spend a relatively large proportion of their disposable income on clothes, cosmetics and diet foods and devote considerable thought and time to their appearance and, for many women, self esteem is inextricably linked to their physical appearance. Furthermore, as the growing incidence of anorexia nervosa and bulimia attests, the preoccupation with weight in particular can become exceedingly destructive. Wolf's analysis of the extent to which such preoccupations contribute to economies that are driven by market forces is also indisputable.

However, I believe that her apocalyptic analysis of women's concern with their physical appearance is unbalanced because she fails to take a number of linked associations sufficiently into account. First, I believe she does not consider the extent to which market forces of the type she documents currently affect men, particularly younger men, as well as women. This issue will be returned to later.

Second, I think she ignores the extent to which physical appearance today is as much related to style, as it is to sexual desirability, or indeed normative or conventional notions of beauty. Who, for example, could regard the 1980s and early 1990s with their rapidly changing and frequently simultaneous fashions of punk, new romantics, power dressing, supermodels, grunge and waif models as imposing conformist, or indeed in the case of the last two categories, overtly sexual models of beauty?

Linked to the simultaneous existence of a number of opposing styles of beauty, is a third consideration which I would argue Wolf does not take sufficiently into account. This is the claim made by many women that most of the time what motivates their choice of clothes, hairstyle and cosmetics is the particular image or style they identify with, and which they enjoy wearing, rather than the wish to look overtly sexually desirable. Finally I think Wolf ignores the extent to which physical attractiveness has, throughout the ages, for men as well as women smoothed the path of personal destinies, quite irrespective of a beauty industry.

Beauty and sexuality as currency

> There once was a king whose *beautiful*, golden-haired wife . . .
> Psyche's great *beauty* caused her to be worshipped . . .
> Cinderella's *beauty* . . . amazes everyone at the ball
> An old queen . . . had a very *beautiful* daughter . . .
> Quotations from Fairy tales (Stein and Corbett, 1991)

Throughout the ages, as the quotations from the fairy tales above indicate, heroines and to a lesser extent heroes, have been portrayed as physically attractive. Furthermore, as empirical studies have shown time and again, physical attractiveness contributes to success in the educational, social and occupational spheres. In job interviews, for example, physical attractiveness is frequently linked to success. In general, however, this finding is shown to hold more powerfully for women than for men (Unger and Crawford, 1992).

Of course, most of us do not consciously discriminate in favour of those whom we perceive to be attractive and it may be that one of the reasons for the success of good-looking people is that as attractive children they found social skills easier to acquire than their less attractive peers. Nevertheless that there is a link, however tenuous, between physical appearance and success is indisputable. Consequently if women and, to a lesser extent, men expend time, money and energy on their appearance they may be less in the grip of an unthinking and blind adherence to a beauty myth than to a realistic acceptance of the importance of physical appearance.

The extent to which it is possible to overtly manipulate both their appearance and their sexuality in order to succeed with the opposite sex (or indeed with their own sex in the case of those who are not heterosexual) obviously varies from individual to individual, and for particular individuals across times and contexts. Nevertheless, it is my belief that few of us, particularly when young, have *never* behaved in the manner that the politician Edwina Currie talked about in the quotation following:

> I like being with men. I like working with men. I like pulling out all
> the stops and trying to figure out how to get my own way, how to get
> what I am after. And if that means being slightly underhand and teas-
> ing them, or flattering them or whatever, I don't give a damn. I'll just
> do it. It's often a very calculating and manipulative way of going about
> things, but I've always done that.
> Edwina Currie (1988)

The wimp and the rake

> Mad, bad and dangerous to know.
> Reputedly said by Lady Caroline Lamb about Lord Byron with whom she was having
> a passionate, and for her, destructive affair.

While the dual madonna/whore image discussed above is frequently referred to in texts on gender it is seldom, if ever, analogized to the other sex.
The analogue does, however, exist and can certainly be identified as running
through western literature and art. In this case, the dichotomy pivots around
women's images of men with at one pole, the safe, caring and unexciting
image of the good husband and at the other, the dangerous, sexualized and
tantalizing figure of the elusive lover.

In the eighteenth century Mozart opera, Donna Anna, despite the ten-
der and loving protection offered by Don Alfredo, is obviously fascinated
by the notorious and evil Don Giovanni. Similar conflicts between the safe and
the sensual characterize many nineteenth century novels – Jane Eyre rejects
the saintly St John for the saturnine Mr Rochester; Anna Karenina leaves her
bureaucratic and conventional husband for a dashing army officer; Emma
Bovary, unsatisfied by the domestic virtues of the good Dr Bovary, seeks
excitement in affairs with men who may be irresistible but are clearly irrespon-
sible as well. In twentieth century novels and films women continue to be torn
– Scarlett O'Hara between the virtue of Ashley and the glamour of Rhett Butler;
Lady Chatterley caught in the conflict of money and class on the one hand and
danger and sex on the other. In the film *Straw Dogs* the heroine, bored by her
worthy academic husband, turns for excitement to men who are not only more
obviously virile but are also incipiently violent. In a film made almost two
decades later the same tensions surface – Isabella Rosellini in *Blue Velvet*
remains in thrall to the sinister figure played by Dennis Hopper despite the
entreaties of the handsome but conventionally small-town figure played by
Kyle Maclachan.

In a somewhat similar vein, it has been suggested that the unreconstructed
male chauvinist offers women more excitement and satisfaction than is offered
by the caring and compassionate 'new' man. Not surprisingly, however, the
protaganists of this viewpoint tend to be men and, less commonly, women
who write from an overtly anti-feminist stance (Lyndon, 1992a, Thomas, 1993,
and Stassinopolous, 1973).

Contemporary trends

Changing images of women

> Let's talk about sex: How to have a brilliant time in bed
> Title of article in *19*, July, 1993

A visit to any newsagent will offer convincing evidence that in recent
years the media have offered very different images of the sexes to those of
even 10 years ago. The most obvious change is in the overt discussion of
sexuality in women's magazines. Whereas mainstream women's magazines in
the past referred obliquely to sexuality, and with the presumption that sexual

initiatives would come from men, things are very different now. For example, *Shout*, which has replaced the long-running teenage magazine for girls *Jackie*, offers advice on taking the initiative with boys. Magazines like *19* and *More*, which are directed at slightly older readers, carry articles which not only advise women on ways of taking the sexual initiative but also discuss sexual practices and techniques very explicitly (Keenan, 1992, *Shout*, 1993).

Although women's magazines continue to focus on relationships with men, beauty and, in the case of those directed at older readers, household issues, they all, unlike magazines of previous years, now take for granted that women are also concerned with their careers and working lives. Some magazines, like *Cosmopolitan*, frequently feature articles on working life, but, in general, most women's magazines do not devote a great deal of space to such articles.

There is, however, little doubt that the content of women's magazines has been influenced by feminism even if they seldom carry articles written from an explicitly feminist standpoint. For, as Wolf herself points out, women's magazines today frequently deal with issues that were high on the feminist agenda in past decades, such as rape, abortion, women-battering, economic independence and sexual self-expression. Furthermore, their tone has shifted in that images which run counter to traditional sex-typing are discussed with approval. For example, in an article about female musicians in an issue of *Elle*, Liz Evans (1993) writes:

> In the 90s, a generation of female musicians has arrived, women and girls who are not content with taking a back seat to their leather-clad, ego-touting brothers . . . Smashing down the barriers which have stereotyped female performers . . . these women are using word, music and images to express their different personalities . . . (and draw in) teenage girls across America (who) link up through mailing lists and fanzines . . . to resist male intimidation and form new bands.

In addition to these changes in mainstream women's magazines, the last few years has also seen the emergence of magazines both in the UK and in America like *Playgirl* and *For Women*, devoted to the kind of coverage of sexuality, in both words and picture, which is as *For Women* (1993) puts it 'what they don't show you in *Cosmo*'. While only a minority of women may ever buy magazines like these, most women presumably know of their existence because their arrival was widely covered in the mass media and the knowledge that women now have a female equivalent of male magazines like *Penthouse* and *Playboy* contributes to a general acceptance of what Wolf calls women's 'sexual self-expression'.

Moving away from magazines to newspapers, there is no doubt that despite the retention of page 3 girls in some tabloids, references to women in terms of their sexual and physical attributes have decreased. This has been accompanied by considerable changes in the range of material which women write about in both tabloid and broadsheet newspapers.

There have also been changes in the presentation of women in mainstream films in that, despite the backlash to feminism found in films such as *Fatal Attraction, Pretty Woman* and *Presumed Innocent,* (Smith, J., 1993) women are more likely than they were in the past to play the role of active and powerful protagonists (as for example in the *Alien* series and *Thelma and Louise*). Women directors are also beginning to make their mark, and although successful women directors are the exception a number of them, for example Gillian Armstrong *My Brilliant Career,* Jane Campion *Angel at My Table, Sweetie* and *The Piano,* and Beeban Kidron *Used People,* have recently demonstrated that films looking at the world through the eyes of female rather than male protagonists can become not only critical but also box office successes.

Change has also come to the television screen. This change lies mainly in the variety of different images of women that are now on offer ranging from counter-stereotypical images like tough policewomen and cynical cab drivers to more conventional wives, sweethearts and mothers. Turning away from the manner in which women are portrayed, to what women do on the small screen, we can see a similar extension of opportunities. Women are no longer confined to reading the news, singing and dancing or acting as seductive assistants on game and quiz shows. Instead they host shows, feature as comedians, analyse the news, deploy cameras, are employed as technicians, direct and produce.

Clearly, then, the media offer young women a great many more images and role models than were on offer to past generations. In a world which features Madonna, Victoria Wood, Ruby Wax, Sarah Dunant and Margaret Thatcher, the notion that women are necessarily more passive and less enterprising than men, socially and sexually cannot be sustained. Nevertheless, some younger women continue to feel that, for them, what Nancy Friday (1991) calls 'The Rules' still exist. These rules spell out that while it may be permissable and acceptable for exceptional women to be where the action is, if the average young woman raises her head too far above the parapet, the personal consequences may not necessarily be all that rewarding. Such women believe that men, and for that matter other women, do not really like pushy women and as a result they monitor their own self-presentation and sometimes modify their aspirations.

Furthermore, while women may see media representations of women with children successfully pursuing careers, the lack of adequate child-care facilities, combined with the implicit assumption that finding alternative child-care is the women's rather than the man's responsibility, results in some mothers, who are affluent enough to have the choice about working, feeling as bewildered as those interviewed by Rosalind Coward (1993, p. 191):

> Will the children be deprived if I work? Will I go mad if I don't? Is the local school good enough for my child? What will happen to the kids when they leave home? More important, what will happen to me?

Young women from less affluent backgrounds can show equal scepticism about the reality of the opportunities ostensibly on offer to women these days. For example the schoolgirl, interviewed by Sue Lees (1986, p. 131), when asked about her future said:

> ... I see myself pushing a pram. I don't see myself working actually. Either at home or queuing at the Labour Exchange, something like that ... A girl in my class she's got a baby who's a couple of months old. I don't see myself working.

Contemporary images of men

> What has changed are the surfaces of lads themselves, the way they carry their masculinity. Individuality is on offer, incited through commodities and consumer display. From jeans: red tabs, designer labels, distressed denim. To hair: wedges, spiked with gel, or pretty hard boys who wear it long, set off with a large earring.
> Mort (1987, p. 193)

> In the June 1993 issue of *GQ* (Gentlemen's Quarterly):
>   Clothes Minded: If you really want to get smart
>   Indian Summer: The tropical look to beat the heat
>   Less is More: The Latest in Affordable Fashion ...
> In the May, 1993 issue of *Arena: The Award-Winning Magazine for the Young Dude*:
>   20 pages of essential spring fashion
>   A collector's guide to Denim

Not surprisingly the changes in media representations of women have been accompanied by analogous though rather less dramatic changes in the images of men. One of the most noticeable aspects of the change has been the acceptance that men, as well as women, are interested both in their appearance and in what they wear. These assumptions can be seen in the emergence of magazines for men like *GQ* and *Arena* which are centrally concerned with fashion. It is now also generally accepted that when a man openly expresses an interest in fashion, this is not a pointer to his sexuality but to his sense of style, and articles have begun to appear about male, as well as female, supermodels (Quick, 1993).

The notion that men as well as women care about their physical appearance has opened a set of lucrative marketing niches. Little boys can be induced to persuade their parents to buy them expensive trainers; adolescent boys to buy anti-dandruff shampoos and anti-spot creams and lotion; young men to buy clothes with designer labels and older men to spend more money on aftershave lotions and colognes for men. In the terminology used in chapter 4 of this book, for many men physical appearance has become an important component of their self-concept. And for a very small but increasing, minority of men burgeoning doubts and worries about their physical appearance assume grave enough dimensions to lead to eating disorders such as anorexia (Mair, 1993).

Men, as well as women, are now increasingly offered disparate physical images and styles. Furthermore, the number and rapidity of change in styles and fashions confer a freedom on men to experiment with different self-presentations and liberate young men from feeling that an interest in self-presentation is necessarily a statement about their sexuality. In other words, expressing an open interest in clothes, hairstyles and physique is no longer taken, as it was in the very recent past, to be an indication of homosexuality. Frank Mort (1987, p. 204) puts it this way:

> Haircuts, the cut of jeans, ways of walking and being are points of comparison between young men . . . The effect of all this is to open up a space for some new *visual codes of masculinity*. What's cool now is not the assertion of a fixed masculine identity but a self-conscious assemblage of style. (my italics)

Mort was writing in 1987 before the recession cut the disposable income of a generation of young school leavers. Nevertheless, the trends he describes continue and within the straitjacket of austerity and even poverty, the traces of the style revolution of the 1980s has not been obliterated. Men, as well as women, have been given the freedom to experiment with their personal appearance.

Sexual images of men have changed too, partly as a result of the increasing sexual sex-expression now permitted to women. As a result, the 80s and 90s have not only seen the arrival of the male supermodel but also the advent of the male stripper. The American group, the Chippendales, have in particular fascinated the tabloid press in the UK and it has regularly featured stories about them and their would-be imitators (Daily Mail, 1993).

Although magazines, advertisements and commercials, albeit chiefly in the service of market forces, now offer men a range of alternative physical images and styles, the portrayal of men in mainstream films and television series has not changed appreciably and sex-typing is still strong. The hero still tends to be stereotyped as active, virile and often tough. The image of the 'new' man has, however, influenced media representations of individual men in four ways.

First, as already mentioned above, he is permitted a degree of narcissism about his appearance, as for example in the famous scene in *American Gigolo* where Richard Gere displays his extensive wardrobe. Second, allied to his interest in his appearance, he is allowed to be the object of female gaze, as women have traditionally been the object of male gaze, for example in the cases of male models and strippers. Third, he is permitted to look after children provided he is, at the same time, tough enough to take the world on (*Kramer vs Kramer, Three Men and a Baby*). Finally, he is more likely than he was in the past to talk about his feelings although when he does so he needs to have some sort of rationale for this behaviour, for example to help his sister in *Prince of Tides* or because he is a foreigner, as in *Green Card*.

It seems to me, however, that the emphasis on style and presentation of self notwithstanding, that there is less flexibility in the manner in which men are portrayed on the media than there is for women. Women are routinely portrayed in what were previously male preserves such as medicine, law, science and the police force while men are relatively less frequently portrayed as nurses (except in documentaries), hairdressers, beauticians, primary school teachers, personal assistants and secretaries. In line with what has already been noted, however, they are now more frequently shown as single parents.

I believe this gender difference is due to the historic inequalities in status between male and female occupations which makes counter-stereotyped images more psychologically threatening to men than to women. This is why, sexuality aside, men like Julian Clary are presented more ironically and more ambivalently than women like Madonna. Women may not like Madonna but she presents a credible role model. Men may like Julian Clary but he does not provide a credible role model for them.

Pornographic images

Like beauty, pornography is in the eye of the beholder.
Richard Green (1987, p. 427), in a review article on psychological aspects of pornography.

Justice Potter Stewart's admission to the 1970 Presidental Commission on Pornography that: 'although he couldn't define it, he knew it when he saw it'.
Williams (1990, p. 17)

In this section on pornography we will centre on the three issues that it seems to me are of direct relevance to gender:

1. Are there gender differences in the use which is made of pornography?
2. Does taking part in the production of pornography inevitably debase the women who do so?
3. Is there any evidence that pornography contributes to men's abuse of women?

Before moving into these areas let us look at some background factors.
As Dennis Howitt and Guy Cumberbatch (1990) point out, pornography is notoriously difficult to define. The word itself has a Greek derivation from

the term *pornographios* which means 'writing about harlots', or prostitutes, (Williams, 1987) but it is a relatively modern word in English usage and did not enter Webster's Dictionary until 1864 when it was defined both with reference to prostitution and also with reference to licentiousness and orgies (Howitt and Cumberbatch, 1990). It has retained both these connotations in modern times: the second connotation, the notion that pornography is designed to arouse sexuality, being the aspect most generally accepted as lying at the core of pornographic material while the first connotation, the aspect concerned with the degradation of women in particular, being the one most commonly associated with it by feminists.

Turning for the moment to the first aspect, it can be seen immediately that defining pornography in terms of its ability to arouse sexuality does not immediately differentiate it from what could be termed 'erotica', and while people in favour of censorship wish to ban pornographic material they seldom talk of extending the ban to erotica. Thus the term pornography tends to be differentiated from erotic material in that pornographic depictions of sexuality are defined as being 'explicit' (Howitt and Cumberbatch, 1990). This notion of sexual explicitness has more recently been further refined with the use of the terms 'hard' and 'soft' core.

The distinction between the terms hard and soft core tend to focus on one of two dimensions. First, the degree of explicitness, for example whether sexual intercourse is simulated or is actually filmed or videotaped and second, the degree to which the material is either violent, or demeaning and degrading to women/and or children (Howitt and Cumberbatch, 1990).

If there has been little concensus about defining pornography amongst experts, there is equally little concensus amongst the general public about what they regard as pornographic material. For example, in one large and representative sample of the public who were asked to classify adverts by the Advertising Standards Authority, seven per cent classified a drawing by the early twentieth century artist Gustav Klimt, which was used in a perfume advert, as obscene and two per cent classified it as harmful (Howitt and Cumberbatch, 1990). It is not likely, however, that the 80 per cent of respondents to a *Cosmopolitan* survey who said that 'page 3' photos were pornographic (Howitt and Cumberbatch, 1990) would have judged the Klimt drawing obscene. Neither is it to be expected that the nine per cent in the Advertising Standards Survey who disapproved of the Klimt drawing would necessarily wish to ban page 3 photos.

Who uses pornography?

The depiction of eroticism and sexuality in words and images is hardly a contemporary phenomenon; the Japanese, for example, have a long tradition of erotic prints and the celebration of sexuality in stone carvings is common in India (Siann, 1985). Indeed it was the discovery in the mid-nineteenth century, when Pompeii was excavated, of sexually explicit artefacts, such as erect stone phalluses at street corners and paintings of sexual intercourse on vases and walls that reintroduced the word 'pornography' to general usage in Europe.

In Europe, however, the production of explicitly sexual images seems to have occured mainly in the mid-nineteenth century. It has been suggested that the development of pornography is linked to the then prevailing middle-class morality which displaced both the licentiousness of the eighteenth century aristocracy and the repressive and inflexible morality of earlier Christian teaching. At that time there was a deep chasm between the respectable and the not respectable. Thus while discussion of sexuality and eroticism was repressed and any evidence of sensuality in women was roundly condemned in the middle class, prostitution, child prostitution and male prostitution flourished in the less salubrious areas of cities.

When Pompeii was excavated it became apparent that explicit depictions of sexuality had been on display in the public places of the cities of what the Victorians regarded as a great civilization. Faced with this contradiction, the guardians of morality lodged all the items recovered from Pompeii which they considered to be obscene in locked rooms from which women, children and the uneducated were excluded. Expensive catalogues with Latin and Greek quotations were produced and as Gillian Rogerson and Wilson put it:

> in this way pornography was born as a genre available to bourgeois men who could declare their interest was scholarly.
> Rogerson and Wilson (1991)

It is not surprising then, given these circumstances and the prevailing moral climate, that sexually explicit images and pornography in the west reflected almost exclusively the sexuality of male heterosexuals. This bias in terms of sexuality continued until the middle years of this century. Today, however, while much pornography, particularly that concerned with violence towards women, reflects the same bias, more and more films, magazines and videos are being produced with different sexual orientations. As a result, pornography is no longer bought or rented almost exclusively by heterosexual males but is also bought and rented by heterosexual women, lesbians and gay men.

Indeed it is now estimated that in the USA 40 per cent of the X-rated video rental market is female, and it is also estimated that two out of three women in France and Germany watch video porn regularly (McClintock, 1992). Furthermore, sex magazines for women are proliferating both in the UK and the USA (Smith, C., 1993).

Working with pornography

Heterosexual and lesbian pornographic films, performances, photographs and videos cannot, of course, be produced without the participation of women. Unger and Crawford, writing from a feminist perspective, argue that such women are inevitably humiliated and exploited. They also report they may be forced, abused and tortured. For example, at a hearing in Los Angeles, one witness testified that women suffered permanent physical injuries as a result of posing for photographs depicting sadomasochistic images (Unger and Crawford, 1992).

Other feminists, writing about women who take part in the production of pornographic material, take issue with the proposition that the 'sex-workers', as they call them, concerned in the production of pornography inevitably suffer adversely. Instead they claim:

> . . . most sex-workers . . . complain bitterly about the stigmatization of women who work in the sex industry by anti-pornography feminists . . . (describing) why they choose the work they do and the type of control they feel it gives them over their lives, as well as the feelings of victimization caused not so much by how they are treated at work as by their fears of arrest, low pay, poor working conditions, inadequate health care and social stigmatization.
> Segal and McIntosh (1992)

Because they wanted to continue working in the industry, but in such a way that they were in control and benefited financially, a group of women who had been starring in pornographic films set up a film company in 1983 to make pornography for women. This trend for women to make, as well as star in, porn film continues mostly in the USA with the production of pornography aimed at both the heterosexual and lesbian market increasing (Williams, 1990).

The effects of pornography

In the last few years, partly because of the increasing availability of pornography and partly because of a growing public awareness of changes in sexual morality, concern about the effects of pornography have been voiced with growing frequency in the United Kingdom (Itzin, 1993) and as a result the Government commissioned a report on pornography and its effects. Let us look briefly at the type of research on which this was based and the conclusions contained in the report, this will be followed by two opposing views held by feminists on pornography.

The impacts and influences of pornography

> Evidence of the adverse effects of pornography is far less clear cut than some earlier reviews imply. Inconsistencies emerge between very similar studies and many interpretations of these have reached almost opposite conclusions.
> Dennis Howitt and Guy Cumberbatch (1990) in a Report commissioned by the Home Office.

Evidence as to the effects of pornography, particularly its impact on women, has been sought in a number of ways. Demographic surveys have investigated the extent of changes in the level of sex crimes following the liberalization of laws about pornography and sex shops, particularly in the Scandinavian countries. Studies have been carried out on the use of pornography by convicted sex offenders. Interviews have been carried out with the victims of sex crimes concerning the extent to which they believed that the men carrying out the crimes used pornographic material. Finally, a number of empirical studies have been carried out in laboratories, and sometimes with student populations outside laboratories, in which subjects who viewed pornographic films and videos were compared with controls who viewed other material. Such studies have most typically compared subjects and controls on attitudes to rape and to women in general before and after viewing the videos and films. Earlier laboratory studies, however, made before the imposition of ethical controls, compared the extent to which subjects and controls were prepared to insult, or aggress against, women after viewing the material (Siann, 1985).

Any attempt to review such evidence is fraught with difficulty. To begin with the manner in which material is labelled pornographic or not varies over time and over investigation. Statistics, too, are notoriously unreliable. For example, the extent to which reported figures on rape and sexual assault actually reflect any trend is problematic because, for many reasons, notably the extremely unsympathetic treatment which has been meted out to them by both police and courts, women are often reluctant to report such crimes. The results of laboratory studies may be unreliable because they have been conducted mainly on undergraduates who are not necessarily representative of the population at large and who may give responses that reflect what they think the investigators want to find. Finally, as the quotation at the beginning of this section indicates, there is considerable divergence in the way different investigators interpret similar results.

Bearing these considerations in mind, Cumberbatch and Howitt, in the review commissioned by the Home Office, concluded that the available evidence did not permit the conclusion that the effect of pornography was such that its elimination would result in a diminution of sexual attacks on women and children. Fundamentally they argued that this is because it is unlikely that pornography is the only determinant of such attacks. They also point out that it is a distortion of history to believe that there is anything peculiarly modern about sexual abuse and sexually violent attacks which could be linked to the increasing availability of pornography. Furthermore, they note, that while some studies do show that sex offenders frequently use pornography, other studies show that sexual problems are more likely to occur in people who have been exposed to pornography relatively late in life. They also point out that there appear to be no adverse effects on the majority of people who use pornography.

Their conclusions are in accord with a number of other researchers in the area, for example, the American psychiatrist Richard Green (1987).

Other researchers, notably the American social psychologist, Neil Malamuth (1987), argue that while the direct effects of pornography are difficult to prove, indirectly, by contributing to a social climate which treats people, particularly women, as objects for the sexual gratification of others, pornography must be implicated in sex offences.

In recent years the subject of pornography has more than any other illuminated divisions within the ranks of feminism. On the one hand, it has been argued that pornography cannot be held responsible for women's subordinate status while, on the other, it has been argued that pornography is pre-eminent in men's domination of women.

Feminists against censorship

Pornography may mirror the sexism of society, but it did not create it. Pornography as we know it – mass produced for a mass audience – is a recent invention. Women's oppression, unfortunately, came long before porn.
Feminists against Censorship (1992) Rogerson and Wilson (1991, cover notes)

Feminists who reject the censorship of sexually explicit material fear that censorship would contribute to what they see as a growing diminution in civil liberties for the population as a whole. Furthermore, those feminists whose political sympathies are on the left and the liberal left question the growing collaboration between feminists campaigning for the abolition of pornography with fundamentalist right wing social movements. However, radical feminists have recently sought to distance themselves from the fundamentalist right (Itzen, 1993).

Anti-censorship feminists also claim, as the quote above implies, that women's historic domination by man can hardly be ascribed largely to pornography but that pornography simply mirrors gender inequalities. Banning pornography, they argue, would not eliminate remaining economic and social gender inequalities. They also contend that feminists who are concerned in the main with the banning of pornography divert both their own and public attention from the more fundamental aspects of gender inequality.

Finally a minority of lesbian feminists have argued for the right of lesbians to view representations not only of what they call *vanilla* sex, gentle erotica, but also depictions of lesbian sex with sadomasochistic overtones (Segal, 1989, Tong, 1989).

Feminists for censorship

Pornography is the theory. Rape is the practice
Anti-pornography slogan attributed to Robin Morgan
Segal (1989, p. 106)

> In the system of male domination explicated in pornography, there is
> no way out, no redemption.
> Andrea Dworkin (1992, p. 223)

Radical feminists argue that men are not only inherently violent but also
that it is through violence, in the form of rape or its threat, that they control
women. It was this viewpoint, according to Lynne Segal (1992), that led radical
feminists to focus on pornography in the 1980s.

According to radical feminists because men are able to terrorize women
by the threat of rape, they utilize this control not only in their behaviour but
also symbolically in the way they talk about women and in the way they
represent them in pornography. The best known exponent of their viewpoint,
Andrea Dworkin (1992) sees the direct aim of pornography as follows – the
women's sex is 'appropriated', her body is 'possessed', she is 'used and de-
spised'. The penis becomes, in pornography as in life, the 'symbol of terror'
and it is only when pornography no longer exists that women will be free.

While Dworkin sees pornography as a form of black propaganda for all
women, confirming them in their subservience, she also sees it as spurring on
those men who are insecure about their sexuality and thus pornography pur-
veys messages to both sexes which amplify women's subjugation. Dworkin
also argues that, because pornography is premised on inequality, it can be
thought of as a violation of civil rights and in the USA Dworkin and her
collaborators, both within the radical feminist movement and within the fundamentalist right, continue to campaign to have it declared illegal (Tong, 1992).

Gender and violence

> Down in the gutter, down in the ditch.
> You better back off. Back off bitch.
> Face of an angel with the love of witch.
> Guns 'N' Roses © 1991 Warner Chappell Music Ltd. Reproduced by permission of
> International Music Publications Limited.

> . . . after millennia of male war against them, women are fighting back
> on every front.
> Marilyn French (1992, p. 211)

Throughout this book there have been references to sexual antagonism,
mainly with respect to misogyny – the dislike or hatred of men for women –
and with respect to the rejection of men by radical feminists. However, while
misogyny has been found to some extent in most societies and at most times,
and while the great majority of men and women feel antagonism towards the
other sex as a group occasionally, I do not believe that sexual antagonism
characterizes the human race. I also believe that, as the earlier sections of this

chapter demonstrate, the great majority of contemporary media representations of the sexes are not such as to stir up antagonism between the sexes or,
in the case of men, to encourage aggressive sexuality designed to humiliate
and debase women.

Nevertheless, while contemporary media representation and values may
not, for the most part, reflect or amplify sexual antagonisms, as the discussion
below will indicate, men who assault women appear to endorse the kind of
traditional values which celebrate machismo and resonate with the dichotomous 'madonna/whore' vision of femininity.

Sexual offences and rape

A little bit of rape is good for man's soul.
Norman Mailer, 1972, in Starr (1980)

Rape and sexual assault do not characterize all known societies and anthropological records show a number of pre-industrial societies in which sexual
coercion was, or is, unknown. Peggy Sanday (1979), who examined the differences between 'rape-free' and 'rape-prone' societies, argues that male dominance and the forcible sexual control of women evolve as societies become
more dependent on the destructive capacities of men and less dependent on
female fertility. In this way she relates sexual violence to cultural variables, a
link which will be further developed below.

However, while rape and sexual assault might not be universal, in recent
times they have been absent in only a very tiny minority of societies. They
have certainly been characteristic of most societies when at war and
the rape of women, and sometimes children and men, by victorious forces
has been authoritatively documented from the time of the religous cru-
sades (Brownmiller, 1975) to the present – for example, the horrific sexual
crimes associated with ethnic cleansing in former Yugoslavia.

There also appears to be some evidence that rape and sexual assaults
are increasing across western societies (Johnson, 1988) in contemporary times
although such trends are difficult to validate because victims are frequently
reluctant to report the assaults they have suffered. Comparability over time is
also difficult to establish because the manner in which sexual assaults and rape
are defined has differed across societies and from time to time (Unger and
Crawford, 1992). For instance, it is only very recently that forced intercourse
in marriage has been defined as rape in the UK.

In recent years a large number of surveys have been conducted documenting the extent to which women have suffered from rape and sexual
assaults. One American study (Koss, 1989) carried out with over 3000 women
college students reported that 15 per cent of the respondents had experienced
rape and 12 per cent attempted rape. This and similar studies also revealed
that large numbers of women have not reported sexual assaults, or indeed

rapes, that have been perpetrated on them by acquaintances, particularly when the attacks have occurred when they were out with the men concerned. This last kind of rape has been termed 'date rape'.

As a result of these studies, there have been a number of initiatives aimed not only at supporting women who have been raped but also at identifying risk factors. The studies attempting to identify who is at risk have not been particularly successful, but they have served to dispel the myth that women who are raped are different in terms of psychological attributes and sexual conduct from other women On the contrary, it would appear that all women in western society are potentially equally at risk (Unger and Crawford, 1992).[1]

Attempts to characterize males who sexually assault and rape women have been somewhat more successful and a number of attributes have been identified. The single best predictor appears to be that rapists have peers who condone and encourage sexual conquests (Ageton, 1983). Rapists are also more likely to come from families with a history of violence and to have had an early and varied sexual history (Unger and Crawford, 1992).

Not surprisingly, in view of the wide prevalence of rape, a number of perspectives have been offered accounting for it and the section below will explore some of the approaches, bearing in mind that they are not necessarily mutually exclusive.

Accounting for rape and sexual assaults

Evolutionary and biological approaches
Chapter 2 discussed a particular essentialist perspective, the socio-biological which explains gender differences in terms of innate differences in the nature of men and women that derive from evolutionary development. Rape, from this perspective, is seen as arising from a biologically based sex-drive, stronger in men than in women, which serves to guarantee the reproduction of the species. It is argued that males have a stronger sex-drive because natural selection favours males who copulate with numerous females, while females achieve reproductive success through limiting their copulation to males who are committed to help care for females and their offspring.

Theorists, operating from this perspective, also point out that by virtue of their greater physical strength males are well equipped to further preservation of their species in this way (McCammon *et al.* 1993).

While rape is certainly made possible by the male's greater physical strength this approach does not explain satisfactorily why some men rape and others do not. In particular, this perspective would lead to the proposition that rapists differ from non-rapists because they are more sexually frustrated. There is no evidence, however, to support this because studies show that most rapists have sexual partners and an active sex life at the time of their offence (Scully, 1990).

This socio-biological approach also has difficulty in accounting for the fact that rape is not universal and that its incidence appears to be linked to the status and power of the sexes within particular societies. For instance, rape has not been reported in societies in which the status differentiation between the sexes is non-existent or very slight (Lepowsky, 1990).

Psychopathological Approaches

Rape is a pseudosexual act, complex and multidetermined, but addressing issues of hostility (anger) and control (power) more than passion (sexuality).
Norman Groth (1980, p. 2)

It has been argued that people who commit sexual crimes do so because they are suffering from psychopathological conditions or mental illness. However, studies of convicted rapists do not show any evidence that they are more prone to mental illness than the rest of the population (Unger and Crawford, 1992).

A variant of the psychopathological approach was proposed by Norman Groth (1980), who argues that rape and sexual assault springs from psychodynamic roots and, rather than being fuelled by sexual motivation, is fuelled by a desire to exert domination. He developed a typology of rapes, each of which is based on some form of emotional problem concerned with the need to subordinate the victim. This typology included the anger rape – the rapist is extremely angry with the victim and rape is the ultimate expression of his anger; the power rape – the rapist is motivated by a desire to possess or demonstrate power over the victim, typically because he feels an underlying insecurity about his masculinity; and the sadistic rape – in which the rapist derives pleasure from humiliating the victim.

However, not all sexual assaults are inevitably driven primarily by aggression and the need to humiliate and dominate. In the case of date rape, in particular, it has been suggested that sexual rather than aggressive motives tend to be salient (Unger and Crawford, 1992). Furthermore Diane Scully (1990) who conducted intensive interviews with 114 convicted rapists disputes Groth's contention that, in the case of convicted rapists, rape is invariably the expression of aggression. Instead she reports that many of her sample reported that sexual motivation was a major component of their offence. There is, however, no doubt that many men who sexually assault and rape are extremely resentful and angry individuals. Moreover the manner in which such men sexually assault women, and not infrequently men, humiliates and degrades their victims to an unbearable extent.

Cultural/feminist approaches

Theorists writing about rape from a cultural perspective point to the absence of rape in societies where there is gender equality and argue that, where females are treated with respect and where they have high prestige, rape and sexual assault do not occur. They also note that in such societies attitudes towards sex are relaxed and, while sexual conduct is governed by custom, it is characterized by sensuality and enjoyment rather than by repression (Lepowsky, 1990). Consequently there is minimal association of sex with violence.

Feminists, like cultural theorists, also tend to link sexual assaults and rape to cultural values, both with respect to women and with respect to sexuality, arguing that, as in all aspects of gender relations, rape and sexual assaults reflect power and prestige imbalances between the sexes. They also argue that the phenomenon of gang rape, like rape in war, tends to foster and reinforce a particular kind of male bonding which draws its sustenance from traditional or sex-typed beliefs about male behaviour. There is evidence to support this contention in the fact that rapists are likely to have close friends who have also been involved in sexual assaults.

The extent to which men who carry out sexual assaults and rape endorse traditional views of masculine superiority has been shown by a number of studies. For example, the intensive interviews Diane Scully (1990) conducted with rapists showed that these men not only harboured a general distrust of women, but they also had extremely repressive views about women's sexuality. Their views supported the double standard whereby male sexuality is perceived as natural and to be celebrated, but overt female sexuality is seen as unnatural and characteristic of immoral and loose women. They also showed a strong identification with the traditional male role. Scully argues that rapists and sexual offenders differ from other men, not in terms of psychopathology or emotional problems, or family background, but in the extent to which they endorse values which enhance the status of men and diminish the status of women.

The men that Scully interviewed frequently rationalized and excused their behaviour by reference to what have been called 'rape myths'. For example, that all women secretly yearn to be raped, that women who invite men to their home are 'asking for it', and that women who wear clothes that are revealing are fair game. Thus they attempted to justify their assaults by reference to the double standard – their victims were the kind of immoral and loose women who deserved what they got.

Social learning appoaches
Related to, and in many ways reinforcing, the cultural perspective is an approach which sees sexual assault and rape as at the extreme pole of the sex-typing of masculine behaviour which was, and to a lesser extent still is, reflected in the media.

Arguing in this vein, Ellis (1989) claims that men learn aggressive behaviour to women, including rape, through four processes. First, the sex-violence linkage whereby in slasher and horror films and even in some music videos violence and sexuality become inextricably associated. Second, through modelling, in that rapists frequently have friends and associates who have committed sexual offences. Third, through 'desensitization', a term which is used to describe the lessening of sensitivity to the pain of others, which is said to occur through repeated exposure to scenes of aggression and violence in the media. Finally, Ellis points to the extent to which society still teaches young men stereotypes and sexist beliefs such as the 'rape-myths' referred to above.

Ellis' work indicates that sexual assault and rape are frequently linked to violence. However, not all violence perpetrated by men against women is sexual although, as the discussion below will indicate, violent men – like rapists – are men who tend to view women in a highly negative and disparaging manner.

Violence

Women should be struck regularly, like gongs
Noel Coward 1930, in Starr (1991), p. 129.

It is a well-known fact that you can strike your wife's bottom if you wish, but you must not strike her face . . . Reasonable chastisement should be the duty of every husband if his wife disobeys.
George Mackay, Sheriff of Kinghorn, Scotland, 1975, p. 134.

Battered women

Domestic violence, or violence against spouses or partners, clearly varies enormously from a slap or a push to the use of knife or gun. Although, as we shall see, women as well as men perpetrate domestic violence, and although domestic violence is also found in homosexual and lesbian relationships, in the very great majority of cases of domestic violence it is the men who abuse women. In addition, the more extreme cases of abuse tend to be carried out by men on women and the women are not infrequently pregnant which creates risks for the unborn child as well as the mother (Unger and Crawford, 1992).

As the quotes above indicate, male chastisement of their wives or partners has, even in the very recent past, had a degree of social acceptance (Dobash and Dobash, 1980) and until recently police were reluctant to become embroiled in such incidents because of the widely held endorsement of the husband's dominant position in the household. Partly as a result of such attitudes, there has been widespread underreporting of male domestic violence against women.

There are, however, a number of other reasons why women have, until recently, been reluctant to report such abuse. To begin with, women have frequently reacted to such abuse with guilt and shame rather than with rage and anger. Guilt, that they have not been able to sustain that most important component of women's traditional role, a happy family life, and shame at making public such inadequacies. At a more practical level, until modern times most women, particularly those with children, have been economically dependent on their husbands. In addition, until very lately many abused wives had no refuge that was safe from pursuing husbands or partners.

Men who abuse women do so in a society where, until recently, there was a tacit acceptance of the husband's right to chastise his wife. Nevertheless only a minority of men do batter their partners and consequently there must be other factors contributing to this behaviour. A great many studies have been conducted seeking to identify these factors and there is some agreement on the characteristics of such men.

They tend to have a history of alcohol of alcohol abuse and to have both witnessed and experienced physical violence in their homes as children. In addition they appear, on the whole, to have poor social skills, to lack assertiveness, to be socially isolated and to have low self-esteem. They are also likely to endorse traditional sex roles. The picture that is built up by the research is of depressed men with poor coping skills who feel inadequate at many levels and who have grown up in an abusive domestic climate. Consequently, particularly when their inhibitions are lowered by drink, they are liable to lash out at the most immediate target, particularly if they feel that she is threatening their already low self-esteem, for example, by being unfaithful.

While more abused women now leave their husbands or partners, others remain and some who leave return. It has been suggested that such women do not leave abusive relationships because of a feminine tendency towards masochism. In other words it was suggested that women who stayed in abusive relationships do so largely because they derived some sort of emotional satisfaction from suffering (Goldstein, 1983). There is, however, little evidence to sustain such a view. Women who remain in abusing relationships have been shown to differ from other women not in terms of their personal attributes, but in terms of their perception of the lack of alternative strategies.

Thus from extensive interviews with battered wives, Lenore Walker (1984) developed the concept of 'the battered woman's syndrome' to explain why women remain with abusive men and why they sometimes see murdering their partners as the only solution. Subject to continual control from their partners, with no avenue of escape because of their economic dependency they feel totally impotent and helpless. Furthermore, they often fear that their reports of their partners brutality may not be believed, and they also fear that if they do leave, their partners will find them and kill or injure them and their children. A fear that is, in fact, frequently justified.

Physical abuse is often accompanied by psychological abuse and consequently, as their husbands continue to ridicule and degrade them, the women feel even more helpless. In this kind of situation it is not surprising that some women become unable to take the initiative and leave.

However it is not only heterosexual women who are subject to violence from their partners. American studies suggest that the level of violence in lesbian relationships is not very different from the level in heterosexual relationships. One study by Brand and Kidd (1986) of heterosexual and lesbian relationships found 27 per cent of the heterosexual relationships and 25 per cent of the lesbian relaionships to be violent. Consequently violence in domestic situations cannot be seen only as a gender issue.

Battered men

When aggression is related to gender, however, it is not always the woman who is the victim. A very small minority of cases of domestic violence involve male victims. In some of these instances, when the man is very severely injured or even killed, this is the end product of what has been described above as the 'battered wife syndrome' when the woman, at the end of her tether, resorts to extreme violence herself.

At a less serious level, what has been termed 'courtship' violence is reported in American studies to be carried out almost equally by women and men. The term is used to cover a continuum of behaviour ranging from verbal abuse, through screaming, yelling and name-calling to severe physical violence which occasionally includes the use of weapons. Such discord is reported as usually relating to jealousy, disagreements about drinking and sexual refusal.

A national survey in the USA of almost 5000 college men and women, (2600 women and 2100 men) indicated that approximately 37 per cent of men and 35 per cent of women had inflicted some sort of violence in heterosexual relationship. It is thought that these figures mirror the rates in non-student populations in the USA (White and Koss, 1991). However, while there may be similar incidences of violent and aggressive behaviour for the sexes, Rhoda Unger and Mary Crawford (1992) suggest that the motives differ. Women are more likely to report being aggressive in self-defence while men report that they are aggressive to instil fear. Furthermore, women are more likely to report being emotionally upset by the violence and are also more likely to be seriously injured. Courtship aggression in both sexes is associated with a previous history of aggression and for women it is associated with having been exposed to aggression at home.

Violence in courtship seldom results in severe injury although both victims and offenders frequently feel emotionally upset for some time. Verbal aggression is, not surprisingly, much more common. Although courtship violence has received a great deal of attention in the USA it is not at all clear whether it is a serious social problem either there or anywhere else. It is, however, perfectly feasible to suppose that people, who are violent during courtship, are likely to have been violent as children and are likely to be violent later in life. It is equally feasible, and indeed supported by some preliminary studies, (Roscoe and Benaske, 1985) that women who are abused in marriage are also likely to have been abused in relationships before marriage as well. There is a great deal of evidence indicating stability over time in aggressive behaviour (Siann, 1985).

Summary

This chapter has indicated that contemporary representations of women and men in the media differ considerably from historic images and stereotypes, particularly in the case of women. Women are now provided with a very varied range of role models and a woman's right to sexual self-expression is now generally accepted. While there have been some changes in the representation of men, particularly with respect to men in the role of fathers, there tends to be fewer portrayals of men in what were traditional female spheres than of women in what were traditionally male spheres.

While the media, in general, do not celebrate machismo, some television programmes and feature films still do. Furthermore, a significant proportion of pornography endorses men's right to treat women, and sometimes children and other men, as objects for their own sexual gratification.

Men who rape and assault women are likely to endorse traditional views of the sexes. In particular they are likely to regard overt sexuality in women as unacceptable. Male violence to women, however, cannot be ascribed simply to media and cultural stereotypes. Indeed while violence between the sexes is predominantly carried out by men on women, such violence cannot be regarded as explicable only in terms of gender antagonism.·

Notes

1. Articles in the media now reflect this general conclusion particularly with respect to 'date' and 'acquaintanceship' rape (*More*, 10–23 June, 1992).

Afterword

Like most people, as I was growing up, when I thought about gender I tended to focus on the differences between men and women. I feel this book shows that contemporary society conditions us to think in this way. However, the more I researched and read about gender issues the more I moved to a position which focused on convergence rather than divergence. This is because I believe that human identity is socially constructed and consequently the more similar conditions, power and resources become for men and women in any society, the more appropriate it will be to think about individuals as people rather than as members of two essentially different groups.

References

ABU-LOGHOD, L., 1983, in Tavris and Wade (1984).

ADAMS, J., 1984, Women at West Point: a three-year perspective, *Sex Roles*, **11**, 525–41.

ADAMS, K.A., 1980, Who has the final word? Sex, race and dominance behavior, *Journal of Personality and Social Psychology*, **38**, 1–8.

ADLER, A., 1954, *Understanding Human Nature*, Greenwich, CT: Fawcett Premier, 110.

AGETON, S.S., 1983, *Sexual Assault among Adolescents*, Lexington, MA: D.C. Heath.

ALLEN, R., 1992, Analysing representations in BONNER, F. GOODMAN, L., ALLEN, R., JAMES, L. and KING, C., 1992, *Imagining Women: Cultural Representations and Gender*, Cambridge: Polity.

ANDREAS-SALOME, L., 1987, *The Freud Journal*, London: Quartet.

ANGELOU, M., 1992, Women's work, in *And Still I Rise*, London: Virago.

ANKNEY, C.D., 1992, Sex differences in relative brain size: the mismeasure of women, too?, *Intelligence*, **16**, 229–36.

ARCHER, J., 1984, Gender roles as developmental pathways, *Journal of Social Psychology*, **23**, 245–56.

ARCHER, J. and LLOYD, B., 1985, *Sex and Gender*, Cambridge: Cambridge University Press.

ATKINSON, J., 1982, Review essay: Anthropology, *Signs*, **8**, 2, 236–58.

BAKER, C. and DAVIES, B., 1989, A lesson on sex roles, *Gender and Education*, **1**, 1, 59–76.

BANDURA, A. and HUSTON, A.C., 1961, Identification as a process of incidental learning, *Journal of Abnormal and Social Psychology*, **63**, 311–18.

BANDURA, A. and WALTERS, R.H., 1963, *Social Learning and Personality Development*, New York: Holt, Rhinehart and Winston.

BANDURA, A., ROSS, D. and ROSS, S.A., 1963, A comparative test of the status envy, social power, and secondary reinforcement theories of identificatory learning, *Journal of Abnormal and Social Psychology*, **67**, 527–34.

BANKS, M., BATES, I., BREAKWELL, G., BYNNER, J., EMLER, N. JAMIESON, L. and ROBERTS, K., 1992, *Careers and Identities*, Milton Keynes: Open University.

BEE, H., 1992, *The Developing Child*, 6th Edn, Glasgow: Harper-Collins.

BELOFF, H., HEPBURN, A., MACDONALD, M. and SIANN, G., 1993, Convergences and divergences: gender differences in the perception of feminism and feminists, paper presented at the British Psychological Society, Annual Conference, Blackpool, April 5–7.

BEM, S.L., 1987, Gender schema theory and its implications for child development: raising gender-aschematic children in a gender-schematic society, in Walsh (1987).

BENJAMIN, J., 1988, *The Bonds of Love*, London: Virago.

BERGER, J., 1990, *Ways of Seeing*, Harmondsworth: Penguin. BETTELHEIM, B., 1984, quoted in Tavris and Wade (1984).

BEUTELL, N.J. and BRENNER, O.C., 1986, Sex differences in work values, *Journal of Vocational Behavior*, **28**, 29–41.

BILLIG, M. CONDER, S., EDWORDS, D., GONE, M., MIDDLETORY, D. and RADLEY, A., 1988, *Idealogical Dilemmas: A Social Psychology of Everyday Thinking*, London: Sage.

BINET, A. and SIMON, T., 1912, *A method of Measuring the Development of the Intelligence of Young Children*, Lincoln: III, Courier.

BIRKE, L., 1986, *Women, Feminism and Biology: The Feminist Challenge*, Brighton: Wheatsheaf.

BLACKWELDER, R.E. and SHEPHERD, B.A., 1981, *The Diversity of Animal Reproduction*, Baca Ratan, Florida: CRC Press.

BLANCHARD, R. *et al.*, Gender dysphoria, gender reorientation, and the management of transsexualism, *Journal of Counseling and Clinical Psychology*, **53**, 295–304.

BLEIER, R., 1984, *Science and Gender: A critique of biology and its theories on women*, New York: Pergamon.

BLEIER, R., 1988, Science and the construction of meanings in the neurosciences, in ROSSER, E.V. (Ed.) *Feminism within the science and health care professions*, New York: Pergamon Press.

BLOCK, J.H., 1976, Debatable conclusions about sex differences, *Contemporary Psychology*, **21**, 517–22.

BLUMSTEIN, P.W. and SCHWARTZ, P. 1983, *American Couples: Money, Work, Sex*, New York: Morrow.

BLY, R., 1993, *Iron John*, Longmead, Dorset: Element.

BONAPARTE, M., 1953, *Female Sexuality*, New York: International Universities Press, 87.

BORGES, J.L. *et al.* (Eds), 1966, *The Book of Fantasy*, London: Transworld.

BORJA-ALVAREZ, T., ZARBATANY, L. and PEPPER, S., 1991, Contributions of male and female guests and hosts to peer-group entry, *Child Development*, 62, 1079–90.

BOWIE, C. and FORD, N., 1989, Sexual behaviour of young people and the risk of HIV infection, *Journal of Epidemiology and Community Health*, **43**, 1, 61–5.

BRAND, P.A. and KIDD, A.H., 1986, Frequency of physical aggression in heterosexual and female homosexual dyads, *Psychological Reports*, **59**, 1307–13.

BREMER, J., 1959, *Asexualisation*, New York: MacMillan.

BROWNMILLER, S., 1975, *Against Our Will: Men, Women and Rape*, Harmondsworth: Penguin.

BULLOCK, A. and STALLEYBRASS, O., 1982, *The Fontana Dictionary of Modern Thought*, Glasgow: Fontana.

BURGESS, A.W. (Ed.), 1989, *Rape and Sexual Assault*, Vol II, New York: Garland.

BUTLER, J., 1990, *Gender Trouble: Feminism and the Subversion of Identity*, London: Routledge.

CAPLAN, P., 1987, *The Cultural Construction of Sexuality*, London: Tavistock.

CAPLAN, P.J., MACPHERSON, G.M. and TOBIN, P., 1985, Do sex-related differences in spatial abilities exist?, *American Psychologist*, **40**.

CHAPMAN, R. and RUTHERFORD, J. (Eds), 1988, *Unwrapping Masculinity*, London: Lawrence and Wishart.

CHESTERTON, G.K., 1910, in *What's Wrong With the World*, part 4, ch. 14, quoted in AUGARDE, T. (1992) (Ed.) Oxford Dictionary of Modern Quotations.

CHODOROW, N., 1979, Feminism and difference: gender relation and difference in psychoanalytic perspective, *Socialist Review*, **46**, 42–6.

COHEN, D., 1990, *On Being a Man*, London: Routledge.

COHEN, G. and FRASER, E.J.P., 1992, Female participation in mathematical degrees at English and Scottish universities, *Journal of the Royal Statistical Society*, **155**, 2, 241–58.

COLE, E., 1938, *Education for Marriage*, quoted by JACKSON, M., Facts of Life, or the eroticization of women's oppression? sexology and the social construction of sexuality, in Caplan (1987).

COLES, J., 1993, An Unsuitable Job for a Woman, Guardian 2, 5.5.93, 8–9.

COLES, R., 1985, quoted in Unger and Crawford (1992).

CONNER, J.M. and SERBIN, L.A., 1985, Visual-spatial skill: is it important for mathematics?, in CHIPMAN, S.F., BRUSH, L. and WILSON, D.M. (Eds) *Women and Mathematics: Balancing the Equation*, Hillsdale, NJ: Erlbaum.

CONRAN, S., 1991, *Down with Superwoman*, Harmondsworth: Penguin.

COWARD, R., 1993, *Our Treacherous Hearts*, first published 1992, London: Faber & Faber.

COWDEN, J., 1969, Adventures with South Africa's black eagles, *National Geographic*, **136**, 533–43.

CRAWFORD, M., HERRMANN, D.J., HOLDSWORTH, M., RANDALL, E. and ROBBINS, D., 1989, Gender and beliefs about memory, *British Journal of Psychology*, **80**, 391–401.

CROMPTON, R., 1992, *Just William*, London: Pan, p. 132.

CULLINGFORD, C., 1984, *Children and Television*, Aldershot, Hampshire: Gower.

CUMBERBATCH, G., 1990, *Television Advertising and Sex Role Stereotyping*, Broadcasting Research Council.

CUMBERBATCH, G. and HOWITT, D., 1989, *A Measure of Uncertainty: Effects of Mass Media*, London: Libbey.

CURRIE, E., 1988, in YOUNG, S., 1988, *Feminism and the Politics of Power*, in

GAMMON, L. and MARSHMENT, M. (Eds) *The Female Gaze: Women as Viewers of Popular Culture*, London: The Women's Press.

D'ANDRADE, R.G., 1966, Sex differences and cultural institutions, in Maccoby (1966).

DALY, M., 1984, *Pure Lust*, London: Women's Press.

DAILY MAIL, 1993, Sorry, chaps, you're not as sexy as a US male: Britons banned from muscling in on Chippendales, 6.5.93, 3.

DAMON, W., 1977, *The Social World of the Child*, San-Francisco: Jossey-Bass, 242.

DARLING, C.A. and DAVIDSON, J.K., 1986, Coitally active university students: sexual behaviors, concerns and challenges, *Adolescence*, **21**, 402–19.

DE BEAUVOIR, S., 1984, *The Second Sex*, Harmondsworth: Penguin.

DEUTSCH, H., 1973, *Confrontations with Myself*, New York: Norton.

DICKISON, E., 1900, *Selected Poems*, Dover: New York.

DOBASH, R.E. and DOBASH, R., 1980, *Violence Against Wives*, London: Open Books.

DOODY, M.A., 1992, Women beware men, *London Review of Books*, 23 July, 3–8.

DORNER, G., ROHDE, W., STAHL, F., KRELL, L. and MASIUS, W.G., 1975, A neuro-endocrine predisposition for homosexuality in men, *Archives of Sexual Behavior*, **4**, 1–9.

DOWLING, D., 1981, *The Cinderella Complex: Women's Hidden Fear of Independence*, New York: Summit.

DUNBAR, R., 1985, Stress is a good contraceptive, *New Scientist*, **17**, January, 16–18.

DURKIN, K., 1986, Sex-roles and the mass media, in Hargreaves and Colley (1986).

DURNDELL, A., 1992, Gender, technology and schooling: Britain and Eastern Europe, *School Science Review*, **73**, 265, 131–6.

DURNDELL, A., SIANN, G. and GLISSOV, P., 1990, Gender differences and computing in course choice at entry to higher education, *British Educational Research Journal*, **16**, 2, 149–62.

DURRELL, L., 1963, *Justine*, London: Faber & Faber.

DWORKIN, A., 1980, Taking Action, in LEDERER, L. (Ed.) *Take Back the Night*, New York: Morrow.

DWORKIN, A., 1992, *Pornography: Men Possessing Women*, London: Women's Press.

EAGLY, A.H., 1987, *Sex differences in social behavior; a social role interpretation*, Hillsdale, NJ: Erlbaum.

EAGLY, A.H. and WOOD, W., 1991, Explaining sex differences in social behavior, a meta-analytical perspective, *Personality and Social Psychology Bulletin*, **17**, 3.

EICHENBAUM, L. and ORBACH, S., 1982, *Outside In, Inside Out*, Harmondsworth: Penguin.

EISENBERG, N. and LENNON, R, 1983, Sex differences in empathy and related capacities, *Psychological Bulletin*, **93**, 100–31.

ELLIS, H., 1913, *Studies in the Psychology of Sex*, Vols I-VI, Philadelphia: Davis.

ELLIS, L., 1989, *Theories of Rape: Inquiries into the causes of sexual aggression*, New York: Hemisphere.

EPELBOIN, S. and EPELBOIN, A., 1979, Female circumcision, *People*, **6**, 1.

Equal Opportunities Commission, 1992, *Women and Men in Britain 1992*.

EHRHARDT, A.A. and BAKER, S., 1974, Fetal androgens, human central nervous system differentiation and behavior sex differences in FRIEDMAN, R.C., RICHART, R.M. and VAN DER WIELE, R.C. (1974).

EHRHARDT, A.A. and MEYER-BAHLBERG, H.F.L., 1981, Effects of prenatal sex hormones on gender-related behavior, *Science*, **211**, 1312–18.

ERIKSON, E., 1963, *Childhood and Society*, New York: Norton.

ERIKSON, E., 1968, *Identity, Youth and Crisis*, New York: Norton, 278.

EVANS, G. and POOLE, M., 1991, *Young Adults: Self Perceptions and Life Contents*, London: Falmer.

EVANS, L., 1993, Rebel Yell, *Elle*, July, 36–8.

FAGOT, B., 1978, The influence of sex of child on parental reactions to toddler children, *Child Development*, **49**, 554–8.

FALUDI, S., 1992, *Backlash: The Undeclared War against Women*, London: Vintage.

FARRELL, C., 1978, *My Mother said: The way young people learned about Sex and Birth Control*, London: Routledge and Kegan Paul.

FAUSTO-STERLING, A., 1992, *Myths of Gender: Biological Theories about Men and Women*, 2nd Edn, New York: Basic Book and Glasgow: Harper-Collins.

FEINGOLD, A., 1988, Cognitive gender differences are disappearing, *American Psychologist*, **43**, 95–103.

FEINMAN, S., 1981, Why is cross-sex-role behavior more approved for girls than boys?, *Sex Roles*, **17**, 621–36.

FINE, G.A., 1987, One of the boys: women in male-dominated settings, in Kimmel (1987b).

FISHER, H., 1992, *Anatomy of Love; The Natural History of Monogamy, Adultery and Divorce*, London: Simon & Schuster.

FOR WOMEN 1993, **1**, 11, cover.

FOSTER, M., 1993, *Daphne du Maurier*, London: Chatto & Windus.

FOUCAULT, M., 1979, *The History of Sexuality, Vol. 1: An Introduction*, London: Allen Lane.

FREEMAN, D., 1983, *Margaret Mead and Samoa, The Making and Unmaking of an Anthropological Myth*, Cambridge, Mass: Harvard University Press.

FRENCH, M., 1992, *The War Against Women*, London: Hamish Hamilton.

FREUD, S., 1923, The infantile genital organisation, in Strachey (1977a) and Strachey (1977b).

FREUD, S., 1925, *Some Psychical Consequences of the Anatomical Distinction between the Sexes* in Strachey (1977a).

FREUD, S., 1931, *Female Sexuality* in Strachey (1976).

FREUD, S., 1933, *Femininity* in Strachey (1965).

FREUD, S., 1940, *An Outline of Psychoanalysis*, New York: Norton.

FREUD, S., 1955, The Psychogenesis of a case of homosexuality in a woman, in Strachey (1977a).

FREUD, S., Reprinted 1983, *Totem and Taboo*, London: Routledge.

FRIDAY, N., 1991, *Women on Top*, London: Hutchinson.

FRIEDMAN, R.C. *et al.* (Eds), 1974, *Sex Differences in Behavior*, New York: Wiley.

FRODI, A., MACAULEY, J. and THORNER, P.R., 1977, Are women always less aggressive than men? A review of the experimental literature, *Psychological Bulletin*, **84**, 4, 634–60.

GALLIVAN, J., 1991, Gender bias in students' ratings of essays, *Journal of Social Behavior and Personality*, **6**, 1, 119–24.

GARBER, M., 1993, *Vested Interest: Cross-Dressing and Cultural Anxiety*, Harmondsworth: Penguin.

GESCHWIND, N., 1982, Left-handedness: Association with immune disease, migraine, and developmental learning disorder, *Proceedings of National Academy of Sciences*, **79**, 5097–100.

GILBERT, S. and GUBAR, S., 1979, *The madwoman in the attic: The woman writer and the nineteenth century*, New Haven: Yale.

GILLIGAN, C., 1982, *In a Different Voice*, Cambridge, MA: Harvard University Press.

GOLDBERG, P.A., 1968, Are women prejudiced against women?, *Transaction*, **5**, 28–30.

GOLDEN, C., 1987, Diversity and variability in women's sexual identities, in Boston Lesbian Psychologies Collective (Eds) *Lesbian Psychologies*, Urbana, IL, University of Illinois Press, 30.

GOLDFOOT, D.A. and NEFF, D.A., 1987, Assessment of behavioral sex differences in social contexts, in REINISCH, J.M. ROSENBLUM, L.A. and SAUNDERS, S.A. (Eds) *Masculinity/femininity: Basic Perspectives*, New York: Oxford University Press.

GOLDSTEIN, D., 1983, Spouse abuse, in GOLDSTEIN, A. (Ed.) *Prevention and Control of Aggression*, New York: Pergamon.

GOULD, S.J., 1981, *The Mismeasure of Man*, New York.

GRADDOL, D. and SWANN, J., 1989, *Gender Voices*, Oxford: Blackwell.

GRAVES, R., 1927, in *Pygmalion to Galatea*, in *Poems*.

GREEN, R., 1987, Exposure to explicit sexual materials and sexual assault: a review of behavioral and social science research, in Walsh (1987).

GREER, G., 1991, *The Female Eunuch*, Glasgow: Paladin.

GRIFFIN, C., 1989, 'I'm not a Woman's Libber but . . . :' Feminism, Consciousness and Identity, in SKEVINGTON, S. and BAKER, D. (Eds) *The Social Identity of Women*, London: Sage.

GRIMM, D.E., 1987, Towards a theory of gender: transsexualism, gender, sexuality and relationships, *American Behavioral Scientist*, **31**, 66–85.

GROTH, N., 1980, *Men Who Rape: The Psychology of the Offender*, New York: Plenum.

GUNS 'N' ROSES, 1991, *Back Off Bitch*, London: David Geffin Company, MCA.

GUNTER, B., 1986, *Television and Sex Role Stereotyping*, London: Libbey.

HAMER, D.H., HU, S., MAGNUSON, V.L., HU, N. and PATTATUCCI, A.M.L., 1993, A linkage between DNA markers on the X chromosome and male sexual orientation, *Science*, **261**, 16–7–93, 321–7.

HRDY, S.B., 1989, Daughter or sons, *Natural History*, **4**, 88, 64–82.

HARE-MUSTIN, R. T. and MARACEK, J., 1990, *Making a Difference: Psychology and the Construction of Gender*, New Haven: Yale University Press.

HARGREAVES, D.J. and COLLEY, A.M. (Eds), 1986, *The Psychology of Sex Roles*, London: Harper & Row.

HARKNESS, S. and SUPER, C.M., 1985, The cultural context of gender segregation in children's groups, *Child Development*, **56**, 219–24.

HARTNETT, O. and BRADLEY, J., 1986, Sex roles and work, in Hargreaves and Colley (1986).

HAWKE, C.C., 1950, Castration and sex crimes, *American Journal of Mental Deficiency*, **55**, 220–26.

HEALEY, E.C., 1993, personal communication.

HEARN, J. and MORGAN, D. (Eds), 1990, *Men, Masculinities and Social Theory*, London: Unwin-Hyman.

HEBDIDGE, D., 1979, *Subcultures: The Meaning of Style*, London: Methuen.

HERDT, G.H. and DAVIDSON, J., 1988, The Sambra Turnim-man: Sociocultural and clinical aspects of gender formation in male pseudo-hermaphrodites with 5 alpha-reductose deficiency in Papua New Guinea, *Archives of Sexual Behavior*, **17**, 33–56.

HITE, S., 1976, *The Hite Report*, MacMillan: New York.

HOLLIDAY, L., 1978, *The Violent Sex: Male Psychobiology and the Evolution of Consciousness*, Guernsville, California: Bluestocking Books.

HOLLWAY, W., 1989, *Subjectivity and Method in Psychology: Gender, Meaning and Science*, London: Sage.

HORNER, M.S., 1972, Toward an understanding of achievement-related conflicts in women, *Journal of Social Issues*, **28**, 157–75.

HORNEY, K., 1967, *Feminine Psychology*, New York: Norton.

HOROWITZ, G. and KAUFMAN, M., 1987, Male sexuality: toward a theory of liberation, in KAUFMAN, M. (Ed.) *Beyond Patriarchy, Essays by Men on Pleasure, Power and Change*, Toronto: Oxford University Press.

HOUSMANN, A.E., 1896, *The Shropshire Lad*, 54 in AUGARDE, T. (1992) (Ed.) Oxford Dictionary of Modern Quotations.

HOW TO CHAT UP BOYS 1993, in *Shout*, 28 June – 8 July.

HOWITT, D., 1982, *The Mass Media and Social Problems*, Oxford: Pergamon.

HOWITT, D. and CUMBERBATCH, G., 1990, *Pornography: Impacts and Influences*, Home Office Research Unit.

HUSTON, A.C., 1985, The development of sex typing: themes from recent research, *Developmental Review*, **5**, 1–17.

HYDE, J.S., 1981, How large are cognitive differences? A meta-analysis using w^2 and d, *American Psychologist*, **36**, 8, 892–901.

HYDE, J.S., 1990, Meta-analysis and the psychology of gender differences, *Signs*, **16**, 11, 55–73.

HYDE, J.S. and LINN, M.C., 1988, Gender differences in verbal ability: a meta-analysis, *Psychological Bulletin*, **104**, 53–69.

IMPERATO-McGINLEY, J. and PETERSEN, R.E., 1976, Male pseudo-hermaphrodism: the complexities of male phenotypic development, *American Journal of Medicine*, **61**, 251–72.

IMPERATO-McGINLEY, J., PETERSEN, R.E., GAUTIER, T. and STURLA, E., 1979, Androgens and the evolution of male-gender identity among male pseudo-hermaphrodites with 5 alpha-reductose deficiency, *New England Journal of Medicine*, **300**, 1233–7.

INSTITUTE of MANAGEMENT, 1992, *The Key to the Men's Club*, Newbury Close, Bristol: IOM Books.

IRIGARY, L., 1985, *The Sex Which Is Not One*, trans. Catherine Porter, Ithaca, NY: Cornell University Press, 32.

ITZIN, C. (Ed.), 1993, *Pornography: Women, Violence and Civil Liberties*, Oxford: OUP.

JACKLIN, C.N., 1981, Methodological issues in the study of sex-related differences, *Developmental Review*, **1**, 266–73.

JAGGAR, A., 1983, *Feminist Politics and Human Nature*, Totowa, NJ: Rowman and Allanheld.

JAMIESON, F., 1982, *The political unconscious: Narrative as a socially symbolic act*, Ithaca, NY: Cornell University Press.

JARMAN, D., 1993, *At your Own Risk: A Saint's Testament*, London: Vintage.

JEFFERY, P., 1976, *Frogs in a Well: Indian Women in Purdah*, London: Zed.

JOHNSON, M.M., 1988, *Strong Mothers, Weak Wives*, Berkeley: University of California Press.

JOHNSON, O.R. and JOHNSON, A., 1975, Male/female relations and the organisation of work in a Machiguenga community, *American Ethologist*, **2**, 634–48.

JOHNSON, R.N., 1972, *Aggression in Man and Animals*, Philadelphia: Saunders.

JONES, M., 1993, Learning to be a Father, in FRENCH, S. (Ed.) *Fatherhood*, Virago: London.

JUNG, C.G., 1953, Anima and Animus, in *Two Essays on Analytic Psychology: Collected works of C.G. Jung*, Vol. 7, New York: Bollinger Foundation.

KABBANI, R., 1986, *Europe's Myth of Orient*, London: Pandora.

KAKAR, S., 1990, *Intimate Relations: Exploring Indian Sexuality*, Harmondsworth: Penguin.

KANTER, R.M., 1977, *Men and Women of the Corporation*, New York: Basic.

KEDENBERG, D., 1979, Testosterone and human aggressiveness: an analysis, *Journal of Human Evolution*, **8**, 407–10.

KEENAN, J., 1992, What men think we do wrong in bed, *More*, 24 June – 7 July.

KELLER, E.F. and MOGLEN, H., 1987, Competition and feminism: conflicts for academic women, *Signs*, **12**, 493–511.

KELLY, A. (Ed.), 1987, *Science for Girls*, Milton Keynes: Open University.

KELLY, G., 1955, *The Psychology of Personal Constructs*, 2 vols, New York: Norton.

KIMMEL, M.S. (Ed.), 1987, *Changing Men: New Directions in Research on Men and Masculinity*, London, Sage.

KIMURA, D., 1992, Sex differences in the brain, *Scientific American*, September.

KINSEY, A.C., POMEROY, W.B. and MARTIN, C.E., 1948, *Sexual Behaviour in the Human Male*, Philadelphia: Saunders.

KINSEY, A.C., POMEROY, W.B., MARTIN, C.E. and GEBBARP, P.H., 1953, *Sexual Behaviour in the Human Female*, Philadelphia: Saunders.

KITZINGER, C., 1987, Introducing and developing Q as a feminist methodology: a study of accounts of lesbianism, in Wilkinson (1987).

KITZINGER, C., 1991, Feminism, psychology and the paradox of power, *Feminism and Psychology*, **1**, 1.

KITZINGER, C., 1992, Sandra Lipsitz Bem: feminist psychologist, *The Psychologist*, May.

KOHLBERG, L., 1966, A Cognitive-developmental analysis of children's sex-role concepts and attitudes, in Maccoby (1966).

KOHLBERG, L., 1981, *The Philosophy of Moral Development: Essays on Moral Development*, San Francisco: Harper & Row.

KOSS, M.P., 1989, Hidden rape: Sexual aggression and victimization in a national sample of students in higher education, in Burgess (1989).

KRASNOFF, A.G., WALKER, J.T. and HOWARD, M., 1989, Early sex-linked activities and interests related to spatial abilities, *Personality and Individual Differences*, **10**, 1, 81–5.

KREUZ, L.E. and ROSE, R.M., 1972, Assessment of aggressive behavior and plasma testosterone in a young criminal population, *Psychosomatic Medicine*, **34**, 321–2.

KRONENBERG, F., 1990, Hot flushes: Epidemiology and physiology, in FLINT, M. KRONENBERG, F. and UTIAN, W. (Eds) Multidisciplinary perspectives on menopause. *Annals of the New York Academy of Sciences*, **592**, 52–86.

LANCASTER, J.B., 1973, In praise of the achieving female monkey, *Psychology Today*, 30ff.

LAWRENCE, D.H., 1971, *Fantasia of the Unconscious*, Harmondsworth: Penguin, p. 87 and p. 10.

LEES, S., 1986, *Losing Out: Sexuality and Adolescent Girls*, London: Hutchinson.

LEPOWSKY, M., 1990, Gender in an egalitarian society: a case study from the Coral Sea, in Sanday and Goodenough (1990).

LERNER, A.J., Lyrics from *My Fair Lady*, London: Chappell & Co, 50 New Bond Street, W1.

LEVAY, S., 1993, *The Sexual Brain*, London: MIT Press.

LEVER, J., 1976, Sex differences in the games children play, *Social Problems*, **23**, 478–87.

LEVI-STRAUSS, C., 1970, *The Elementary Structures of Kinship*, London: GYRE and Sportiswood.

LEWIS, C., 1986, Early sex-role socialization, in Hargreaves and Colley (1986).

LIEBERT, R.M. and SPRAFKIN, J., 1988, *The Early Window, Effects of Television on Children and Youth*, 3rd Edn, New York: Pergamon.

LINDEMALM, G. *et al.*, 1986, Long-term follow-up of sex change in 13 male-to-female transsexuals, *Archives of Sexual Behaviour*, **15**, 187–210.

LLOYD, B. and DUVEEN, G., 1992, *Gender Identities and Education: The Impact of Starting School*, London: Harvester Wheatsheaf.

LINN, M.C. and PETERSEN, A.C., 1985, Emergence and characterization of sex differences in spatial ability: a meta-analysis, *Child Development*, **56**, 4, 1479–98.

LORBER, J.A. and FARRELL, S.A., 1991, *The Social Construction of Gender*, London: Sage.

LOTT, B., 1981, A feminist critique of androgyny. Towards the elimination of gender attributes for learned behavior, in MAYO, C. and HENLEY, N.M. (Eds) *Gender and Non-Verbal Behavior*, New York: Springer-Verlag, 178.

LOTT, B., 1990, Dual natures or learned behavior: the challenge to feminist psychology, in Hare-Mustin and Maracek (1990).

LYNDON, N., 1992a, *No more Sex Wars*, London: Sinclair-Stevenson.

LYNDON, N., 1992b, Women: Who do they think they are?, *The Times*, 14.9.92.

LYNDON, N., 1992c, Who gives a damn about the battered man?, *The Times*, 15.9.92.

MACCOBY, E.E. (Ed.), 1966, *The Development of Sex Differences*, Stanford: Stanford University Press.

MACCOBY, E.E. and JACKLIN, C.N., 1974, *The Psychology of Sex Differences*, Stanford: Stanford University Press.

MADDOX, J., 1992, How to publish the unpalatable, *Nature*, **358**, 187.

MAHFOUZ, N., 1991, *Palace Walk*, London: Doubleday.

MAILER, N., 1991, *The Deer Park*, London: Paladin.

MAIR, A., 1993, Dying for Beauty, *I-D.*, June, 17–18.

MALAMUTH, N.M., 1987, Do sexually violent media indirectly contribute to anti-social behavior?, in Walsh (1987).

MALINOWSKI, B., 1962, *Sex, Culture and Myth*, New York: Harcourt, Brace and World.

MAMET, D., 1984, *Glengary Glen Ross*, London: Methuen.

MARTIN, E., 1987, *The woman in the body. A cultural analysis of reproduction*, Boston: Beacon.

MASSON, J., 1990, *Against Therapy*, Glasgow: Fontana.

MATHEWS, M.H., 1987, Sex differences in spatial competence: the ability of young children to map 'primed' unfamiliar environments, *Educational Psychology*, **7**, 2, 77–90.

MATTSSON, A., SCHALLING, D., OLWEUS, D., LOW, H. and SVENSSON, J., 1980, Plasma testosterone, aggressive behavior and personality dimensions in young male delinquents, *Journal of the American Academy of Child Psychiatry*, **19**, 476–90.

McCALL, D.K., 1979, Simone de Beauvoir, the second sex and Jean-Paul Sartre, *Signs*, **5**, 2, 210.

McCAMMON, S., KNOX, D. and SCHACHT, C., 1993, *Choices in Sexuality*, Minneapolis/St Paul: West.

McClintock, A., 1992, Gonad the Barbarian and the Venus Flytrap, in Segal and McIntosh (1992).

McEwan, I., 1982, *The Comfort of Strangers*, London: Picador.

McGirk, T., 1993, He wanted to kill our babies for being girls, *The Independent*, 8–4–93, 11.

McRobbie, A. and Garber, J., 1976, Girls and subcultures: an exploration, in Hall, S. and Jefferson, T. (Eds) *Resistance Through Rituals*, London: Hutchinson.

Mead, M., 1935, *Sex and Temperament in Three Primitive Societies*, New York: William Morrow.

Mead, M., 1971, *Male and Female*, Harmondsworth: Penguin.

Meigs, A.S., 1976, Male pregnancy and the reduction of sexual opposition in a New Guinea Highland society, *Ethnology*, **15**, 4, 393–407.

Mernissi, M., 1971, *Beyond the veil: Male–female dynamics in a modern Muslim society*, New York: Wiley.

Miedzian, M., 1992, *Boys Will Be Boys: Breaking the link between Masculinity and Violence*, London: Virago.

Miller, A., 1989, *Death of a Salesman*, Harmondsworth: Penguin.

Miller, J.B., 1986, *Towards a New Psychology of Women*, 2nd Edn, Harmondsworth: Penguin.

Mishel, W. and Grusec, J., 1966, Determinants of the rehearsal and transmission of neutral and aversive behaviors, *Journal of Personality and Social Psychology*, **3**, 197–205.

Mitchell, J., 1974, *Psychoanalysis and Feminism*, London: Allen Lane.

Money, J. and Ehrhardt, A., 1972, *Man and woman, boy and girl*, Baltimore: John Hopkins University Press.

Money, J. and Schwartz, M., 1976, Fetal androgens in the early treated androgenital syndrome of 46XX hermaphroditism: Influences on assertive and aggressive behavior, *Aggressive Behavior*, **2**, 1, 19–30.

Morawski, J.G., 1990, Toward the unimagined: feminism and epistemology in psychology, in Hare-Mustin and Maracek (1990).

Morris, J., 1974, *Conundrum*, New York: Harcourt, Brace, Jovanovich.

Mort, F., 1987, Boy's Own? Masculinity, style and popular culture, in Chapman and Rutherford (1988).

Moyer, K.E., 1974, Sex Differences in Aggression, in Friedman, R.C., Richart, R.M. and Van der Weile, R.C. (1974) 358–9.

Mullen, B., 1993, Meta-analysis, *Thornfield Journal*, **16**, 36–41.

Napheys, G.H., 1878, *The Transmission of Life*, quoted in Starr (1991).

Newson, J. and Newson, E., 1986, in Hargreaves and Colley (1986).

Nietzsche, F., in *The Will to Power*, quoted in Starr (1991).

1992, Date Rape; Could it happen to you?, *More*, 10–23 June, 40–41.

Niven, C., 1992, *Psychological Care for Families: Before, during and after birth*, London: Heinemann.

Nkweto-Simmons, Felly, 1993, personal communication.

Nkweto-Simmonds, F.N., 1987, A history of women's education in Zambia, unpublished MA thesis, University of Warwick.

O'Brien, D., 1977, Female husbands in Southern Bantu societies, in Schlegel, A. (Ed.) *Sexual stratification: A cross-cultural view*, New York: Columbia University Press.

O'Reilly, J., 1992, Year of the Woman? in *The Guardian Weekend*, 24 October, 4–7.

Offer, D., Ostrov, E., Howard, K. and Atkinson, R., 1988, *The Teenage World: Adolescents' Self Image in Ten Countries*, New York: Plenum Press.

Olivier, C., 1989, *Jocasta's Children*, London: Routledge.

Ortner, S.B., 1975, Oedipal father, mother's brother and the penis: a review of Juliet Mitchell's psychoanalysis and feminism, *Feminist Studies*, **2**, 2–3, 179.

Orton, J., 1986, *What the Butler Saw*, London: Methuen.

Ottenberg, C.B., 1959, The changing economic status of women among the Afikpo Ibo, in Bascon, W. (Ed.) *Continuity and Change in African Cultures*, Chicago: University of Chicago Press.

Paglia, C., 1993, *Sexual Personae*, Harmondsworth: Penguin, 37–8.

Paige, K.E. and Paige, J., 1981, *The politics of reproductive ritual*, Berkeley: University of California Press.

Parke, R. and Sawin, D., 1980, The family in early infancy: social interaction and attitudinal analyses, in Pedersen, F.A. (Ed.) *The father-infant relationship: observational studies in the family setting*, New York: Praeger.

Parker, D., 1989, General Review of the Sex Situation, in *Collected Dorothy Parker*, Harmondsworth: Penguin.

Parlee, M.B., 1973, The premenstrual syndrome, *Psychological Bulletin*, **80**, 454–65.

Parlee, M.B., 1976, The premenstrual syndrome, in Cox, S. (Ed.) *Female Psychology*, Chicago: Science Research Associates.

Parlee, M.B., 1985, Psychology of women in the 80s: promising problems, *International Journal of Women's Studies*, **8**, 193–204.

Piaget, J., 1954, *The Construction of Reality in the Child*, New York: Basic Books.

Plath, S., 1985, in Hughes, T. (Ed.) *Selected Poems*, London: Faber & Faber.

Quick, H., 1993, Where are the male super-models?, *I-D.*, June, 24–7.

Radford, T., 1993, Your mother should know, *The Guardian*, 17–6–93, 23.

Rich, A., 1979, *Of Woman Born*, New York: Norton.

Richardson, S., 1980, *Pamela*, Harmondsworth: Penguin.

Roberts, Y., 1992, *Mad about Women: Can There Ever be Fair Play between the Sexes?*, London: Virago.

Rogerson, G. and Wilson, E. (Eds), 1991, *Pornography and Feminism: The Case Against Censorship*, London: Lawrence & Wishart.

Robertson, P., 1992, quoted in *The Guardian Weekend*, 24.10.92, 3.

Rohrbaugh, J., 1981, *Women: Psychology's Puzzle*, London: Sphere, 125.

Roscoe, B. and Benaske, N., 1985, Courtship violence experienced by abused wives: similarities in patterns of abuse, *Family Relations*, 419–24.

Ross, H.S. and Goldman, D.B., 1977, Infants' sociability towards strangers, *Child Development*, **48**, 638–42.

ROSS, M.P., 1989, Hidden Rape: sexual aggression and victimization in a national sample of students in higher education, in Burgess (1989).

ROSSI, A., 1987, On the Reproduction of Mothering: A Methodological Debate, in Walsh (1983).

RUBIN, J.Z., PROVENZANO, F.J. and LURIA, Z., 1974, The eye of the beholder; Parents' views on sex of newborns, *American Journal of Orthopsychiatry*, **44**, 512–9.

RUBIN, R.T., REINISCH, J.M. and HASKETT, R.F., 1981, Postnatal gonadal steroid effects on human behavior, *Science*, **211**, 1318–24.

RUDDICK, S., 1987, Beyond moral theory: Political and legal implications of difference, in KITTAY, E.F. and MEYERS, D.T. (Eds) *Women and moral theory*, Towota, NJ, Rowman and Littlefield.

RUSE, M., 1988, *Homosexuality: A Philosophical Enquiry*, Oxford: Blackwell.

RUSHTON, J.P., 1992, Cranial capacity related to sex, rank, and race in a stratified random sample of 6,325 US military personnel, *Intelligence*, **16**, 401–33.

SALMINEN, S. and GLAD, T., 1992, The role of gender in helping behavior, *The Journal of Social Psychology*, **131**, 1, 13–133.

SANDAY, P.R., 1979, *The Socio-Cultural Context of Rape*, Washington, DC: US Department of Commerce, National Technical Information Services.

SANDAY, P.R., 1981, *Female power and male dominance: On the origins of sexual inequality*, Cambridge: Cambridge University Press.

SANDAY, P.R. and GOODENOUGH, R.G. (Eds), 1990, *Beyond the Second Sex: New Directions in the Anthropology of Gender*, Philadelphia: University of Pennsylvania Press.

SAYERS, J., 1992, in *Mothering Psychoanalysis*, Harmondsworth: Penguin, 145–6.

SCOTT, W., 1990, *The Possibility of Communication*, New York: de Grouter.

SCULLY, D., 1990, *Understanding Sexual Violence: A Study of Convicted Rapists*, Boston: Unwin-Hyman.

SEGAL, L. and MCINTOSH, M. (Eds), 1992, *Sex Exposed: Sexuality and the Pornography Debate*, London: Virago.

SEGAL, L., 1987, *Is the Future Female? Troubled Thoughts on Contemporary Feminism*, London: Virago.

SERBIN, L.A. and O'LEARY, K.D., 1975, How nursery schools teach girls to shut up, *Psychology Today*, **9**, 7, 56–8ff.

SHEPHERD, G., 1987, Rank, gender and homosexuality in Mombasa, in Caplan (1987).

SHOWALTER, E., 1987, *The Female Malady: Women, Madness and English Culture, 1860–1980*, London: Virago.

SHUTE, V.J., 1983, in Kimura (1992).

SIANN, G., 1977, Sex differences in spatial ability in children, unpublished PhD thesis, University of Edinburgh.

SIANN, G., 1985, *Accounting for aggression*, London: Allen & Unwin.

SIANN, G. and KNOX, A., 1992, Influences on career choice: the responses of ethnic minority and ethnic majority girls, *British Journal of Guidance and Counselling*, **20**, 2, 193–204.

SIANN, G. and UGWUEGBU, D., 1988, *Educational Psychology in a Changing World*, 2nd Edn, London: Unwin-Hyman.

SIGNORELLA, M.L., KRUPA, M.H. and JAMISON, W., 1989, Predicting spatial performance from gender stereotyping in activity preferences and self-concept, *Developmental Psychology*, **25**, 1, 89–95.

SMITH, C., 1993, Exposed: the X-rated debate, *The Observer*, 4 July, 151.

SMITH, J., 1993, *Misogynies*, 2nd Edn, London: Faber & Faber.

SMITH, L.S., 1978, Sexist assumptions and female delinquency: an empirical investigation, in SMART, C. and SMART, B. (Eds) *Women, Sexuality and Social Control*, London: Routledge and Kegan Paul.

SMITH, P., 1986, Exploration, play and social development in boys and girls, in Hargreaves and Colley (1986).

SPEARS, R., ABRAMS, D., SHEERAN, P., ABRAHAM, S.C.S. and MARKS, D., 1991, Social judgements of sex and blame in the context of AIDS: Gender and linguistic frame, *British Journal of Social Psychology*, **30**, 37–49.

SPELKE, E., ZELAZO, P., KAGAN, J. and KOTELCHUCK, M., 1973, Father interaction and separation protest, *Developmental Psychology*, **9**, 83–90.

SPENCE, J.T., HELMREICH, R.L. and STAPP, J., 1975, Ratings of self and peers on sex-role attributes and their relation to self esteem and conceptions of masculinity and femininity, *Journal of Personality and Social Psychology*, **32**, 29–39.

SPENDER, D., 1978, The right way to talk: sex differences in language, *Times Educational Supplement*, 3.11.78.

SPENDER, D., 1982, quoted in Lees (1986) 32.

SQUIRE, C., 1989, *Significant Differences – Feminism in Psychology*, London: Routledge.

STARR, T., 1991, *In Her Master's Voice*, Harmondsworth: Penguin.

STASSINOPOLOUS, A., 1973, *The Female Woman*, London: Davis-Poynter.

STEIN, M. and CORBETT, L. (Eds), 1991, *Psyche's Stories: Modern Jungian Interpretations of Fairy Tales*, Vol. 1, Wilmette, Illinois: Chiron Publications.

STEPHENS, J., 1912, The Crock of Gold, Bk 1, Ch. 4 in AUGARDE, T. (1992) (Ed.) *Oxford Dictionary of Modern Quotations*.

STERNGLANZ, S.H. and SERBIN, L.A., 1974, Sex-role stereotyping in children's television programs, *Development Psychology*, **10**, 710–15.

STORR, A., 1970, *Human Aggression*, Harmondsworth: Penguin.

STRACHEY, J. (Ed.), 1965, *New Introductory Lectures on Psychoanalysis*, New York: Norton.

STRACHEY, J. (Ed.), 1976, *The Complete Psychological Works*, Vol. XIX, New York: Norton.

STRACHEY, J. (Ed.), 1977a, *The complete psychological works*, vol. XVIII, New York: Norton.

STRACHEY, J. (Ed.), 1977b, *The Pelican Freud Library*, vol 7., Harmondsworth: Penguin.

TANNEN, D., 1991, *You Just Don't Understand: Women and Men in Conversation*, London: Virago.

TAVRIS, C. and WADE, C., 1984, *The Longest War: Sex Differences in Perspective*, 2nd Edn, San Diego: Harcourt, Brace, Jovanovich.

TAYLOR, M.C. and HALL, J.A., 1982, Psychological androgyny: theories, methods and conclusions, *Psychological Bulletin*, **92**, 2, 347–66.

TERMAN, L.M., 1916, *The Measurement of Intelligence*, Boston: Houghton Mifflin.

THE ENGINEERING COUNCIL, 1993, Newsletter, May, 9.

THE QUOTABLE WOMAN 1993, London: Pavilion.

THOMAS, D., 1993, *Not Guilty: In Defence of Modern Man*, London: Weidenfield and Nicolson.

THOMPSON, S.K., 1975, Gender labels and earty sex role development, *Child Development*, **46**, 339–47.

THURSTONE, L.L., 1938, *Primary Mental Abilities*, Chicago: University of Chicago Press.

TIEFLER, L., 1988, Sexuality, in Kimmel (1987b).

TIGER, T., 1980, On the biological bases of sex differences in aggression, *Child Development*, **51**, 943–63.

TONG, R., Reprinted 1992, *Feminist Thought: A Comprehensive Introduction*, London: Routledge.

TRESEMER, D.W., 1977, *Fear of Success*, New York: Plenum.

TREVARTHEN, C., 1992, personal communication.

TREVARTHEN, C., 1993, personal communication.

TYTLER, D., 1993, Opening the doors at Oxbridge, *Guardian Education*, May 16, 6–7.

UNGER, R.K., 1990, Imperfect Reflections of Reality, in Hare-Mustin and Maracek (1990).

UNGER, R.K. and CRAWFORD, M., 1992, *Women and Gender: A Feminist Psychology*, London: McGraw-Hill.

URBERG, K.A., 1982, The development of the concepts of masculinity and femininity in young children, *Sex Roles*, **6**, 659–88.

USSHER, J.M., 1989, *The Psychology of the Human Body*, London: Routledge.

USSHER, J.M., 1991, *Women's Madness: Misogyny or Mental Illness?*, London: Harvester Wheatsheaf.

VAN DER VELDE, T.H., 1928, *Ideal Marriage: It's Physiology and Technique*, London: Heinemann.

WALKER, L., 1984, *The Battered Woman Syndrome*, New York: Springer.

WALKERDINE, V., 1986, Post-structuralist theory and everyday social practices: the family and the school, in Wilkinson (1986).

WALSH, M.R. (Ed.), 1987, *The Psychology of Women: Ongoing Debates*, New Haven: Yale University Press.

WEEKS, J., 1987, Questions of Identity, in Caplan (1987).

WEINER, A., 1976, *Women of value, men of renown: New Perspectives on Trobriand exchange*, Austin: University of Texas.

WHITE, A., 1989, *Poles Apart? The Experience of Gender*, London: Dent.

WHITE, D. and WOOLLETT, A., 1992, *Families: A Context for Development*, London: Falmer.

WHITE, J.W. and Koss, M.P., 1991, Courtship violence: Incidence in a national sample of higher education students, in Unger and Crawford (1992).

WHITEHEAD, H., 1981, The bow and the burden strap: a new look at institutionalised homosexuality in native North America, in ORTNER, S. and WHITEHEAD, H. (Eds) *Sexual Meanings*, Cambridge: Cambridge University Press.

WIKAN, U., 1977, Man becomes woman: transsexualism in Oman as a key to gender, *Man*, **12**, 2, 304–19.

WILEY, M.G. and ESKILSON, A., 1982, in Unger and Crawford (1992).

WILLIAMS, J.E. and BEST, D.B., 1990, *Sex and Psyche: Gender and Self viewed Cross-Culturally*, London: Sage.

WILLIAMS, J.H., 1987, *The Psychology of Women: Behaviour in a Biosocial Context*, 3rd Edn, New York and London: Norton.

WILLIAMS, L., 1990, *Hard Core*, London: Pandora.

WILKINSON, S. (Ed.), 1986, *Feminist Social Psychology: Developing Theory and Practice*, Milton Keynes: Open University Press.

WILSON, E.O., 1978, *Sociobiology: The New Synthesis*, Cambridge, MA: Harvard University Press.

WITKIN, H.A., DYK, R.B., FATERSON, H.F., GOODENOUGH, D.R. and KARP, S.A., 1962, Psychological Differentiation: Studies of Development, New York and London: Wiley.

WITKIN, H.A., MEDNICK, S.A., SCHULSINGER, F., BAKKESTROOM, E., CHRISTIANSEN, K.O., GOODENOUGH, D.R., HIRSCHHORN, K., LUNDSTEEN, C., OWEN, D.R., PHILIP, J., RUBIN, D.B. and STOCKING, M., 1976, Criminality in XYY and XXY men, *Science*, **193**, 547–55.

WOLF, N., 1990, *The Beauty Myth*, London: Chatto & Windus.

WOLPE, A., 1988, *Within School Walls: The Role of Discipline, Sexuality and the Curriculum*, London: Routledge, 69.

WOOD, J., 1984, Groping towards Sexism: boys' sex talk, in McROBBIE, A. and NAVA, M. (Eds) *Gender and Generation*, London: MacMillan, 57.

WORTH, R., 1992, A Material Whirl in *The Guardian*, 2, 17 November, 8.

YAMAMOTO, T., 1969, Sex Differentiation, in HOAR, W.S. and RANDALL, D.J. (Eds) *Fish Physiology*, Vol 3, New York: Academic Press.

YOUNG-EISENDRATH, P. and WIEDEMANN, F., 1987, *Female Authority*, New York: Guildford.

Index

aborigines 15
abortion 133
activity as male attribute 7, 72, 89
    education 101–2
    Freud 22, 28, 30
    images 162
    psychoanalysis 37–8
    work 104
Adam and Eve 154
Adler, Alfred 31–3
adolescence 50, 82–7, 120, 147
advertisements 151–2, 162
Africa 45, 76–7, 89, 118, 121
aggression as male attribute 44, 89, 110
    chromosomal abnormalities 51
    Freud 31
    hormones 51–3, 62
    New Guinea 124
    social learning 67
    socio-biology 59–60
    violence 173, 174, 176, 177
Aids 15, 17, 85, 143, 147
Allen, Richard 153
alpha-reductose deficiency 48, 62
anal stage 26
androgynes 52–3
androgynized women 46
androgyny 72, 74, 129
anima 30, 33
animus 30, 33
anorexia nervosa 156, 162
Arapesh tribe 124
Australia 15, 82

Balinese 118
Bedouin 123
behaviour 88–90
    biological determinism 41

dimorphism 42, 44–5
    gender differences 6, 8, 21, 105–15
    sexual 143–8
    social learning 65–8
Bem, Sandra 71–6, 115, 131
Bem's Sex Role Inventory (BSRI) 72
Bemba tribe 77
berdache 118
Bible, The 11, 154
biological determinism 7–8, 13, 31, 39,
        41–63
    brain function 57–8
    chromosomes 43, 50–1
    homosexuality 60–1
    hormones 43, 45–9, 51–6
bisexuality 17–18, 21, 28, 46, 146
Bly, Robert 142
brain
    chromosomal abnormalities 50
    homosexuality 60, 97
    hormones 49, 55, 57
    hypothalamus 56, 59, 60
    sex differences 45, 57–8, 62, 92–3, 96,
        98–9
Breuer, Josef 23

castration 38, 44, 52
    anxiety 26, 28, 121, 155
    symbolic 35
celibacy 11
central nervous system 56, 57
Charcot, Jean 22–3
chastity 11, 12, 123, 154, 155
childbirth 31, 53, 119, 120
childhood
    gender differences 33, 39, 41, 93–4
    homosexuality 145
    psychoanalysis 7, 23–4, 25, 34

social behaviour 112–14
  see also children; infancy
children 9, 24, 41, 125, 141, 160
  care facilities 103, 134, 148, 160
  cognitive development 68–71
  pornography 164, 167, 177
  as prostitues 12, 165
  sex typing 79–81, 87
  sexual rituals 121
  social learning 64–7, 70, 73, 87
  stereotyping 151, 152
  violence 167, 170, 174, 175
  see also adolescence; childhood
Chodorow, Nancy 32–3, 112, 128
chromosomes
  abnormalities 45, 49–51, 61–2
  gender differences 43, 45–7, 92
  homosexuality 61
  hormones 46–7
Church 3, 16, 133
circumcision 121–2
Clary, Julian 1, 163
cognitive development 68–71, 73
  gender differences 90, 92–99
commercials 151–2, 162
counter-stereotyping 150, 152
  images 154, 160, 161, 163
couvade 120, 121
criminality 50–1, 167
cross-dressing 1–2, 20–1

Daly, Mary 129, 136
date rape 150, 171
de Beauvoir, Simone 34, 126–7
Deutsch, Helen 30–1, 36
divorce 145
dominance 7, 9, 32, 117–19
  castration 52
  feminism 126–30, 141, 144
  group behaviour 108–9
  pornography 168
  psychoanalysis 36–8
  sex differences 38–9, 72, 107, 110
  social control 122
  violence 169, 171, 174
Dominicam Republic 48–9, 62
dreams 23, 46
du Maurier, Daphne 19
Dworkin, Andrea 136, 169

economic dependency 118, 119, 127, 175
education 92, 99–102, 146
ego 25
Ellis, Havelock 13, 14, 173, 174
employment 152
  adolescence 82–3, 86–7
  child care facilities 103, 133, 148, 160
  feminism 134–5, 148
  images 159, 162
  sexual inequality 3, 100–5, 147–8
  women 12–13, 89, 144, 147–8, 159
Erikson, Erik 29–30
essentialism 6–7, 16, 21, 39, 64, 116
  feminism 129
  homosexuality 59, 60–1
  new men 140–3
  social behaviour 105, 112–14
  socio-biology 59–60
  violence 171
evolutionary theory 60
  sex differences 7, 41, 45, 112, 114
  violence 171
existentialist feminism 126–7

Faludi, Susan 133, 137, 140
fantasies 14, 23, 37, 46, 68, 150
feminists and feminism 8, 24, 116, 143, 148
  backlash 92, 127, 131, 132–42, 155, 159
  biological determinism 7, 31, 62
  existentialism 126–7
  gender differences 29, 33, 37, 99, 102, 112
  homosexuality 146
  images of women 154, 155, 158–9
  pornography 164–8
  post-modern 126, 130–2
  psychoanalysis 31, 34, 36, 127–8, 129
  purdah 122–3
  radical 128, 130–1, 168, 169
  social constructionism 126, 130–2
  social learning 73, 127
  socio-biology 59–60
  violence 133–4, 140, 141, 171–2
fetishes 26

films
  images of men 161–2
  images of women 154, 158–61, 177
  pornography 164–6
  stereotyping 150–1
  violence 174
Foucault, M 131
free association 23
French, Marilyn 133–5, 140
Freud, Anna 24–5, 29
Freud, Sigmund 22–39, 128
  followers and critics 29–34
  homosexuality 38–9
  origins of psychoanalysis 22–4
  psychosexual development 25–7
  relationships with women 24–5
  sex differences 6–7, 27–9

gender constancy 69, 71
gender distinction 5–10
gender identity
  biological determinism 45–52, 62
  psychoanalysis 34–6, 39
  social learning 68–70, 79, 87
gender polarizing lenses 75, 130
gender schema 73–4, 86, 103
gender stability 69
gender typing *see* sex typing
genitalia 12, 29, 38, 90, 121
  abnormal 45, 47–9, 51
  ambiguous 19, 43–4
genital stage 27
Gilligan, Carole 8, 111–13, 128
glass ceiling 102, 104, 133
Goldberg effect 103, 127
gonads 42, 43, 46
group behaviour 108–9
guevedoce 48

Harris survey 21
helpfulness 109–10
hermaphrodites 42, 45–6, 49, 51, 52
homosexuality 14–18, 21, 25, 38–9,
    145–7
  adolescence 86
  androgynized women 46
  chromosomes 61
  essentialist perspectives 58, 60–1
  hormones 146

images of men 161
  pornography 164
  social learning 67–8, 146
  spatial ability 95–7
  transvestism 20
  violence 174
hormones 43–4, 45, 52–7
  abnormalities 45–9, 51, 62
  brain 48, 57–9
  chromosomal abnormalities 50–2
  homosexuality 145
  spatial ability 95–7
  transsexuality 19
Horney, Karen 31, 36
Hua 118
Humphrey, Barry 20
hypothalamus 56, 59–60
hysteria 22–3

id 25
identification 67
images of men 161–3, 177
images of women 150, 154–61
  beauty 155–8
  contemporary trends 158–61, 176–7
  madonna and whore 154–5, 158,
      170
  pornography 163–9
imaginary phase 34
India 77, 164
infancy 34, 64–5, 76, 116–17
  homosexuality 145
  sex differences 29, 33, 93
  social behaviour 111–13
  see also childhood
intelligence 51–2, 58, 92–3
Iroquois 119
Islam (Muslim) 122, 123, 124, 146

Jacklin, Carole Nagy 93, 94, 95
Jung, Carl 30, 31, 34, 142

Kenya 79
Kinsey, Alfred 13, 14, 16
Klinefelter's syndrome 51
Kohlberg, Lawrence 69, 70, 71, 111, 112,
    130
Korea 77
!Kung tribe 45, 76

Lacan, Jacques 34–5
language 6, 9, 35–6, 108
La Rue, Danny 20
latency stage 27
Law of the Father 35–6
lenses of gender 74–5, 87
Lepowsky, Marie 117, 119
lesbians and lesbianism 38–9, 145–6
  brain 59
  feminism 137
  pornography 165, 166, 168
  sexuality 14, 16–18, 21
  violence 174, 175
LeVay, Simon 61
Levi-Strauss, Henri 9
libido (sex drive) 10–14, 25–6, 28, 30–1
Lilith 154
literature 4–6, 77, 82, 158
lordosis 44
Lott, Bernice 72–3, 112
Lyndon, Neil 139, 140, 142

Maccoby, Eleanor 93–5
Madonna (singer) 2, 20, 144, 160, 163
magazines 158–9, 165
marriage 9, 24, 143–5, 147–8
  rape 170
  sexuality 11–16
  transsexuals 19
  Xanith 18
masochism 26, 27–8, 30, 36, 175
  see also sadomasochism
masturbation 12–14, 26, 68
mathematical ability 93, 95, 99, 101, 130
Mead, Margaret 124–5
menarche 120, 121
menopause 29, 53, 55, 56, 62
menstruation 29, 118, 120–2
  hormones 47, 53, 54, 55
meta-analysis 93, 94, 95, 96, 98, 106
mirror phase 34
misogyny 4, 155, 169
Mombasa 18
mood 51, 52, 56, 62
moral development 111–12
Morris, Jan (formerly James) 19
mounting behaviour 44
Mundugumor tribe 124
Muslim (Islam) 118, 122–3, 146

native Americans 118, 119
New Guinea 15, 49, 62, 117–18, 124–5
new men 140–2, 158, 162
newspapers 151, 152, 153, 159, 162

Oedipal phase 35, 37, 128
Oedipus complex 26
oestrogen 43, 56
Oman 18
oral stage 26

parents 23–4, 27–35, 39, 114, 147
  feminism 129
  gender difference in play 93
  of newborn 59–60
  sex stereotyping 77, 101
  sex typing 79, 80, 81
  sexual rituals 120
  social learning 65, 66–7
passivity as female attribute 7, 72, 89, 97
  education 99–100
  feminism 143
  images of women 160
  psychoanalysis 22, 29, 30, 37–8
  social learning 67
  stereotyping 150
penis envy 27–8, 30, 31, 34, 39
personality 7, 28, 29, 34, 124–5
phallic stage 26–8, 30–3
physical appearance 70, 86, 90–2
  feminists 139
  images of men 161–3
  images of women 154–6
  stereotyping 82, 150
Piaget, Jean 68
Plath, Sylvia 36, 37
play 78, 79, 81, 91–2
polymorphous sexuality 26
pornography 38, 163–9, 177
  censorship 164, 168–9
post-feminism 116
post-modernism 35, 127, 130–1
power 10, 13, 15, 89–90, 142
  feminism 127, 131–3, 139–42
  sexual inequality 3–4, 21, 35, 107, 110
  sexual violence 174, 175
  social control 121–2
pregnancy 31, 76, 77, 120
  hormones 46, 52, 56

pre-menstrual tension 54, 56, 62
pseudohermaphrodites 63
psychoanalysis 6–8, 22–40, 121
  dominance 36–8
  feminism 29, 33, 36, 125, 127
  Freud and followers 24–33
  homosexuality 38–9, 145
  origins 22–4
  recent trends 32–6
psychodynamics 111–12, 145
psychosexual stages 25–7, 34, 128
puberty 12, 91, 146
  hormones 43, 47–9, 53
purdah 18, 122–3

race 14, 68, 71, 107, 109–10, 130–2
  brain function 57
  employment 104
radio 151, 152
rape 141, 149, 170–1, 177
  date 149, 171
  feminism 172–3
  pornography 167–9
  psychopathology 172
  social learning 173–4
Red Sea fish 42
Rich, Adrienne 60, 128
role models 65–6, 160, 177
romanticism 11

sadism 26
sadomasochism 166, 168
Samoa 125, 126
Sampson, Deborah (transvestite) 20
Satre, Jean-Paul 126–7
sex drive (libido) 10–14, 25–6, 28, 30–1
sex manuals 13–14
sex role theory 8, 113–14
  see also sex-typing
sex-typing 71–5, 77–9, 113–14, 124–5
  adolescence 86
  childhood 79–81, 87
  education 99–101
  feminism 126
  homosexuality 145
  images 159, 162
  sexual antagonism 150–1
  social learning 69, 70
  toys 98

sexual assault 3, 141, 149, 170–1, 176
  feminism 172–3
  pornography 167, 169–70
  psychopathology 172
  social learning 173–4
sexual organs *see* genitalia
sexual orientation 16–19, 38–9, 51,
    145
  biological determinism 45, 58, 61–2
  pornography 165
  social learning 66–7, 144
sexual rituals 120, 121–2, 123
sexual self-expression 159, 162
Shepherd, Gillian 18
social class 24, 66, 67, 70, 94
  adolescence 84–6
  feminism 136–7
  pornography 164–5
  power 130–2
  sex typing 76, 87
  sexuality 11, 13, 18
  social control 122–3
social constructionist feminism 126,
    130–2
social control 121–3
social interactions 106–8
socialization 64–5, 86, 116, 145
  gender differences 75, 106, 109,
    113–14
social learning 59, 64–71, 87, 151
  children 64–7, 70, 73, 87
  feminism 71, 126
  gender identity 69–70, 79, 87
  gender-schema 73
  homosexuality 67–8, 145
  violence 174–5
socio-biology 7–8, 59–62, 91, 111–13
  violence 110, 169
spatial ability 58, 60, 94, 97–100
Spender, Dale 107, 108
status 4, 9, 109–10, 118–20, 145, 163,
    168
  adolescence 84, 85
  bought in Africa 118
  feminism 131, 133, 140
  sexuality 11, 15–16
  social control 121
  transsexuality 19
  violence 171, 173

stereotyping 1, 76–7, 113–14, 150–3, 177
  adolescence 82
  feminists 131, 137
  sex differences 41, 95–6, 99, 101–4, 111
    images 152, 158, 162
    sexuality 19
    transsexuals 19
    violence 174
Stopes, Marie 13
structuralism 6, 8–10, 21, 114, 116
  feminism 126, 141
subjugation 38–9, 169
submissiveness 7, 9, 154, 155
subordination 7, 9, 84, 127, 128
super-ego 25–8
supermales 50–1
surgery 12, 19–20, 118
Swahili community 18
symbolic order 35

Tchambuli tribe 124–5
television 66, 152, 160, 162, 177
  stereotyping 151–3
temperament 124–5
Terman, Lewis 93
testicular-feminization syndrome 47
testosterone 43, 47–8, 52–4
Thomas, David 139, 140, 142, 147
tokensim 104

toys 76, 80, 98
transference 23
transsexuals 19–20, 21, 47, 118
tranvestites 1–2, 20–1
Trobianders 117
Turner girls 49, 50
twins 60–2

unconscious 23, 25, 30, 34, 35, 39

Vanatinai 15–16, 119
Van der Velde, T H 14
verbal ability 58, 94, 95, 130
  communication 107–8, 110
victimization of women 151
Victorians 12, 122–3, 165
violence 3, 7, 59, 110, 150, 169–77
  chromosomes 50–1
  domestic 174–5
  feminist 133–4, 139, 140, 172–3
  hormones 52–4
  pornography 164, 165

Walkerdine, Valerie 100–1
wild men 140–2
Witkin study 51–2, 96
Wolf, Naomi 155–6, 159
Woolf, Virginia 127

Xanith 18